Xenophon on Violence

Trends in Classics – Supplementary Volumes

Edited by
Franco Montanari and Antonios Rengakos

Associate Editors
Stavros Frangoulidis · Fausto Montana · Lara Pagani
Serena Perrone · Evina Sistakou · Christos Tsagalis

Scientific Committee
Alberto Bernabé · Margarethe Billerbeck
Claude Calame · Jonas Grethlein · Philip R. Hardie
Stephen J. Harrison · Richard Hunter · Christina Kraus
Giuseppe Mastromarco · Gregory Nagy
Theodore D. Papanghelis · Giusto Picone
Tim Whitmarsh · Bernhard Zimmermann

Volume 88

Xenophon on Violence

Edited by
Aggellos Kapellos

DE GRUYTER

ISBN 978-3-11-076372-0
e-ISBN (PDF) 978-3-11-067146-9
e-ISBN (EPUB) 978-3-11-067153-7
ISSN 1868-4785

Library of Congress Control Number: 2019948509

Bibliographic information published by the Deutsche Nationalbibliothek
The Deutsche Nationalbibliothek lists this publication in the Deutsche Nationalbibliografie; detailed bibliographic data are available on the Internet at http://dnb.dnb.de.

© 2021 Walter de Gruyter GmbH, Berlin/Boston
This volume is text- and page-identical with the hardback published in 2019.
Editorial Office: Alessia Ferreccio and Katerina Zianna
Logo: Christopher Schneider, Laufen
Printing and binding: CPI books GmbH, Leck

www.degruyter.com

Contents

Agellos Kapellos
Introduction —— 1

Cinzia Bearzot
The notion of violence (*bia, hybris*) in Xenophon's work —— 11

Paolo A. Tuci
***Apronoētos Orgē*: the Role of Anger in Xenophon's Vision of History** —— 25

P.J. Rhodes
Lawfulness and Violence in Decision-Making in Xenophon's *Hellenica* —— 45

Frances Pownall
Violence and Civil Strife in Xenophon's *Hellenica* —— 67

Edith Foster
Minor Infantry Defeats and Spartan Deaths in Xenophon's *Hellenica* —— 83

Edward Harris
Violence and the State in Xenophon: A Study of Three Passages —— 103

Nathan Crick
The Rhetoric of Violence in Xenophon's *Anabasis* —— 125

Bogdan Burliga
**Xenophon's βίαιος διδάσκαλος:
Thinking War and Empire in the *Cyropaedia*** —— 143

Aggelos Kapellos
The Greek reaction to the slaughter of the Athenian captives at Aegospotami and Xenophon's *Hellenica* —— 161

Andrew Wolpert
Xenophon on the Violence of the Thirty —— 169

Notes on Contributors —— 187
Index of Sources —— 191
General Index —— 203

Aggelos Kapellos
Introduction

This volume examines the issue of violence in Xenophon's works.[1] Students of Xenophon might be interested in such a topic partly because of the evolution of Xenophon's life[2] alongside war and violence, which he defined as 'the irrational application of physical force to unwilling bodies'.[3]

Xenophon was born sometime between 430 and 425 BC. This means that he grew up during the Peloponnesian War. He seems to have served in the cavalry and he may have participated in the Athenian attack on Ephesus in 409, under the general Thrasyllus. Around 407 he may have spent time as a prisoner in Boeotia.[4] As the war was going on, Xenophon may have attended the Assembly meetings where the Athenians discussed and finally decided on the execution of the Athenian generals who had defeated the Spartan Callicratidas at Arginousae.[5]

In 405 the Spartan commander Lysander caught almost the entire Athenian fleet on the beach at Aegospotami in the Hellespont except for nine ships that escaped, among them the Paralus which reached Athens with word of the disaster. It is likely that during that time Xenophon heard about the slaughter of the Athenian captives at Aegospotami.[6] Athens surrendered to Sparta and Lysander and then the Thirty ruled the city violently.[7] Xenophon was in Athens at this time and may have served in their cavalry.

In 401 Xenophon served as a hired hoplite in the army of the Persian prince Cyrus who wanted to unseat his older brother, King Artaxerxes II, and he fought in the battle of Cunaxa. Xenophon's campaigning with Cyrus enabled him to have an immediate experience of the way of life of the Persians and see the workings of their empire. This may have inspired him later to write his *Cyropaedia*, in which he highlighted the virtues of Cyrus the Great, ancestor of the Cyrus under whom

---

1 I am most grateful to Prof. P.J. Rhodes, Prof. C. Bearzot, Prof. A. Wolpert, Prof. I.N. Perysinakis, Dr. E. Foster and Dr. P.A. Tuci for reading this chapter and commenting on it.
2 For this short biographical sketch I draw heavily on Lee, 2017, 15–36. However, also see the footnotes of the papers published here, which contribute to the subject under discussion.
3 For this definition of the term see Crick in this volume p. 126.
4 Cf. Rhodes in this volume about Boeotian institutions and procedures in the *Hellenica*.
5 About Xenophon and the Arginousae trial see Rhodes in this volume.
6 See Kapellos, 2013, 468–469 who investigates the issue of the slaughter of the Athenian captives at Aegospotami and Xenophon's suppression of this incident in his *Hellenica*.
7 About the rule of the Thirty see Wolpert in this volume.

Xenophon served, although he did not abstain from admitting that the vast Persian Empire could not survive without the use of violence.[8]

However, violence also hit Cyrus' Greek mercenaries unexpectedly. The Persians invited Clearchus, Proxenus, and the other generals to a conference at which they seized and executed them. The army selected new generals, Xenophon among them. During his command Xenophon proved himself able to enforce discipline on his men, but when this was not possible he did not hesitate to punish those who disobeyed his orders.[9]

After the Ten Thousand made their way to the Black Sea, Xenophon did not return to Athens. Instead, from 399 to 394, Xenophon served in western Anatolia under Agesilaus against the Persian satrap Tissaphernes and against the Thebans and the Argives in the battle of Coronea. By the late 390's the Spartans gave him a home at Scillus in the Peloponnese and this became the place where he started writing his works. But war and violence did not end, because Thebes arose as the new military power in the Greek world. Athens, Sparta and several Peloponnesian forces fought against Thebes in 362 at Mantinea. In this battle Xenophon lost his son Gryllus, who served with the Athenian cavalry and died even before the main military encounter between the two armies.

Therefore it is legitimate to say that since Xenophon lived in circumstances of war for so many years violence was a common phenomenon for him, so it is not surprising that the word appears so often in his work[10] and accounts of incidents of violence are innumerable in his *oeuvre*. From this experience the subject of the present volume arises.

Violence exists in nature, personal relationships, military life, political relations, incidents of *stasis*, foreign policy, and management of power.[11] Xenophon describes explicitly the violence that took place during the Peloponnesian War,[12] during the rule of the Thirty in Athens,[13] in other *staseis* in the Greek world[14] and in all kinds of military engagements in Greece and Persia.[15] In all cases he implies that violence should be avoided, especially if it originates in anger.[16] He believed that personal influence should be preferred to violence, but when this was not

---

8 About the *Cyropaedia* see Burliga in this volume.
9 See Harris in this volume about Xenophon's behaviour to his men during his generalship.
10 For the occurrence of the word βία in Xenophon's works see Bearzot in this volume.
11 See Bearzot in this volume.
12 See Kapellos in this volume.
13 See Wolpert in this volume.
14 See Pownall in this volume.
15 See Foster and Crick in this volume.
16 See Tuci in this volume.

effective, the threat of violence was necessary.[17] However, it was his contention that officials, among themselves Xenophon himself, could use physical force in order to keep order.[18]

All the papers in this volume address these issues of violence from different aspects. The exclusive focus on this fundamentally important issue is justified, since no previous detailed study exists on the subject.[19]

Bearzot and Tuci offer a lexical analysis of Xenophon's works. Rhodes, Kapellos, Wolpert, Pownall, Foster and Harris (in the third part of his chapter) focus on Xenophon's *Hellenica*. Crick and the second part of Harris' chapter are devoted to the *Anabasis*, and Burliga examines the *Cyropaedia*. Rhodes, Pownall, Foster, and Harris contribute chapters on diverse aspects of public life, civil or military. Crick and Burliga offer chapters on the *Anabasis* and the *Cyropaedia* respectively. Kapellos and Wolpert participate with chapters which analyze particular episodes in the *Hellenica* (see in detail below).

Most of the chapters in this volume focus on the *Hellenica*, because this work records more aspects of violence than the rest of his works. Moreover, the present volume is more concerned with examining violence in practice rather than the theory of violence, and violent practices are more frequently recorded in the *Hellenica*, which is the main historical work of Xenophon.[20]

Some methodological statements about the *Hellenica* must be made at the outset of this enterprise. There is a strong debate and different opinions about whether Xenophon wrote Books 1–2 at a different time from the other Books.[21] In this volume all the contributors argue for a conceptual unity of the *Hellenica*.[22] Of importance for these arguments is the fact that Xenophon presupposed his readers' knowledge of Herodotus[23] and also of Thucydides whose history Xenophon

---

17 See Crick in this volume.
18 See Harris in this volume.
19 Riess, 2012 offers a detailed analysis of violence in Athens and its treatment in lawcourt speeches, curse tablets and old and new comedy. Riess, 2012, 37–38 argues that the Thirty shaped-unknowningly- the notion of homicide in the fourth century. However, he does not focus on Xenophon's account of the Thirty, while he does not take into account Wolpert's account on the violence of the Thirty (2006, 213–223; see now Wolpert in this volume).
20 For history-writing practice in Xenophon's *oeuvre* see Tuplin, 1993, 18–20. Marincola, 2017, 106–115 provides a comparison of the common historiographical themes in the *Anabasis* and the *Hellenica*. For the historiographical dimension of the *Cyropaedia* see Tamiolaki, 2017, 182–189.
21 See Sordi, 1950, 3–53, 1951, 273–348, Tuplin, 1993, Gray, 1991, 201–228, Dillery, 1995, 13–15, Gray, 2004, 132.
22 For a previous approach of this kind to Xenophon's *Hellenica* see Gray, 1989 and Hau, 2016, 216–235.
23 See Tamiolaki, 2008, 33. Cf. Gray, 2012, 1–54.

continued.[24] Xenophon's readers knew at least the bare facts of the Peloponnesian War.[25] So Xenophon chose which events to record, imposing his own ideas of what was important, and he chose a particular approach to those events.[26] The authors of this volume attempt to shed more light on Xenophon's *oeuvre* by performing a careful close reading of the texts themselves.[27] The papers take a lexical and semantic approach to the study of violence from different aspects.

The body of this volume begins with a contribution by Cinzia Bearzot ('The notion of violence (*bia, hybris*) in Xenophon's work'), which considers the notion of violence in Xenophon's *Hellenica*, making also a comparison with the complex of Xenophon's writings. Xenophon disapproved of the open violence of those in power (individual or states) and the exercise of their roles in inappropriate forms, not only on an ethical basis but also from the perspective of political opportunity. Several cases show that the use of violence carries with itself political weakness (this is the case, for example, with the Thirty Tyrants); good rulers like Agesilaus and Jason, though able to practice violence, are shown to prefer mildness and persuasion. Moreover, those who practice violence are exposed to a justified reaction: violent and arrogant behavior not only produces a bad ethical and political judgment but also provokes arrogant military punitive responses that find their justification precisely in the violent practices. Indeed, in the destiny of the states (as in the case of Athens, defeated in the Peloponnesian War) it is possible to recognize the divine punishment of violence exerted by the stronger over the weaker. Opposed to *nomos* and the virtues of moderation and equilibrium in the exercise of power, violence is part of the forms of degeneration of political relations and constitutes a factor with significantly negative consequences on the relationship between rulers and ruled, between hegemonic powers and subdued states, without however even benefiting those who practice it.

Paolo Tuci ('*Apronoētos Orgē*: Anger in Xenophon's *Hellenica*') investigates whether in the *Hellenica* ὀργή generates violent actions. The survey of this concept starts from the death of Teleutias, due to a decision made on the wave of anger: Xenophon, observing that ὀργή is an ἀπρονόητον ἁμάρτημα, remarks that this episode teaches us not to act under the influence of anger. The survey conducted on the cases of anger by individuals and by communities suggests that in Xenophon's *Hellenica* anger is considered an irrational and negative emotion

---

24 See MacClaren, 1979.
25 See Kapellos, 2018, 397.
26 Gray, 1989, 19.
27 Thus all the contributors follow the opinion of Tuplin, 1993, 18 that this is the most important evidence for the interpretation of an ancient literary composition.

which has to be restrained, because it prevents people from acting rationally; if not controlled, it provokes serious consequences. Moreover, Xenophon seems to imply that single individuals can control emotions better than groups and that anger may be an understandable and justifiable reaction to a wrong; in the latter case, anger may not be negative in itself, as long as it provokes a well-thought-out and not an emotional response.

Peter J. Rhodes ('Lawfulness and Violence in Decision-Making in Xenophon's *Hellenica*') seeks to show how far Xenophon's *Hellenica* depicts lawful procedures in decision-making in Greek cities, how far it depicts or implies violent overriding of those procedures. Rhodes argues that, although Xenophon was a man of moderate oligarchic sympathies, and was exiled from Athens from the 390's to the 350's, he is more apt to give detailed accounts of procedures in Athens than in other states: procedures abused in the late fifth century, and procedures used correctly but with unexpected results in the fourth century. For Sparta his only comparable set piece shows the personal machinations which led to the acquittal of Sphodrias after his raid on Attica in 379/8; as there he often focuses on disagreements between individuals, but he often includes short remarks which give an indication of the procedures followed. For the affairs of other cities (Corinth, Argos, Thebes, Phlius, Arcadia, Sicyon) he most often focuses on a change of alignment or régime, and here he is inconsistent in the detail which he gives, influenced partly by his access to detailed information and partly by how he chose to write up an episode.

Frances Pownall ('Violence and Civil Strife in Xenophon's *Hellenica*') investigates the issue of violence and civil strife in Xenophon's *Hellenica*. She remarks that the most egregious acts of violence occur during episodes of civil strife: Critias' murder of Theramenes, mass slaughter committed by both sides during an episode of civil strife at Corinth, the Theban exiles' massacre of their political opponents. In each of these episodes, Xenophon deliberately highlights his descriptions of violence with vivid narrative and careful attention to detail in order to make them particularly memorable. In so doing, Xenophon provides support for one of the underlying themes of the *Hellenica*, the futility and destructiveness of internecine warfare, and also makes a pointed allusion to Thucydides' account of the civil strife at Corcyra.

Edith Foster ('Minor Infantry Defeats and Spartan Deaths in Xenophon's *Hellenica*') investigates the issue of massed deaths in Xenophon's *Hellenica*. At the climax of important campaign narratives, Herodotus and Thucydides tell how enemies surround and defeat groups of a few hundred Spartan hoplites. In Xenophon scenes in which groups of Spartans are surrounded and killed proliferate. While one such disaster is mentioned in Book 1, narrative descriptions of this kind of event become more frequent after the beginning of book 3. Three of these accounts depict tactical successes of light-armed troops against Spartan hoplites and subsequent scenes show how groups of Spartans die as a result of problematic Spartan leadership. This second group of passages seems intended to illustrate the deterioration of Spartan leadership in the period leading up to the disaster at Leuctra and its dangerous inability to guard Sparta thereafter. Xenophon is thus making a deliberate choice to depict Greek massed death with particular attention to Sparta. Foster analyzes Xenophon's language and narrative strategies, asks whether his descriptions of group death develop or react against the paradigms available from Herodotus and Thucydides, compares them to similar descriptions in epic and tragedy, queries the differences between Spartan disaster scenes and those Xenophon created for other nations and concludes by focusing on how such disaster scenes disturb the larger narrative, allowing no relief from violent death between the more prominent battles and political events.

Edward Harris ('Violence and the State in Xenophon: A Study of Three Passages') explores the use of violence within the community in two passages from the *Anabasis* and one from the *Hellenica*, and shows that Xenophon refused to let his men stone individuals as a means of punishment because spontaneous violence was not an alternative form of justice, but instead might result in harsh injustice, and undermined the law and order needed for military discipline and social peace. Then Harris studies the use and abuse of violence by public officials in the Greek *polis* and argues that generals and other officials did not have the absolute right to use force in any circumstances. To keep officials accountable, the army instituted legal procedures and allowed those who felt that they had been mistreated to bring an accusation. While officials in Greek communities did not use the *bakteria* or *skeptron*, which might have been a Spartan habit, to enforce discipline, they had the right to use physical force and to beat the disorderly with *rhabdoi*, but they had to be very careful about the use of force, especially without legal justification. Finally, Harris focuses on Euphron of Sicyon and his assassination in Thebes. In his view, Euphron's career demonstrates that opposition to tyranny could be used both by the proponents of constitutional regimes opposed to democracy and by the advocates of democracy. Even though Xenophon respected the principle that only the officials of the state should have the right to use deadly force, he also recognized that in the case of tyranny there was an exception to this general rule. On the other hand, there is a certain consistency in his views: for Xenophon, the only justification for the use of violence was for the sake of justice and the benefit of individuals and the community. The killing of a tyrant was not only a way to protect democracy; it was mainly a way to restore the rule of law when it was threatened.

Nathan Crick ('The Rhetoric of Violence in Xenophon's *Anabasis*') writes on the *Anabasis* and remarks that we encounter in this work Xenophon as a narrator who is in constant need of self-justification for his actions. This need is particularly acute in his interactions with the villages, cities, and peoples that his army of 10,000 Greeks encounter on their journey back home across the hostile land of the Persian empire. However, what readers find is a subtle and often contradictory logic of justification that rests on a fluid relationship between honor, truth, and power. We see Xenophon's honor in his encounter with the Macrones when he offers a pledge to the gods not to attack them and to pay for all the food and gifts offered to his army. Xenophon relates honor to truth, in which recognition of the facts combines with an ability to keep one's word — even if that word is a threat — to persuade others to act without compulsion. We see this in Xenophon's negotiations with the people of Cotyora, when he effectively demands that they act as 'friends' and allow his men into the city, threatening that otherwise they will be attacked as enemies by a superior force. But, finally, he also believes in the principle of power which means not only physical force but also the capacity to act in concert under a unified command and thus stands in stark contradiction to the code of honor. This is expressed when Xenophon considers founding a city in the Euxine, despite his promises to the people of Sinope that his army was only briefly residing in the area before traveling back to Greece. Crick's paper explores these competing tensions and shows how Xenophon selectively calls upon different principles to justify his acts of violence or coercion in different circumstances.

Bogdan Burliga ('Xenophon's βίαιος διδάσκαλος: Thinking War and Empire in the *Cyropaedia*') explores the theme of maintaining power and the use of violence in the *Cyropaedia* and looks at it as a highly realistic piece, arguing that in this respect the tale of Cyrus is implicitly a tale about empire and hegemony. Cyrus' process of building the empire presupposes conquests, which means expansion, conflicts, wars, annexation of territories, with various forms of subordination and subjugation, including physical violence, enslavement and the killing of those who refuse to obey: before the subjects are turned into a consenting and applauding flock, they must either be conquered by force or be terrorized by the threat of force. Xenophon usually tries to avoid focusing on shocking accounts and things that eventually and inevitably happened when Cyrus constructed his ideal kingdom. Nevertheless, we have plenty of glimpses that atrocities occurred. As in similar cases in the *Agesilaus* and the *Hellenica*, Xenophon permits his readers — from time to time — to see terrifying details of battle. These details help the reader to acknowledge that this is what real power and authority, even the most just, are about. Xenophon, although he never promoted violence, remained a man without illusion about the inevitability of conflicts that presuppose and allow the use of violence. Xenophon always remained a man of practical mind, interested in specific issues (technical ones or the duties of commanders) that warfare generates, rather than engaged in *theoria* — philosophical speculations on the nature of armed conflicts and power. On the other hand, assuming for sure that as a disciple of Socrates he either witnessed and heard many debates on this topic or knew other people's books (e.g. Thucydides), it seems to be obvious that he had his own, precise views on this matter. Burliga pays attention to passages of this work that shed some light on how Xenophon perceived the phenomenon of war and imperialism in more abstract, general terms. Additionally, his investigation of these passages makes it possible to judge Xenophon's views against the background of political thought at the time, as reconstructed now from historiography, oratory and philosophical writings of the sophists.

Aggelos Kapellos ('The Greek reaction to the slaughter of the Athenian captives at Aegospotami and Xenophon's *Hellenica*') argues that Xenophon leads his readers to realize that the Greeks would not have reacted against the slaughter and that Xenophon has not omitted reporting such a reaction. Xenophon clarifies the problematic relation of the Athenians and the other Greeks before the battle of Aegospotami. Thus the Spartans and their allies considered the killing of the Athenian prisoners an act of justice. Athens' allies were against her before the defeat at Aegospotami while the Athenians knew the real feelings of the Greeks for them. Arrian corroborates Xenophon's narration. Xenophon implicitly explains the non-reaction of the Greeks to the captives' slaughter by reporting several Athenian and Spartan crimes in such a way as to prove that violence tended to become banal, while when pity was shown it was all the more remarkable. Adeimantus proves that there could be some Greeks who would disagree with extreme acts of violence, but these were the exception. Philocles' brutal slaughter proves that Xenophon was sensitive and perceptive in detecting human reactions to violence, but he was also realistic since he makes a distinction even in the *Agesilaus* between his hero who remained humane and his men who maltreated the prisoners.

Andrew Wolpert ('Xenophon on the Violence of the Thirty') warns against attempts to normalize the rule of the Thirty or their violence. Although the rule of the Thirty is especially well documented, with some striking chronological discrepancies in the sources, there is a danger of overemphasizing these differences and downplaying the similarities. He compares Xenophon's *Hellenica* with Lysias' speech *Against Eratosthenes* and [Aristotle]'s *Athenaion Politeia* to show that the accounts are largely in agreement on the nature of the oligarchy even though their authors held different political viewpoints. Lysias' depiction of the Thirty as morally bankrupt individuals who committed atrocities against the Athenian people for the most part matches the description of their rule found in the other accounts. The *Athenaion Politeia* provides the most favorable assessment of Theramenes by presenting him as an opponent of the extreme policies of the other oligarchs even before the Thirty gained control of Athens and by distancing him from some of the more brutal acts of the oligarchy. In both Xenophon and [Aristotle] the Thirty become bolder as they accumulate greater power, and as their violence escalates the opposition grows, causing them to resort further to violence. Theramenes is unsuccessful in his attempts to restrain his colleagues, and he is killed so that he cannot hinder the Thirty from ruling as they please. Xenophon is more equivocal in his assessment of Theramenes, provides a more vivid account of the violence perpetrated by the Thirty, includes speeches of the partisans and combatants of the warring factions and emphasizes the moral implications of the conflict. The reader is sympathetic to Theramenes because of the way Xenophon portrays him at his trial and execution and for standing up to Critias, but Xenophon also draws attention to Theramenes' weaknesses and raises questions about his character, which falls far short of Thrasybulus'. After Theramenes' execution, the violence continued to escalate just as in Lysias and the *Athenaion Politeia*. However, Xenophon reveals how the Thirty made the Three Thousand complicit in their murders and how this in turn created dissension among the men of the city even after the Thirty were deposed and the Ten elected. Wolpert concludes that authoritarian regimes are inherently violent. Repression and opposition were inevitable once the Thirty refused to extend power beyond a narrow clique of individuals.

Thus this volume attempts to provide a comprehensive study of the subject of violence in Xenophon's works and to demonstrate the coherence and consistency of his thought on it. I hope that that this work will prove to be a worthwhile contribution to classical scholarship since it attempts to: (1) shed further light on the literary character of Xenophon's *oeuvre*; (2) offer new interpretation of passages and themes; and (3) put emphasis on passages that scholars have not pointed out and which offer important insights to the thought of Xenophon.

I am most grateful to the editors, in particular Professor A. Rengakos (University of Thessaloniki) for the publication of this volume in the excellent series *Trends in Classics*. Moreover, I express my warm thanks to the contributors for our excellent cooperation and to Professor P.J. Rhodes for his actual support in seeing this volume concluded. Finally, I wish to thank the anonymous readers for their comments.

I may be allowed to dedicated this book to the memory of my father Sotirios Kapellos.

Bibliography

Dillery, J. (1995), *Xenophon and the History of his Time*, London/New York.
Gray, V.J. (1989), *The Character of Xenophon's* Hellenica, London.
Gray, V.J. (1991), "Continuous History and Xenophon, *Hellenica 1–2.3.1*" in: *AJP* 112, 201–228.
Gray, V.J. (2004), "Xenophon" in: *Narrators, Narratees and Narratives in Ancient Greek Literature: Studies in Ancient Greek Narrative*, vol. 1, I. de Jong/R. Nunlist/A. Bowie (eds), Leiden, 129–46.
Gray, V.J. (2012), *Xenophon's Mirror of Princes*, Oxford.
Hau, I. (2012), *Moral History from Herodotus to Diodorus Siculus*, Edinburgh 2016.
Kapellos, A. (2013), "Xenophon and the execution of the Athenian captives at Aegospotami" in: *Mnemosyne* 66, 464–472.
Kapellos, A. (2018), "Lysander and the execution of the Athenian captives at Aegospotami" in: *Mnemosyne* 71, 394–407.
Konstan, D. (2006), *The Emotions of the Ancient Greeks: Studies in Aristotle and Classical Literature*, Toronto.
Lee, J.W.I. (2017), "Xenophon and his Times" in: *The Cambridge Companion to Xenophon*, M. Flower (ed.), Cambridge, 15–36.
Marincola, J. (2017), "Xenophon's *Anabasis* and *Hellenica*" in: *The Cambridge Companion to Xenophon*, M. Flower (ed.), Cambridge, 103–118.
McClaren, M. (1979), "A supposed lacuna at the beginning of Xenophon's *Hellenica*" in: *AJP* 100, 228–238.
Riess, W. (2012), *Performing Interpersonal Violence: Court, Curse, and Comedy in Fourth-Century BCE Athens*, Berlin/Boston.
Sordi, M. (1950, 1951), "I caratteri dell'opera storiografica di Senofonte nelle Elleniche" in: *Athenaeum* 28, 3–53 and 29, 273–348.
Tamiolaki, M. (2008), "Les *Helléniques* entre tradition et innovation. Aspects de la relation intertextuelle de Xénophon avec Hérodote et Thucydide" in: *CEA* 45, 15–52.
Tamiolaki, M. (2017), "Xenophon's *Cyropaedia*: Tentative Answers to an Enigma" in: *The Cambridge Companion to Xenophon*, M. Flower (ed.), Cambridge, 174–194.
Tuplin, C.J. (1993), *The Failings of Empire: A Reading of Xenophon* Hellenica 2.3.11–7.5.27, Stuttgart.
Wolpert, A. (2006), "The violence of the Thirty Tyrants" in: *Ancient Tyranny*, S. Lewis (ed.), Edinburgh, 213–223.

Cinzia Bearzot
The notion of violence (*bia, hybris*) in Xenophon's work

The notion of *bia* expresses first of all physical violence, not only human violence but also that of natural forces; that of *hybris* rather concerns violence perpetrated by somebody who intends to prevail over others, driven by irrational passions and by lack of sense of measure, and possibly to humiliate and dishonour his victims.[1] Both are often opposed to notions such as *sophrosyne, phronesis, gnome* (everything that expresses discipline, reflection, self-control, and opposes the uncontrolled expression of pure force) or as *peitho* (an alternative to violence to obtain adhesion by others).

An analysis of the use of *bia* (adj. *biaios, biazomai*) and of *hybris* (vb. *hybrizo*) in Xenophon[2] reveals that the author carefully considers the role played by violence in human relations and in domestic and foreign policies. Moreover, it highlights a strong coherence between the moral and the political perspective, which emphasizes not only the illegitimacy but also the ineffectiveness of violence.

1 Violence in nature, in personal relationships, in military life

1.1

Bia as the uncontrollable violence of nature is present in a passage of the *Hellenica* (5.4.17) which refers to the strong wind that the Spartan king Cleombrotus, retreating from Boeotia in the winter of 379/8, met along the road and that caused much damage, including the loss of mules, luggage and weapons by Spartans (πολλὰ μὲν γὰρ καὶ ἄλλα βίαια ἐποίησεν).

---

[1] Chantraine, 1968, respectively 174–175 and 1150. On the notion of violence see Riess, 2012, 1–9 (120–125 for *hubris*). A fresh discussion on the notion of *hubris*, based on *Anab.* 5.8.1, is provided by Phillips, 2016; see also Harris in this volume. I do not consider in this paper the notion of *orge*, which is studied by Tuci in this volume.
[2] For a fine-tuning of the overall problem on Xenophon, see Flower, 2017.

https://doi.org/10.1515/9783110671469-002

1.2

More often, however, the notion of *bia* is applied to the vast field of human relations. A special case is that of sexual violence. In *Hell.* 6.4.7 Xenophon evokes the story of the virgin daughters of Skedasos, violated by the Spartans, who died by suicide and were buried at Leuctra, where the Spartans were defeated in 371 (ἔνθα τὸ τῶν παρθένων ἦν μνῆμα, αἳ λέγονται διὰ τὸ βιασθῆναι ὑπὸ Λακεδαιμονίων τινῶν ἀποκτεῖναι ἑαυτάς). Here the verb *biazo, biazomai* is used in the technical sense employed also in Attic law, which envisaged a *dike biaion* (besides a *graphe hybreos* for crimes against the person).[3] In this same sense *bia* and *biazo, biazomai* recur in the vicissitude of the beautiful prisoner Panthea, threatened with violence by her jailer Araspas and defended by Cyrus (*Cyr.* 6.1.33–34).[4] The idea of sexual violence, exercised by those who are in power, is expressly rejected in *Hier.* 1.33 and 7.6, as opposed to relationships based on friendship and consensus.[5] An allusion to this aspect is probably to be seen in 2.1.30, where Virtue scolds Vice for doing "violence" to his friends and followers during the night, then letting them consume the day sleeping.

Hybris is violence trampling on basic rights in *Hell.* 6.5.46, where Procles of Phlius reminds the Athenians of the help given them by the Spartans against the Thebans who wanted the destruction of Athens and asks them not to let the Spartans be ruined and destroyed (μήτε ὑβρισθῆναι μήτε ἀπολέσθαι), who had defended the right of the Seven against Thebes to be buried worthily. Similarly, in *Hell.* 6.5.47 Procles himself evokes another mythical episode, that of the Heraclids, whom the Athenians did not allow to be overpowered by Eurystheus.[6] In both cases Procles appeals to mythical vicissitudes to encourage the Athenians to remain faithful to their tradition, which is to prevent acts of *hybris* against the defeated enemy and against the stranger in difficulty.[7]

Legal issues are very frequent in Xenophon. In *Cyr.* 1.2.2 and 1.2.6, *bia* is included in a series of crimes (*klope, harpage, apate, kakologia, moicheia*, house violation, beatings, insubordination…); moreover, the illegality of the use of force

---

[3] For an update on this issue see Harris, 2004, 41–83 (= 2006, 97–332).
[4] On this episode see Azoulay, 2004, 413–418.
[5] Azoulay, 2004, 396–398. See Brillante, 1998, 7–34.
[6] On Procles' speech see *ACD* 40–41 (2004–2005 = *Studi Havas*), 17–32; Marincola, 2010, 273–277; Baragwanath, 2012, 316–344; Pontier, 2013, 178–184. On the use of speeches in Xenophon see Buckler, 1982, 180–204; Gray, 1989, 79–140; Pontier, 2001, 395–408; Tamiolaki, 2014, 121–137; Baragnawath, 2017, 279–297.
[7] For the latter case, see also *Mem.* 3.5.12: πολλοὶ δὲ ὑπὸ κρειττόνων ὑβριζόμενοι κατέφευγον πρὸς ἐκείνους.

is theorized, through the opposition *nomimon/dikaion* and *anomon/biaion*, also in the presence of a good objective (*Cyr.* 1.3.17: the context alludes to judicial evaluation, and not by chance the conclusion is that the court must judge according to the law, since what is under the law is right: ἐπεὶ δὲ ἔφη τὸ μὲν νόμιμον δίκαιον εἶναι, τὸ δὲ ἄνομον βίαιον, σὺν τῷ νόμῳ ἐκέλευεν ἀεὶ τὸν δικαστὴν τὴνψῆφον τίθεσθαι).[8] In *Mem.* 2.1.5 we find a mention of the violence which can be suffered by the adulterer caught *in flagrante* (ὑβρισθῆναι), who, as we know, according to Athenian law could be killed with impunity: in this case, it is a *hybris* foreseen by law.

1.3

The role of *bia* in military life is particularly present in the *Anabasis*, where it can characterize relations with enemies (it is *bia*, in fact, that one must expect from the enemy: *An.* 3.1.21; *Mem.* 2.6.9),[9] relations between commander and soldier (*An.* 1.3.2; 5.7.8; 5.8.1; 5.8.3; 5.8.19; 5.8.22–23; 6.6.15; 6.6.25; 7.3.3; 7.8.11),[10] the exercise of force in overcoming a fortified position or in resolving a siege (1.4.4; 3.4.12; 7.1.19), the methods of prevailing over the enemy and the treatment of the same (1.4.5; 5.5.11; 5.5.16; 5.5.18; 5.5.20; 7.1.31; see *Cyr.* 3.3.69; 5.4.51). In the *Anabasis* we find only in one case a general reflection on the theme of violence: in 7.7.24 Xenophon, addressing the Thracian king Seuthes, affirms that the words of men who practise the truth have greater power than the violence of others (οἶδ' ἂν φανεροὶ ὦσιν ἀλήθειαν ἀσκοῦντες, τούτων οἱ λόγοι, ἤν τι δέωνται, οὐδὲν μεῖον δύνανται ἀνύσασθαι ἢ ἄλλων ἡ βία); in fact, their threats are more effective in reducing the interlocutor to reason, and their promises more credible. Here, in the context of a short *speculum principis*,[11] the theme of the ineffectiveness of pure violence is introduced, a topic that is very dear to Xenophon, as we shall see.

1.4

In personal relationships, as regards friendship *bia* is opposed to the notions of benefit (*euergesia*) and of pleasing (*hedone*), which generate *charis* (*Mem.*

---

8 Rapp, 1988, 57–47.
9 *An.* 1.8.27; 3.1.14; 3.1.29; 6.4.2; *Cyr.* 5.2.28; 7.1.3. refer to the serious violence which arises in situations of war.
10 Ferrario, 2014, 190–201. On 5.8.1 see Phillips, 2016.
11 Lendle, 1995, 471.

3.11.11).¹² Trustful relationships, in fact, are established on the basis of benefit (*euergesia*) rather than with *bia* (*Cyr.* 8.7.13); a friend cannot be won by deception or force, as is done with the enemies (*Mem.* 2.6.9).

However, the situation often does not appear so clear: *bia* can sometimes be used with friends, with good intent, next to persuasion (*peitho*: see *Mem.* 2.4.6); on the other hand, even with adversaries *bia* is not the only viable path, since they can also be undone with *techne* (*Eq. mag.* 5.14). The opposition between *bia* and the notions of *euergesia*, *charis*, *peitho*, *techne*, which introduce effective alternatives to the use of violence, remains in any case confirmed.

In turn, *hybris* can play a relevant role in the degeneration of personal relationships (Spithridates offended by Pharnabazus in *Ages.* 3.3; Gadatas offended by the Assyrian king in *Cyr.* 5.4.35; Abradatas and the *hybris* of the Assyrian king in *Cyr.* 6.1.45). Its inappropriateness is underlined by its frequent opposition with *sophrosyne*: for instance, in *Ap.* 19.5, where Socrates claims never to have made violent (*hybristes*) a person capable of self-discipline (*sophron*), and therefore not to be a corrupter; or in *Mem.* 1.2.19, where in turn Xenophon defends Socrates from the accusation of not teaching *sophrosyne* to his students who turned out to be *hybristai*, underlining that even the sage can become violent if he does not keep his soul "trained".¹³ In the same sense is *Cyr.* 2.4.5, which underlines the lack of ostentation in Cyrus' clothing (ἐν τῇ Περσικῇ στολῇ οὐδέν τι ὑβρισμένῃ).¹⁴

Hybris therefore must be opposed to education, as emerges from *Lac.Pol.* 3.2 and 5.6, on the subject of Lycurgan education and of Spartan banquets;¹⁵ from *Cyr.* 5.2.18, on Persian banquets (and see 8.1.53), and from *Cyn.* 12.9, on such activities as are instrumental in removing shameful and violent attitudes from body and soul (τὰ μὲν αἰσχρὰ καὶ ὑβριστικὰ). In *Hier.* 10.2, *hybris*, in men as in horses, is precisely the result of a bad education, too condescending.¹⁶

In this regard, men who occupy senior positions can play an important exemplary role. Agesilaus is presented as a paradigm of *arete* for those who want to educate themselves to religious piety, justice, self-discipline and continence, since imitating those who are pious, just, moderate and continent will prevent them from becoming impious, unjust, violent and unrestrained (*Ages.* 10.2: τίς γὰρ ἂν ἢ θεοσεβῆ μιμούμενος ἀνόσιος γένοιτο ἢ δίκαιον ἄδικος ἢ σώφρονα ὑβριστὴς

---

12 Azoulay, 2004, 281–326, 374.
13 For this opposition between *hybris* and *sophrosyne* see also *Ages.* 10.2; *Mem.* 3.10.5; *Cyr.* 3.1.21; 3.1.27; 8.1.30; 8.4.14; 8.6.16. Cf. Fisher, 1992, 111–117.
14 The pf. part. pass. ὑβρισμένος, referred to things, means "arrogant, ostentatious": see *LSJ* s.v.
15 Lipka, 2002, 137 and 156.
16 On the contribution of education to the creation of a new social "order", so as to overcome disturbances and disorders, see Pontier, 2006, 313–336.

ἢ ἐγκρατῆ ἀκρατής;).[17] The practice of *sophrosyne* by those who can *hybrizein* and choose not to do so, therefore, is of a great educational value (*Cyr.* 8.1.30: ὅταν γὰρ ὁρῶσιν, ᾧ μάλιστα ἔξεστιν ὑβρίζειν, τοῦτον σωφρονοῦντα, οὕτω μᾶλλον οἵ γε ἀσθενέστεροι ἐθέλουσιν οὐδὲν ὑβριστικὸν ποιοῦντες φανεροὶ εἶναι). On the other hand, the commander's negligence towards his soldiers discourages the best and makes *hybristai* the mediocre (*Cyr.* 5.5.42).

2 Violence in political relations

Violence is also a category of political relations, both internal and external, as well as of the behaviour of individuals.[18] This emerges particularly in the *Hellenica*, in which the historical character of the work makes frequent application of the term to political relations.[19] But there are also interesting references in other works.

2.1 Internal policy

Speaking of relations in domestic politics, in several passages of the *Hellenica* the violence of the regime of the Thirty Tyrants is mentioned.[20] In *Hell.* 2.3.19 Theramenes admonishes Critias for the fact that they are building a regime which, despite being violent (and indeed for this reason), is weaker than its subjects (ἔπειτα δ', ἔφη, ὁρῶ ἔγωγε δύο ἡμᾶς τὰ ἐναντιώτατα πράττοντας, βιαίαν τε τὴν ἀρχὴν καὶ ἥττονα τῶν ἀρχομένων κατασκευαζομένους). In these same manifestations of violence, we may notice *Hell.* 2.4.17, in which Thrasybulus invites his men to take revenge for the violence they suffered (πάντες ὁμοθυμαδὸν ἀνθ' ὧν ὑβρίσθημεν τιμωρώμεθα τοὺς ἄνδρας ἔπειτα δ', ἔφη, ὁρῶ ἔγωγε δύο ἡμᾶς τὰ ἐναντιώτατα πράττοντας, βιαίαν τε τὴν ἀρχὴν καὶ ἥττονα τῶν ἀρχομένων κατασκευαζομένους), and 2.4.23, when, after the battle of Munichia, those of the Three Thousand who were guilty of violence for collaborating with the Thirty, fearing the reactions of the democrats (ὅσοι μὲν γὰρ ἐπεποιήκεσάν τι βιαιότερον καὶ ἐφοβοῦντο), called for resistance.[21]

---

17 Ferrario, 2014, 240–250.
18 Lintott, 1982, 82–124; Fisher, 1992, 121–142.
19 D'Huys, 1987, 210: "ancient historiography accords a major role to *political violence*".
20 On the Thirty Tyrants' *hubris* see Riess, 2012, 126–130.
21 Tuplin, 1993, 43–47; Tamiolaki, 2013, 32–39.

Moreover, violence is a characteristic feature of *stasis*. The theme recurs in particular in the case of Phlius.[22] In *Hell.* 5.3.12 the exiles from Phlius, after taking refuge in Sparta, accuse their fellow citizens of having done violence to them, depriving them of political rights and property (ἐδίδασκον ὡς οὗτοι μὲν εἴησαν οἱ βιαζόμενοι ταῦτα ... οὗτοι δὲ οἱ πριάμενοί τε τὰ σφέτερα καὶ βιαζόμενοι μὴ ἀποδιδόναι). In *Hell.* 5.3.13 the Spartans acknowledge that the Phliasians hostile to the exiles have behaved arrogantly (ὑβρίζειν) and therefore they mobilize in favour of the latter. In this case *bia* and *hybris* materialize above all in the deprivation of political and civil rights, which denies the equal status of citizens. It is noteworthy that the violence of the Phliasian democrats serves as a justification for a military intervention that in itself would constitute an interference in the exercise of autonomy by Phlius.

Elsewhere *bia* can be employed in countering popular will, as in the case of Midias, who occupied the fortress of Skepsis with force and let in the Spartan Dercylidas, being aware that he was unable to stop him without opposing the citizens' will with violence (*Hell.* 3.1.21: γνοὺς δὲ ὁ Μειδίας ὅτι οὐκ ἂν δύναιτο κωλύειν βίᾳ τῶν πολιτῶν, εἴασεν αὐτὸν εἰσιέναι).

In *Mem.* 2.6.24 too, though the text has not a historical character, internal politics is seen as a possible occasion for violence: in fact, in this passage we find that people who want honours and charges in order to steal money, use violence (*biazesthai*), and enjoy life are called *adikoi* and *poneroi*, incapable of working in harmony with others, as the community dimension requires.

2.2 Foreign policy

Bia and *hybris* are often present also in the context of international relations and affect relationships both with enemies and, more delicately, with allies.

As for enemies, it is worth signalling passages such as *Hell.* 4.1.2, recalling Agesilaus' activity in Phrygia in 395, where the king ensures his control of cities in part by force, in part by spontaneous adhesion (πόλεις δὲ τὰς μὲν βίᾳ, τὰς δ' ἑκούσας προσελάμβανε), or such as *Hell.* 6.1.15, where Polydamas of Pharsalus describes Jason as very able to escape, prevent or overcome by force the enemy (ἄνδρα ὃς φρόνιμος μὲν οὕτω στρατηγός ἐστιν ὡς ὅσα τε λανθάνειν καὶ ὅσα φθάνειν καὶ ὅσα βιάζεσθαι ἐπιχειρεῖ οὐ μάλα ἀφαμαρτάνει). Violence emerges here as an element of international relations substantially taken for granted.

---

[22] Dillery, 1995, 130–138; Fisher, 2000, 83–123, 110–111; Pontier, 2006, 363–377; Fontana, 2014, 187–241; Hau, 2016, 228–231.

As for allies, *bia* can refer to an imperialistic system characterized by the oppression of the Greeks. For instance, in *Hell.* 6.3.8 Autocles, in the context of his harsh attack on Spartan imperialism at the Sparta congress of 371, mentions the harmosts as responsible for keeping the cities subdued with violence (καὶ τούτων τῶν ἀρχόντων ἐπιμελεῖσθε οὐχ ὅπως νομίμως ἄρχωσιν, ἀλλ' ὅπως δύνωνται βίᾳ κατέχειν τὰς πόλεις).[23] The same happens with *hybris* in *Hell.* 2.2.10, where the Athenians, besieged by the Spartans by land and sea, evoke the pains inflicted by them διὰ τὴν ὕβριν on the small Greek cities, fearing, for a sort of *nemesis*, the same fate. Particularly interesting is *Hell.* 6.1.7, where Jason of Pherae considers *bia* as a possible mode of relationship with the allies, but disputes the opportunity in utilitarian terms: he declares to Polydamas that he would prefer to win Pharsalus over by voluntary adhesion rather than by compulsion (opposition *biasthentes* / *peithentes*), because the use of violence leads to less solid results both for the *hegemon*, being always threatened, and for the ally itself, kept in a state of weakness.[24]

Regarding the opposition between *bia* and persuasion already mentioned, this occurs elsewhere in Xenophon also. A good example is *Mem.* 1.2.10, where, as a reply to the accusations made against Socrates of encouraging young people to despise the institutions and of making them *biaioi*,[25] Xenophon introduces a long reflection on the fact that those who cultivate *phronesis* do not resort to the use of force, knowing quite well that violence generates enmities and dangers and that persuasion, on the other hand, achieves the same results through friendship and without leading to dangerous situations: the former causes hatred, the latter benevolence. The use of violence is therefore typical not of those who cultivate *phronesis*, but of those who possess strength (*ischys*) without wisdom (*gnome*). This passage develops an opposition between *phronesis, gnome, peitho, philia* on the one hand, and *bia, ischys, echthra, misos*, on the other, emphasizing not only the unlawfulness of violence, but also its uselessness for achieving the desired result, which makes it an inadequate method for the wise ruler.[26] The passage closely recalls the speech of Jason, considered above. And it is precisely to the example of Jason that Xenophon refers to stress that violence is not always

---

[23] Gray, 1989, 123–131; Riedinger, 1991, 149–152; Bearzot, 2004, 63–72. For an analysis of the trilogy of speeches for the peace of 371 see Schepens, 2001, 81–96.
[24] For the alternative *bia/peitho* in relationships with allies see also *Cyr.* 5.5.45.
[25] See *Mem.* 1.2.12–13, about Alcibiades, called *biaiotatos* and *hybristotatos*.
[26] Dorion, 2000–2011, I, 83.

the best means to obtain results, and that Jason resorted rather to rapidity of action (*Hell.* 6.4.21).[27] Not very different is what emerges e.g. from *Ages.* 1.20, where the Spartan ruler remembers his wish to secure his enemies more with mildness (*praotes*) than with violence (*bia*), even in the utilitarian perspective of being able to use their resources, if left intact. Once more, the contrast between *bia* / *anomia* and *peitho* / *nomos* is developed in the *Memorabilia* (1.2.41 ff.), in the famous discussion between Pericles and Alcibiades on violence and legality: in the different constitutional contexts we find *anomia*, not *nomos*, when the stronger forces (verb *anankazo*) the weaker to do what he wants not by persuasion, but by violence.[28] The exercise of force by those in power is therefore intrinsically contrary to legality. *Basileis* and *archontes* are such not because they obtain power through violence or deception (verbs *biazo*, *exapatao*), but because they know how to rule, as they have the *episteme* necessary for *archein*: *bia* and *apate* are here juxtaposed to each other as a motive for illegitimacy of power (*Mem.* 3.9.10).[29]

The theme is present also in the *Poroi*, a work in which the issue of hegemony is central. It first appears at 5.5, where, by challenging those who believe that hegemony can be more easily acquired by war than by peace, Xenophon evokes the era of the Persian Wars, when the Athenians became *hegemones* not by doing violence to the Greeks (*biazomenoi*), but by benefiting them (*euerghetountes*). Similarly, in 5.7 Xenophon notes that it is precisely because of the benefits received (*euergetoumenoi*, *eupaschontes*), and not because of the violence suffered (*biasthentes*), that the Thebans and the Spartans kept relaxed relations with the Athenians, allowing them to enjoy hegemony. In both cases good international relations and a recognized and stable hegemony are based on the rejection of violence as a tool for managing relations between states and on the quest for consensus through the granting of benefits.[30]

Hell. 5.2.34 is of particular historical interest for the federal context: the ambassador Cligenes of Acanthus, in his attempt to convince the Spartans to make war against Olynthus, recalls the possible threat represented by an alliance between Olynthus and Thebes and evokes the Spartan concern for the violent subjugation of Boeotia as a whole by the Thebans (καὶ ὑμεῖς γε τότε μὲν ἀεὶ προσείχετε τὸν νοῦν πότε ἀκούσεσθε βιαζομένους αὐτοὺς τὴν Βοιωτίαν ὑφ' αὑτοῖς εἶναι).

---

27 On the paradigmatic character of the figure of Jason see Dillery, 1995, 171–176; Pownall, 2004, 99–103; see moreover Sordi, 1951, 329–332; Higgins, 1977, 110–111.
28 Dorion, 2000–2011, I, CLX, 105–109.
29 Dorion, 2000–2011, II, 1, 360–361.
30 Gauthier, 1976, 196–215.

Here the theme of *bia* alludes to the relations between *hegemon* and individual communities in a federal context, in a vision hostile to federalism such as that of Cligenes and of the Spartans themselves.[31] The case of the Olynthians is mentioned once more in *Hell*. 5.2.38, where the Spartan Teleutias explains to the dynast of Elymia, Derdas, the need to curb the *hybris* of the Olynthians, who were in full imperialistic expansion.

Once more in the federal sphere, some attention is devoted to the *hybris* of the Thebans and, in particular, to their claim to challenge the hegemony of Sparta, with the series of slights mentioned at 3.5.5, just before the outbreak of the so-called Boeotian war in 395 (ἐλογίζοντο δὲ καὶ καλὸν καιρὸν εἶναι τοῦ ἐξάγειν στρατιὰν ἐπ' αὐτοὺς καὶ παῦσαι τῆς εἰς αὐτοὺς ὕβρεως). This claim increases after the victorious battle of Haliartus (3.5.24: των δὲ πραχθέντων οἱ μὲν Λακεδαιμόνιοι ἀθύμως ἀπῆσαν, οἱ δὲ Θηβαῖοι μάλα ὑβριστικῶς).[32]

I should like to highlight, in conclusion, that some abuses can be distinguished from actual *bia* but are, however, no less dangerous. For example, in *Hell*. 3.2.31 the Spartans refuse to recognize the Eleans' possession of Epeum, which they had bought with money, convinced that to buy something from the weakest is not better than to take it by violence (γνόντες μηδὲν δικαιότερον εἶναι βίᾳ πριαμένους ἢ βίᾳ ἀφελομένους παρὰ τῶν ἡττόνων λαμβάνειν). In *Hell*. 7.3.9 one of the assassins of Euphron of Sicyon, while defending himself, recalls that the ruler had tried to corrupt citizens with money and that, by doing this, he had caused them dishonour, as well as damage.[33] On the contrary, those who suffer violence by weapons (οἱ μὲν ὅπλοις βιασθέντες) do not appear *adikoi*. In both cases corruption, or what is interpreted as such, appears more serious than pure violence. Moreover, elsewhere Xenophon deplores more insidious forms of open violence: for example, at *Symp*. 8.20 he warns that in interpersonal relations persuasion (*peitho*) may be worse than violence (*bia*), because it can corrupt the soul of those who let it prevail.[34]

2.3 Management of power

There are numerous passages in which Xenophon emphasizes the uselessness of violence in the management of personal power and the need to repress it both

---

[31] Bearzot, 2004, 45–46.
[32] Tuplin, 1993, 62. On the subject of the *phronema* the Thebans, parallel of their *hybris*, see Bearzot, 2004, 52–56.
[33] Winter, 2016, 2–14.
[34] Huß, 1999, 393–394, suggesting a comparison with Lys. 1.32.

personally and in those of lower condition: some of them we have already met, and we do not need to discuss them once more.

In general, violence does not benefit the powerful (*Hier.* 7.7) and indeed exposes them to retaliation on the part of the inferior (*Hier.* 4.3, 10.4); thus the execution by Cyrus the Younger of two notables in *Hell.* 2.1.9 is stigmatized as a form of *hybris*. Like Agesilaus, a good leader must express his dignity through *gnome*, not with *hybris* (*Ages.* 11.11); moreover, thanks to his virtue, he was able to reverse Greek-Persian relations so that the Greeks, first forced to *proskynesis*, were later honoured by those from whom they suffered violence (τοὺς μὲν πρόσθεν προσκυνεῖν Ἕλληνας ἀναγκαζομένους ὁρῶν τιμωμένους ὑφ' ὧν ὑβρίζοντο).

Punishing those who want to do violence (τοὺς ὑβρίζειν βουλομένους) is among the actions that the holder of absolute power must perform, if he wants to maintain power, even if he arouses hatred (*Hier.* 8.9). And in two cases it is emphasized that the sovereign must punish those who commit *hybris*: in *Oec.* 4.8 *hybris* is, together with *chalepotes* and *ameleia*, among the defects of the governor whom the sovereign punishes; in *Cyr.* 8.6.16 the satraps are brought back to *sophronizein*, if they commit *hybris*.

***

Xenophon therefore considers negatively the open violence (*bia*) of those in power (individuals or states) and its exercise in inappropriate forms of their role (*hybris*), not only on an ethical basis, but also from the perspective of political opportunity. From various cases it emerges that the exercise of violence brings with it political weakness (this is the case, for example, with the Thirty Tyrants).[35] Good rulers such as Agesilaus and Jason, although able to practice violence, show that they prefer mildness (*praotes*) and persuasion (*peitho*), and so also do good military leaders on the model of Cyrus, starting from Xenophon himself.[36] The one who practices violence, in fact, reveals the lack of the virtue of *sophrosyne* (moderation and self-control) and of the other virtues that can justify power by generating admiration and consent; but above all he exposes himself to a justified reaction, because violent and arrogant behaviour not only produce a bad ethical-political judgment, but also expose those guilty of it to punitive military interventions, which find their justification in the violent practice. Consequently,

---

35 For the violence of the Thirty see Wolpert and Pownall in this volume.
36 Bibliography on the virtues of the good leader in Xenophon is quite extensive: I refer in particular, for the military aspect to Riedinger, 1991, 227–243; Hutchinson, 2000; Buxton, 2017, 323–337; also, Azoulay, 2004; Gray, 2011; Buxton, 2016, Hau, 2016, 223–228.

the accusation of violence also lends itself to a pretentious use in political propaganda to justify military interventions, in the context of the debate on "justified war".[37] Significant in this regard is the case of Phlius, where the pro-Spartan exiles and the Spartans themselves invoke the *bia* and the *hybris* of the Phliasian democrats to justify their attack against the city. Indeed, in the destiny of states (as in the case of Athens, now defeated in the Peloponnesian war and with the thought turned to the small towns which were victims of its arrogance) can be recognized the divine punishment of violence exercised by the stronger again the weaker.[38]

Opposed to *nomos* and to the virtues of moderation and balance in the exercise of power (in particular to *sophrosyne*), violence is part of the forms of degeneration of human and political relations and constitutes a factor with strongly negative consequences on the relationship between rulers and ruled, between hegemonic states and subjugated states, without however even benefiting those who practise it. In fact, it is considered by Xenophon not only illegitimate, but also ineffective;[39] to achieve the desired results it is better to turn to virtues such as respect for legality and self-control, capable of arousing consensus. The strong coherence between the moral perspective and the political perspective that is highlighted by the analysis conducted here on the subject of violence in the complex of Xenophon's work,[40] from the *Hellenica* to the Socratic works and to the various treatises, constitutes a contribution to the affirmation of a new political and cultural climate: while it shows that it completely overcomes the sophistical theorizing of the right of the strongest in the interpretation of political relations, it advocates adherence to new values in the coexistence of Greeks on both an internal and an international level.[41]

---

37 Sordi, 2001; Giovannini, 2007, 137–218; Bertoli, 2009, 7–30.
38 Sordi, 1950, 341; Rood, 2004, 353, Hau, 2016, 222.
39 Violence is after all considered useless also in the treatment of animals, such as horses (*Eq.* 9.5 and 9.7).
40 In line with what is highlighted by Pownall, 2004, 65–112; see Ferrario, 2017, 57–83, especially 79–82.
41 Kane, 1990, 1–11.

Bibliography

Azoulay, V. (2004), *Xénophon et les grâces du pouvoir. De la charis au charisme*, Paris.
Baragnawath, E. (2012), "A Noble Alliance: Herodotus, Thucydides, and Xenophon's Procles" in: *Thucydides and Herodotus*, E. Foster/D. Lateiner (eds), Oxford, 316–344.
Baragnawath, E. (2017), "The Character and Function of Speeches in Xenophon" in: *The Cambridge Companion to Xenophon*, M.A. Flower (ed.), Cambridge, 279–297.
Bearzot, C. (2004), *Federalismo e autonomia nelle Elleniche di Senofonte*, Milano.
Bertoli, M. (2009), "La "guerra giusta" in Tucidide: argomenti giuridici, argomenti religiosi" in: *Aevum* 83, 7–30.
Brillante, C. (1998), "*Charis, bia* e il tema della reciprocità amorosa" in: *QUCC* 59, 7–34.
Buckler, J. (1982), "Xenophon's Speeches and the Theban Hegemony" in: *Athenaeum* 60, 180–204.
Buxton, R.F. (2017), "Xenophon on Leadership: Commanders as Friends" in: *The Cambridge Companion to Xenophon*, M.A. Flower (ed.), Cambridge, 323–337.
Buxton, R.F. (ed.) (2016), *Aspects of Leadership in Xenophon* (Histos Suppl. 5), Newcastle upon Tyne.
Chantraine, P. (1968), *Dictionnaire étymologique de la langue grecque*, Paris.
D'Huys, V. (1987), "How to Describe Violence in Historical Narrative. Reflections of the Ancient Greek Historians and Their Ancient Critics" in: *AncSoc* 18, 209–250.
Dillery, J. (1995), *Xenophon and the History of His Times*, London.
Dorion, L.A./Bandini, M. (eds) (2000–2011), *Xénophon, Mémorables*, I–II, 1–2, Paris.
Ferrario, S.B. (2014), *Historical Agency and the 'Great Man' in Classical Greece*, Cambridge.
Ferrario, S.B. (2017), "Xenophon and Greek Political Thought" in: *The Cambridge Companion to Xenophon*, M.A. Flower (ed.), Cambridge, 57–83.
Fisher, N. (1992), *Hybris. A Study in the Values of Honour and Shame in Ancient Greece*, Warminster.
Fisher, N. (2000), "*Hybris*, Revenge and *Stasis* in the Greek City-States" in: *War and Violence in Ancient Greece*, H. van Wees (ed.), London/Swansea, 83–123.
Flower, M.A. (ed.) (2017), *The Cambridge Companion to Xenophon*, Cambridge.
Fontana, F. (2014), *Tra autonomia locale e dinamiche regionali. Storia di Fliunte dall'VIII al IV secolo a.C.*, Bari.
Gauthier, P. (1976), *Un commentaire historique des Poroi de Xénophon*, Paris.
Giovannini, A. (2007), *Les relations entre États dans la Grèce antique du temps d'Homère à l'intervention romaine, ca. 700-200 av. J.-C.*, Stuttgart.
Gray, V. (1989), *The Character of Xenophon's* Hellenica, Baltimore.
Gray, V. (2011), *Xenophon's Mirror of Princes: Reading Reflections*, Oxford.
Harris, E.M. (2004=2006), "Did Rape Exist in Classical Athens? Further Reflections on the Laws about Sexual Violence" in: *Dike* 7, 41–83 (= *Democracy and the Rule of Law,* New York, 97–332).
Hau, L. (2016), *Moral History from Herodotus to Diodorus Siculus*, Edinburgh.
Higgins, W.E. (1977), *Xenophon the Athenian. The Problem of the Individual and the Society of the Polis*, Albany.
Huß, B. (1999), *Xenophons Symposion. Ein Kommentar,* Stuttgart/Leipzig.
Hutchinson, G. (2000), *Xenophon and the Art of Command*, London/Pennsylvania.
Lendle, O. (1995), *Kommentar zu Xenophons* Anabasis, Darmstadt.

Lipka, M. (2002), *Xenophon's Spartan Constitution. Introduction, Text, Commentary*, Berlin/New York.
Lintott, A. (1982), *Violence, civil strife and revolution in the classical city, 750–330 BC*, London/Canberra.
Marincola, J. (2010), "The Rhetoric of History: Allusion, Intertextuality, and Exemplarity in Historiographical Speeches" in: *Stimmen der Geschichte: Funktionen von Reden in der Antiken Historiographie*, D. Pausch (ed.), Berlin/New York, 259–289.
Phillips, D.D. (2016), "Xenophon & the Muleteer: Hubris, Retaliation, and the Purposes of Shame" in: *The Topography of Violence in the Greco-Roman World*, W. Riess/G.G. Fagan (eds), 19–59.
Pontier, P. (2001), "Place et fonction du discours dans l'oeuvre de Xénophon" in: *REA* 103, 395–408.
Pontier, P. (2006), *Trouble et ordre chez Platon et Xénophon*, Paris.
Pontier, P. (2013), "L'utilisation de l'histoire dans les discours politiques de Xénophon, de Marathon à Platées" in: *DHA* Suppl. 8, 165–187.
Pownall, F. (2004), *Lessons from the Past. The Moral Use of History in Fourth-Century Prose*, Ann Arbor.
Rapp, H. (1988), "The Notion of Justice in Xenophon's *Cyropaedia*" in: *Philosophy of Law in the History of Human Thought, IVR12th World Congress*, S. Panou et al. (eds), Athens, 57–47.
Riedinger, J.-C. (1991), *Étude sur les* Helléniques. *Xénophon et l'histoire*, Paris.
Rood, T. (2004), "Xenophon and Diodorus: Continuing Thucydides" in: *Xenophon and His World. Papers from a Conference Held in Liverpool in July 1999* (Historia Einzelschriften, 172), C.J. Tuplin (ed.), Stuttgart, 314–395.
Sordi, M. (1950, 1951), "I caratteri dell'opera storiografica di Senofonte nelle *Elleniche*" in: *Athenaeum* 28, 3–53 and 29, 273–348.
Sordi, M. (ed.) (2001), *Il pensiero sulla guerra nel mondo antico* (CISA, 27), Milano.
Tamiolaki, M. (2013), "Emotions and Historical Representation in Xenophon's *Hellenika*" in: *Unveiling Emotions II. Emotions in Greece and Rome: Texts, Images, Material Culture*, A. Chaniotis/P. Ducrey (eds), Stuttgart, 15–53.
Tamiolaki, M. (2014), "A l'ombre de Thucydide ? Les discours des *Helléniques* et l'influence thucydidéenne" in: *Xénophon et la rhétorique*, P. Pontier (ed.), Paris, 121–137.
Tuplin, C.J. (1993), *The Failings of Empire. A Reading of Xenophon* Hellenica 2.3.11–7.5.27 (Historia Einzelschriften, 76), Stuttgart.
Winter, J. (2016), "Reinterpreting Xenophon's Speeches: Euphron's Killer to the Theban Council (*Hellenica* 7.3.7–11)" in: *Auctor. A Journal for Postgraduates in Classics* 1, 2–14.

Paolo A. Tuci
"*Apronoētos Orgē*": the Role of Anger in Xenophon's Vision of History

1 Introduction

Within a study globally dealing with the subject of violence in Xenophon, a special place should be devoted to the topic of ὀργή, which is usually translated as "anger".[1] In Thucydides this term is very important, because it is strongly characterised by its opposition to γνώμη and thus, even before assuming the meaning of anger, it denotes a natural impulse, an altered state of mind that restricts the use of reason and may lead to the performance of irrational deeds.[2] Also in Xenophon, continuator of Thucydides, this term should be an interesting key to better understanding the author's mind and his value system.

The present paper aims at exploring what is, according to Xenophon, the role played by ὀργή in history. As a consequence, it is natural that, also given the prescribed spatial limits, this paper will be focused mainly (but not exclusively) on the *Hellenica*, because that is the more strictly historical work composed by Xenophon. Nevertheless, the last paragraph will broaden the enquiry to the other works of Xenophon, in order to check whether the framework provided by the *Hellenica* can be confirmed or not. More precisely, the purpose of the survey is to investigate whether anger generates violent actions, what are the causes and the

---

[1] In recent years much attention has been drawn to emotions in the ancient world: see e.g. both books (Konstan, 2006) and collections of papers (Chaniotis, 2012, Chaniotis/Ducrey, 2013, and Cairns/Nelis 2017), which however do not take into consideration Xenophon (with the exception of Tamiolaki, 2013 in Chaniotis/Ducrey, 2013). Further bibliography in Zaccarini, 2018, 473 n. 2. Concerning the wide bibliography about anger in ancient Greek world, see mainly: Harris, 2001 (about the ideology of anger control); Braund-Most, 2004 (with papers about anger in various contexts); Konstan, 2006, 41–76 (mainly an analysis of Aristotle's theory of anger, with a partition of this emotion in three classes: contempt, arrogance and arrogant abuse, pp. 45–46); see also the Introduction of A. Kapellos in this book; Kalimtzis, 2012 (a study of the literary, cultural and philosophical development of the nature of anger); see also Ludwig, 2009, 298–301. Concerning violence, it is worth mentioning Riess, 2012, who also deals with anger (115–119, in a forensic context; 254–260 and 319–328 in Greek comedy), but does not devote attention to Xenophon.
[2] For the opposition between ὀργή and γνώμη in Thucydides see the famous 2.65.1 but also 2.22.1; 2.59.3; 2.65.3–4, 8; 3.42.1. See Müri, 1947, 262–264, 274–275; Huart, 1968, 50–57, 154–162; Fantasia, 2003, 327, 455; Tsamakis, 2006, 168 n. 22; Wohl, 2017, 449–452.

https://doi.org/10.1515/9783110671469-003

consequences of this emotion and which are the subjects more vulnerable to it. Besides, it will be particularly significant to evaluate what is Xenophon's historical and moral point of view on ὀργή: from the historical point of view, what the consequences of actions are, produced under the influence of anger and, from the moral point of view, whether Xenophon has a positive or negative opinion on it.

In the *Hellenica* the noun ὀργή and the verb ὀργίζομαι appear slightly more than twenty times, mainly concentrated in the third and fifth books.[3] The core passage is 5.3.7, in which Xenophon expresses his opinion about anger, using these terms four times: it is a theoretical consideration, following the narration of Teleutias' death, which was due precisely to a decision made on a wave of anger. In 381, during the war between Sparta and Olynthus, Teleutias, angry (ὀργισθείς) because the Olynthian horsemen had killed more than a hundred Spartans, rapidly (ταχύ) led his hoplites against the enemy, but in the battle that followed he was defeated and killed (5.3.5–6). After this episode, Xenophon observes (5.3.7):

> Now I claim that men can learn (παιδεύεσθαι) from such experiences, and they can learn especially that it is not right to punish anyone in anger (ὀργῇ κολάζειν) – even a slave, since masters who are angry (ὀργιζόμενοι) often themselves suffer greater evils (μείζω κακά) than they inflict on their servants. And it is a complete and utter mistake to attack an enemy with anger rather than with judgment (τὸ μετ᾽ ὀργῆς ἀλλὰ μὴ γνώμῃ προσφέρεσθαι ὅλον ἁμάρτημα). For anger acts without foresight (ἡ μὲν γὰρ ὀργὴ ἀπρονόητον), whereas judgment (ἡ δὲ γνώμη) has in view a way to harm one's enemy without suffering any hurt from him in return.[4]

In this important passage, the lexical field of ὀργή occurs several times and it is expressly opposed to γνώμη. Xenophon remarks that anger is ἀπρονόητος, a crucial adjective, as will be shown, but not easy to translate: it means "improvident", in the sense that it leads to action without πρόνοια, without foresight, not considering consequences beforehand. Moreover the author, having a clearly didactic purpose, observes that no action should be driven by anger, because otherwise major κακά will arise, and that his audience should learn (παιδεύω) from what happened to Teleutias. It is interesting that previously the same Teleutias was praised by Xenophon, because he was greatly appreciated by his soldiers (5.1.3–

---

[3] For a very brief introduction to these passages see Gish, 2012, 175 n. 24; Tamiolaki, 2013, 42 n. 162.
[4] The translations of the passages from the *Hellenica* are by Marincola, 2009.

4):⁵ this element further emphasizes the fact that even a single moment of blurring of reason could cause fatal consequences. This case is therefore different from that of Phoebidas, who similarly died in a hazardous assault (5.4.43–45), but who was usually considered a man neither λογιστικός nor φρόνιμος (5.2.28); conversely, Teleutias in other circumstances is praised because he attempted a feat which may seem to have been undertaken ἀφρόνως, but actually was the result of a serious ἀναλογισμός, as proven by the successful outcome of his deed (5.1.19–24). Xenophon, who is a subtle and sensitive portrait-painter, is thus suggesting that irrational passions have to be avoided in key decision-making moments. Within this framework, *Hell.* 5.3.7 is particularly relevant because it both concerns a case in which ὀργή produces a violent action and provides Xenophon's theoretical perspective on the (bad) consequences of anger: decisions taken under the influence of ὀργή are dangerous because the mind is blurred by an irrational passion.⁶

Now we must assess whether the theoretical evaluation of 5.3.7 can be confirmed by the analysis of other cases of ὀργή in passages in the *Hellenica* (and, eventually, in other works). In this survey I shall separate cases of anger experienced by individuals and by communities.

2 Ὀργή of individuals

In addition to Teleutias, feelings of anger are attributed to five individuals, listed below.

Before the battle of Arginusae, Callicratidas went to Cyrus in order to ask him for money to pay his forces, but he was told to wait two days: Callicratidas, "annoyed (ἀχθεσθείς) by the delay and angered (ὀργισθείς) by his unsuccessful visits to Cyrus, said that the Greeks were most wretched, since they flattered barbarians for the sake of money and that [...] he would, to the extent he was able, attempt to reconcile Athenians and Spartans" (1.6.7). In this case, anger does not produce a violent action, but only an intention that afterwards was not implemented: in

---

5 On these shifting viewpoints in Xenophon's *Hellenica*, see for example Azoulay, 2004, 17 n. 38. On Xenophon's remark in *Hell.* 5.3.1 about Teleutias, see also Tuci, 2010, 81–82.
6 Concerning Xen.*Hell.* 5.3.7 and the case of Teleutias' death, see: Sordi, 1950, 19; Higgins, 1977, 113; Gray, 1989, 132–133; Riedinger, 1991, 239–240; Tuplin, 1993, 46, 93–94; Dillery, 1995, 219–220; Harris, 2001, 319; Azoulay, 2004, 209 n. 188; Konstan, 2004, 119; Pizzone, 2004, 312–313 (cf. 307–324); Konstan, 2006, 70; Gray, 2010, 558; Tamiolaki, 2012, 571–572; Tamiolaki, 2013, 44–45; Hau, 2016, 220; Pelling, 2017, 255; Buxton, 2017, 335. See also the paper of E. Foster in this book.

fact, shortly after, Callicratidas assaulted the pro-Athenian city of Methymna (1.6.13) and led the Spartans in the battle of Arginusae against the Athenian fleet (1.6.28). Thus ὀργή produces an irrational reaction on the spot, but then it has no specific consequences in terms of actual violence.[7]

An example of self-control is that of Pausanias in 403: after he arrived near the Piraeus, in order to disturb the plans of Lysander, the Athenian democrats had a minor engagement with him, but Pausanias prevailed; Xenophon comments that not even at that moment did he grow angry (οὐδ' ὣς ὠργίζετο) with the men of the Piraeus (2.4.35). The historian here is praising a commander who has a plan, i.e. to differ from Lysander, and who, in order to achieve his goal, is able to control his own emotions, even the anger prompted by the fact that he had to fight against those whom he was indirectly going to support. Ὀργή in itself would have produced a violent reaction against the men of the Piraeus, blurring Pausanias' mind and diverting him from his plan, but he was able to control himself and to act according to reason and not to ὀργή.[8]

In 399, since the commander of Cebren, unlike other cities in Asia Minor, refused to admit Dercylidas within the walls, the latter, enraged (ὀργιζόμενος), prepared to attack the fortress; Dercylidas' emotional reaction was tempered by his religious devoutness and he waited for favourable sacrifices (3.1.17); instead, Athenadas, an otherwise unknown Sicyonian commander, assuming that Dercylidas was wasting time, tried a sortie in order to interrupt the water supply to the Cebrenians, but was driven back and killed. Apparently, while Athenadas was subtle but impulsive, Dercylidas, previously marked by the historian as μάλα μηχανητικός (3.1.8), controlled his emotions and had a religious sense stronger than his temporary annoyance.[9]

Another case of ὀργή concerns the Persian satrap Pharnabazus, who, during the Corinthian War, having failed to subjugate the cities of Abydos and Sestos, was angered (ὀργιζόμενος) with the Spartans because of what he had suffered at

---

[7] Higgins, 1977, 11; Gray, 1989, 81–83; Krentz, 1989, 147; Dillery, 1995, 118; Azoulay, 2004, 210. See for example the characterization of Callicratidas' temper in Diod. 13.76.2: he was a young man, very just and straightforward in character, without craftiness and experience of foreign peoples' habits; the kind of man that flares up easily.
[8] Concerning self-control, see Harris, 2001. Moreover, it should be noted that, according to Xenophon (*Hell.* 2.4.32), on this occasion clashes with the enemies made him irritated, since his intervention in Athens was actually in favour of the men of the Piraeus: the verb used in this occasion is ἄχθομαι; this remark suggests that naturally he experienced emotions, but he was to some extent able to control them in order to accomplish a plan.
[9] Tuplin, 1993, 215; Dillery, 1995, 105; Krentz, 1995, 165; Hau, 2016, 221–222, 226; Marincola, 2017, 117.

their hands, and desired above all things (περὶ παντός) to reach their country and take there what vengeance he could (τιμωρήσασθαι ὅτι δύναιτο) (4.8.6). Consequently, Pharnabazus in the next spring sailed to Melos, making it his base to move εἰς τὴν Λακεδαίμονα; then he reached Pherae (in Messenia), Cythera and Corinth, where he exhorted the allies to carry on the war against Sparta and left them all the money he had with him (7-8). The "irrational" part of his purpose was "ἐλθεῖν εἰς τὴν χώραν αὐτῶν" if we understand χώρα in the strict sense of Laconia, but nevertheless Pharnabazus actually reached the Peloponnese: the Persian was full of anger and this is proved by the phrase "περὶ παντός" used to stress how much he sought revenge, but his plan seems anyway to have been meditated and not reckless.[10]

The historical figure to whom ὀργή is most frequently attributed is Agesilaus. While in 396 he was sacrificing at Aulis before leaving for Asia Minor, Theban horsemen interrupted him and threw away from the altar whatever remained; Agesilaus called the gods to witness and, full of anger (ὀργιζόμενος), sailed away (3.4.4). In this case ὀργή is only an instinctive reflex, connected not only with Agesilaus' deep religiosity but also with political considerations (the Thebans' act was aimed at combating Agesilaus' attempt to present himself as a second Agamemnon); but, anyhow, the ὀργή produced no concrete or violent reactions.[11]

In the next passage, anger is attributed to Agesilaus by Tissaphernes, who had violated the oath of peace previously sworn with him: Tissaphernes assumed that Agesilaus was angry (ὀργίζεσθαι) with him and, thus, that he would plan to march against his own residence in Caria (3.4.12). Probably Agesilaus was actually upset, but again he could control his emotions and use this occasion to his advantage, heading in the opposite direction and unexpectedly attacking Phrygia. While Tissaphernes thought that Agesilaus would act in blindness from rage, he behaved with cleverness and cunning.[12]

The third case involves the citizens of Phlius, who, since Agesilaus was besieging their city, in 379 asked him for permission to send an embassy to Sparta for capitulation: Agesilaus, angered (ὀργισθείς) at being treated as if he did not

---

10 Buckler, 2003, 132–136.
11 References to this episode are also in Xen.Hell. 3.5.5 (see below, § 3), 7.1.34 and Plut.Lys. 27.3 (not in Plut.Ag. 6.6). See Dillery, 1995, 23, 107, 116; Krentz, 1995, 184; Ferrario, 2012, 345–346; Hau, 2016, 226–227; Ferrario, 2017, 75 (who characterizes Agesilaus as "immoderate and impetuous", quoting also Hell. 4.5.6, 4.5.10; from these passages this nature is not apparent to me).
12 Cf. also Xen.Ag. 1.14–17, where the verb ὀργίζομαι also occurs, and Plut.Ag. 9.1–3, who plainly speaks about deception: it was obviously a well-thought-out plan, not an irrational decision driven by rage. See Cartledge, 1987, 231; Hamilton, 1991, 96; Krentz, 1995, 187; Hutchinson, 2000, 149–150.

have full powers, allowed the embassy but also sent his friends to Sparta in order to control the situation (5.3.24). Given that the Spartans entrusted all decisions about Phlius to Agesilaus (§ 25), once more he appears as a good leader: although annoyed, he reacts cleverly obtaining exactly what he wanted.[13]

Lastly, when, after the peace of Athens (371/70), the Mantineians wanted to build a wall around their city, the Spartans sent Agesilaus as an ambassador: they refused not only to summon the assembly, inviting him to speak directly to the ἄρχοντες, but also to interrupt the construction of the wall. Xenophon observes that "although he was angry (ὀργιζόμενος), it did not seem possible to send an army against Mantineia, because the peace had been agreed to on the assumption of autonomy for all cities" (6.5.5). Albeit angry, Agesilaus remains able to reason.[14]

Some concluding remarks. In the passages above, ὀργή is aroused mainly by Greek communities, while only in two cases is it unambiguously aroused by individuals (the ὀργή of Callicratidas is due to Cyrus and that of Agesilaus is against Tissaphernes).[15] Besides, anger is experienced by six individuals, one Persian and five Greeks, all Spartans: this is in itself a rather curious fact. The man to whom ὀργή is most frequently attributed is Agesilaus, but there is no need to infer from this that Xenophon wanted to depict him as particularly irascible. Perhaps this could depend on the good level of knowledge that he had of him and of the personal sphere of his emotions. Having said that, the passages considered show that Xenophon depicts Agesilaus as a wise commander;[16] he is not immune to anger, and in particular to a "just" anger because provoked by impious acts, treachery and the like, but in none of the four cases his reaction is driven by wrath.[17] Two different types of situation may be distinguished: in the first and the last passages, he only has to swallow a bitter pill, and notably in the last one he

---

[13] Hamilton, 1991, 133–134; Tuplin, 1993, 91–93 (who wonders whether his anger is due to the affront to his *amour propre* or to fear that other Spartans could manage the business not in accordance with his plans); Dillery, 1995, 211, 220; Ferrario, 2012, 352–353.

[14] Nielsen, 2002, 475.

[15] Ὀργή against communities: the Olynthians arouse the ὀργή of Teleutias; the Athenians that of Pausanias; the Spartans that of Pharnabazus; the Phliasians and Mantineians that of Agesilaus. In 3.4.4 it is not completely apparent if Agesilaus' ὀργή is directed against the Thebans or Theban boetarchs or the Theban cavalry; and in 3.1.17 whether Dercylidas' ὀργή is against the commander of Cebren or all the citizens.

[16] This is not the place to study Agesilaus' image in Xenophon or to provide an exhaustive bibliography on this issue. See Ferrario, 2012, 344–353 and Ferrario, 2014, 240–254.

[17] Tamiolaki 2012, 571 n. 32 distinguishes cases in which Agesilaus' wrath is "rather justified" (3.4.4, 3.4.12) and others in which it "derives from a personal motive and from his dissatisfaction that his political plans meet with some obstacles" (5.3.24, 6.5.5).

acts with lucid realism, being conscious that he must comply with the principle of αὐτονομία; in the other two cases, his behaviour is not only lucid and rational, but also smart and this enables him to achieve his goal.

Only in two of the passages considered the ὀργή provoked a violent conduct, i.e. a military attack: in those of Teleutias and of Pharnabazus, respectively a Spartan and the only non-Greek on the list. But while in the latter case the satrap retained the use of reason, since he quickly abandoned the Peloponnese when he realized that to remain could be dangerous for several reasons (4.8.7), in the former Teleutias is totally dominated by an irrational anger. It is meaningful that Xenophon inserts his theoretical observation on the consequences of ὀργή in the only case in which the absence of self-control leads to a fatal result. In the other instances, the ὀργή does not generate a violent reaction. Among these, the cases in which self-control is particularly evident are significant: Pausanias, Dercylidas and Agesilaus (at least in the cases concerning Tissaphernes and the Phliasians) were able to constrain their emotions and to use their reason to achieve their goal. Therefore the overall pattern emerging from this paragraph is completely consistent with the theoretical consideration of Xenophon in 5.3.7.

3 Ὀργή of communities

Feelings of anger are ascribed also to some communities (or, at least, they are not assigned to specific individuals).[18] During his navigation in the eastern Aegean Sea, Thrasybulus brought some cities to the Athenian side, while he left the others to the plundering of his soldiers in order to raise money to pay them. When he arrived at Aspendus, the citizens gave him the money required, but his soldiers anyway pillaged the country: the Aspendians, angered (ὀργισθέντες), attacked the Athenian general at night and slaughtered him in his tent (4.8.30). In this case we undoubtedly face a violent reaction prompted by anger: the rage of the Aspendians was somewhat well-founded, since they paid what was requested, but their reaction was emotional and exaggerated. Xenophon does not explicitly say that Thrasybulus was unaware of the sack (which seems to be implied by Diodorus in 14.99.4, who presents it as a private initiative of τινὲς τῶν στρατιωτῶν), but

---

[18] Xen.Hell. 7.4.37 (οὐδεὶς γὰρ οὐδενὶ ὠργίζετο), about mutual rage between the Arcadians and the Thebans, will not be considered, because, being extremely generic, it is not significant.

anyway the consequence of the ὀργή is something considered by him as extremely serious and unfortunate, i.e. the death of a μάλα δοκῶν ἀνὴρ ἀγαθός.[19]

Years later, the Athenians were asked for help by the Thebans: being angry (ὀργιζόμενοι) with the Spartans because of Sphodrias' action, they sent προθύμως against the Peloponnese a fleet of sixty vessels with the *strategos* Timotheus (5.4.63). However, this action was not only well considered, because it opened a new field of conflict, diverting the Spartans from their imperialistic activities, but also well-conducted, since Timotheus, thanks to his mildness in the region of Corcyra, won the favour of the population and then defeated the Spartans at Alyzeia (64–65). Therefore his ὀργή did not blind Timotheus nor prevent him from conducting the military operations wisely.[20]

The Argives as well felt ὀργή, because of the loyalty of the Phliasians towards the Spartans. This happened not long after Leuctra, when conversely many allies deserted Sparta: the Argives, angry (ὀργιζόμενοι) at the loyalty of the Phliasians to the Spartans, invaded in full force and ravaged the territory of Phlius, but the Phliasians did not yield even on that occasion (7.2.4). The sympathy of Xenophon is clearly with the Phliasians: in § 1 he asserts that "if a small city has accomplished many fine deeds, it is even more fitting to make them known",[21] and in § 4 he repeatedly emphasises their loyalty even in hard circumstances and the fact that their small force defeated the Argives' larger army. Conversely, the Argives are negatively marked, for their shameful defeat, for the fact that they despise loyalty and that they act ὀργιζόμενοι. This ὀργή leads to an almost disproportionate violence, since the Argives invaded the small territory of Phlius πανδημεί.[22] In the following year the hatred of the Argives and also of the Arcadians against the Phliasians recurs, and Xenophon observes that it is motivated not only by the fact that they ὠργίζοντο αὐτοῖς, but also because the Phliasian territory lays between Argos and Arcadia (7.2.10).

While ὀργή is attributed only once to the Aspendians, the Athenians and the Argives, it recurs on two other occasions for the Spartans (globally four occurrences), on which they are angry with the Eleians and the Thebans. In 3.2.21–23, concerning the war between the Spartans and the Eleians, Xenophon lists the

---

19 Tuplin, 1993, 80–82; Dillery, 1995, 197; Pownall, 2004, 78. I am aware of the fact that Xenophon's judgment on Thrasybulus is not undisputed (see e.g. Hobden/Tuplin, 2012, 36 and Tamiolaki, 2012, 568–569), but an interpretation of it in a negative way seems to me unlikely and inconsistent with the global characterisation of Thrasybulus in *Hellenica* (see e.g. Sordi, 2000, 182–191 and Sordi, 2011, 16–17).
20 On Sphodrias' coup see Parker, 2007, 13–33.
21 Tuci, 2010, 79–81.
22 Gray 1989, 166; Dillery, 1995, 131; Flower, 2017, 307.

reasons for which the former "had long been angry" (πάλαι ὀργιζόμενοι) with the latter: (I) the Eleians had made an alliance with the Athenians, the Argives, and the Mantineians; (II) they had forbidden them from taking part in the Olympian games; (III) they had whipped the Spartan elder Lichas in the stadium; and (IV) they had prohibited King Agis from praying for a victory in war (§§ 21–22). "Angered by all these affronts (ἐκ τούτων οὖν πάντων ὀργιζομένοις), the ephors and the assembly resolved to teach the Eleians a lesson in how to behave moderately" (§ 23). Then Agis sent envoys to the Eleians in order to announce that they should ἀφιέναι τὰς περιοικίδας πόλεις αὐτονόμους and, on their refusal, mobilized the army and ravaged their land. This is an example of an extremely motivated and almost "rational" ὀργή (which is nearly an oxymoron), which, moreover, resulted in violence only after diplomatic solutions were attempted. Obviously in this case Xenophon seems clearly pro-Spartan: on the one side, he makes an effort to rationalize the Spartan reasons, justifying them to his audience; on the other side, it should not be forgotten that, naturally, during Spartan hegemony, diplomacy represents another sort of violence. However, we face a case of ὀργή justified by the historian.[23]

Not much different is the case of 3.5.5. At the beginning of the Corinthian War, the Phocians sent an embassy to get help against the Locrians and the Thebans from the Spartans: the latter are said to be glad to seize a pretext (ἄσμενοι ἔλαβον πρόφασιν) for undertaking a campaign against the Thebans, since they were πάλαι ὀργιζόμενοι with them.[24] Here occurs the same phrase (πάλαι ὀργιζόμενοι) that we find in 3.2.21, in order to remark that anger has ancient roots. Besides here as well Xenophon provides a list of the reasons by which ὀργή was caused: (I) the Thebans at Decelea claimed Apollo's tenth; (II) they refused to follow the Spartans against the Piraeus; (III) they persuaded the Corinthians not to

---

23 Higgins, 1977, 112–113; Tuplin, 1993, 64; Pownall, 2004, 95.
24 The Phocian embassy to Sparta is mentioned also in Hell.Oxy. 18.4 and Paus. 3.9.10, with less details and some differences (e.g. in Xenophon and Pausanias the Thebans invaded Phocis before the Phocians sent the embassy to Sparta, while in Hell.Oxy. after it). In Hell.Oxy. it is interesting that the Spartans considered the Phocians' complaints unworthy of belief: this does not contradict Xenophon and actually it is congruent with the fact that he presents the Spartans as happy to obtain an excuse to march against the Thebans (the adjective ἄσμενος is used by both sources, but in different contexts). Pausanias closely recalls Xenophon, mentioning also the Aulis affair; however, he associates the Spartans' ὀργή not with the Thebans, but with the Athenians (3.9.11). On this episode see Buckler, 2004, 397–411, especially 407. See also Riedinger, 1991, 126–128; Tuplin, 1993, 63–64; Krentz, 1995, 195, 197 (according to whom Xenophon is making this situation parallel with that of the Eleian war cf. 3.2.21–31); Ferrario, 2012, 345–346; Schepens, 2012, 213–241.

join in that campaign; (IV) they had prevented Agesilaus from sacrificing at Aulis; and (V) they did not join him for the campaign in Asia. Therefore the Spartans reasoned (ἐλογίζοντο) that it was the right time to lead an army against them and to stop their insolent behaviour; therefore they mobilized the army and sent Lysander to Haliartus. In this case, many features already encountered in the former episode recur: not only the phrase πάλαι ὀργιζόμενοι, but also the fact that Xenophon seems very justificatory towards the Spartans, and that we are facing again an example of "rational" ὀργή; in the present case, this last aspect is even more marked, because the historian uses the verb λογίζομαι, i.e. to calculate, which leads to the rational sphere of behaviour, quite opposite to that of ὀργή. Xenophon in both these episodes seems to be suggesting to his audience that the Spartans showed great patience and waited long before reacting violently.

The exact situation of 3.5.5 is echoed in the speech of the Theban envoy at Athens in 395, but obviously from a different point of view. He says: "When the Spartans called on us to march with them against the Piraeus, then our whole city voted to refuse the Spartan demand to march out with them. So, then, since it is not least on your account that the Spartans are angry with us (ὀργιζομένων ἡμῖν τῶν Λακεδαιμονίων), we consider it just for you to assist our city now" (3.5.8).[25] What is interesting is that the reason for the Spartan anger alleged by the Thebans is quite different from the catalogue of reasons previously listed by Xenophon: obviously they are both tendentious, as the historian in accounting for Spartan behaviour, and the anonymous Theban in presenting an actual benefit made in favour of the Athenians as the only ground for the Spartans' ὀργή.

In conclusion, the ὀργή of communities is directed mainly against Greek communities, while only in one case it is directed against one individual, Thrasybulus, "guilty" for having let his army ravage the country of the Aspendians. Four are communities for which it is said that, at least once, they felt ὀργή, among which the most represented are the Spartans, perhaps again because Xenophon had better knowledge of what moved their emotions.

Under some aspects, the overall picture is similar to what emerged from the analysis of individuals' ὀργή. For example, we find judgments implicitly negative by Xenophon: this occurs in the cases of the ὀργή which caused the death of Thrasybulus, ἀνὴρ ἀγαθός, and which led the Argives against the little city of Phlius, loyal to Sparta (in both circumstances Xenophon's evaluation is not completely "neutral", given his pro-Thrasybulean and pro-Phliasian attitude). On the other side, at least three new data emerge: the aspect of violence is more marked, given

---

[25] See Krentz, 1995, 198–199; Buckler, 2003, 409. Cf. Gray, 1989, 107–112, Rood, 2012, 80–85; Schepens, 2012, 228.

that in all cases considered the ὀργή generates a military action; besides, we have two examples, both concerning Sparta, of ὀργή which seems almost "rational", in the sense that, whilst still being emotional, it is (or is presented by the historian as) well-grounded; lastly, the component of political propaganda, mostly pro-Spartan, is not marginal, since Xenophon on the one side stresses the reasons for the Spartans' actions, thus justifying them, and on the other seems to show the bad faith of the Thebans.

4 Ὀργή in *Hellenica* and in other Xenophon's works

My intention in this paper was to provide not a comprehensive study of anger in Xenophon, but mainly a survey concerning his opinion about the role played by ὀργή in history (the reason why the study has been focused so far on Xenophon's most "historical" work, the *Hellenica*). The enquiry has shown that Xenophon traces two different frameworks: the ὀργή experienced by individuals and the ὀργή of communities. While in the former case the man, if (portrayed as) valiant, can take control over his irrational emotions, in the latter, when Xenophon (being biased?) does not justify the ὀργή as well-grounded, it is harder for communities to restrain this emotion and usually this emotion leads to violence, sometimes also in terms of military attacks. A comparison between the passage with which we started (*Hell.* 5.3.7) and the other occurrences of the terms ὀργή/ὀργίζομαι suggests that, according to the *Hellenica*, generally speaking, ὀργή is a negative emotion in so far as it leads men to act irrationally; it has to be restrained and, if not, it leads to serious consequences. Given this framework, Xenophon seems to imply both that individuals can control their emotions better than groups, and that ὀργή may even be an understandable and justifiable reaction to something wrong. In the latter case, ὀργή would be not negative in itself, but only if it provoked a well-thought-out response and not an emotional one. Clearly, the evaluation of what is right or wrong may be highly discretionary, depending on author's bias; anyhow, it emerges that a certain amount of emotional control is essential.

Xenophon's evaluation of ὀργή as an irrational impulse towards anger that prevents men from acting rationally is very close to Thucydides'. Besides, the two historians share also the opposition between ὀργή and γνώμη (i.e. a well-considered reasoning), an opposition which is more marked in Thucydides, but which occurs once in Xenophon as well, indeed in the crucial theoretical passage of

5.3.7.[26] Also the idea that single individuals seem able to control their emotions better than groups recalls closely Thucydides' thought.[27] Some aspects, however, distinguish Xenophon from Thucydides. Firstly, the notion of ὀργή seems less important in Xenophon, since he counts about twenty occurrences of the substantive and the verb, compared to the about fifty of Thucydides.[28] Secondly, the author of the *Hellenica* employs these terms more in military than, as Thucydides, in political contexts; besides, Xenophon, though considering ὀργή as basically negative, suggests that it may be "acceptable" when caused by well-founded reasons and that in these cases it is not completely negative if it does not blur the ability to react reasonably. But, despite these differences, there is a certain degree of consonance between Thucydides and his continuator.

At this point, we may wonder whether the results achieved concerning ὀργή in the *Hellenica* could be valid more generally if we refer to anger in Xenophon's works. The enquiry could be broadened in two directions, by extending the survey to other Greek terms related to anger and to other works of Xenophon. The first possible extension actually seems not to be very relevant. In fact, a number of synonyms should be taken into account, such as the nouns θυμός, χόλος, μῆνις, though mainly poetic, and the verbs μαίνω and ἄχθομαι,[29] or even the opposite terms related to the semantic field of wisdom, restraint and moderation.[30] Nevertheless, these enquiries, even if systematically conducted, not only would make this paper exceed the prescribed spatial limit, but above all would not lead to any complete and definitive result, because in the *Hellenica* also cases of anger in which there is no specific terminology can be found.[31]

---

26 On the importance of the term γνώμη in the *Hellenica*, see Riedinger, 1991, 227–43 (and 228 n. 3).
27 On Thucydides and crowd see Hunter, 1988, 17–30; Bruno Sunseri, 2011, 24–35; Zumbrunnen, 2017, 475–489. See also Hdt. 5.97.2, with Tuci, 2004, 251–264.
28 But admittedly it should be considered also that the text of Thucydides is much longer than Xenophon's *Hellenica*. Besides, although this does not seem particularly significant, Xenophon uses the verb more often, while Thucydides the substantive.
29 A few examples of interesting occurrences of these terms from Xenophon's *Hellenica*. Μαίνομαι: 3.4.8 (Agesilaus' fury at Lysander's successes). Ἄχθομαι: 2.4.32 (Pausanias' passion against Athenians; cf. 2.4.35, above § 2), 7.1.32 (the Thebans' and Eleians' passion against Arcadians). Cf. also μῖσος (5.2.5: Ismenias' hate against Spartans), which however cannot be considered an exact synonym of anger. The nouns θυμός, χόλος, μῆνις do not occur in Xenophon's *Hellenica*. For a list of emotions-related terms in Xenophon's *Hellenica*, see Tamiolaki, 2013, 21–22.
30 For example, Xen.*Hell*. 5.2.28, where Phoebidas is characterized as a man neither λογιστικός nor φρόνιμος (see above, § 1) hence a man who acts driven by irrational emotions.
31 See e.g. 6.2.19 for individuals (Mnasippus punishes his undisciplined soldiers striking some of them with a staff and others with spike of his spear) and 1.7 for communities (the Athenian

The second possible extension, on the contrary, could be useful. The terms ὀργή/ὀργίζομαι occur some forty times in works other than the *Hellenica* and in this case also we can distinguish instances of anger experienced by groups (rather than communities) and individuals.

As for the first typology (anger proved by groups), we find some cases of anger experienced by soldiers, obviously mainly from the *Anabasis*. E.g. in 1.2.26, soldiers are angry because one hundred of their comrades died under mysterious circumstances close to Tarsus and therefore they took revenge by sacking the city; later Cyrus arranged a meeting with Syennesis, the king of Cilicia, during which they exchanged gifts and Cyrus promised that Cilicia would not be plundered anymore and that Syennesis could take back the captured slaves. Later, in 1.5.11, soldiers were angry with the Spartan commander Clearchus, since he punished a man of Menon's squadron who had an argument with one of Clearchus' soldiers: this episode almost degenerated into an actual fight between soldiers of different squadrons, which was stopped only by the intervention of Cyrus. An example of anger experienced by a community could be mentioned as well: in *Mem.* 1.1.18, Xenophon mentions that the Athenian demos was angry with Socrates, because he tried to prevent the assembly from judging the generals of the Arginusae battle though a single vote; as it is well known, eventually the generals were sentenced to death in exactly the way that Socrates wanted to avoid.[32] In all these cases, anger is presented as something wrong that prevents men from acting rationally: the soldiers were not supposed to sack Tarsus, since there was no proof that the Cilicians had killed their comrades; Clearchus should not punish Menon's soldier, but rather judge the quarrel impartially; and the Athenians should not become angry, driven by irrational impulses, given that, according to Xenophon, Socrates was simply acting in accordance with the law.

As for individuals, Xenophon offers various examples: I will provide only a few instances, among the most interesting cases. In *Anab.* 1.5.8 we find a case of anger that was well grounded and provoked a good outcome: when Cyrus gets irritated because of soldiers' inaction in removing some chariots from slime, even Persian dignitaries cooperated for this purpose, that soon was promptly achieved. Concerning the above-mentioned Clearchus, Xenophon observes that, as previously noted, he used to punish soldiers harshly, sometimes in anger, so much that in some cases afterwards he felt sorry about this (*Anab.* 2.6.9); despite

---

assembly during the trial of the generals of the battle of Arginusae; about ὀργή in this event, see notably Gish, 2012, 161–212).

32 See also Xen.*Hell.* 1.7.15 for the role of Socrates and 1.7.34 for the death sentence. For irregularities and anomalies during the trial see Tuci, 2002, 51–85.

this harshness, his soldiers appreciated him and would choose no other to command them (2.6.11).[33] Besides, we have also examples in which anger is restrained: in a passage of *Cyropaedia*, Cyrus says to Cyaxares that, despite the unfavourable situation, he was not angry with him (*Cyrop.* 5.5.21) and this self-control produced positive effects; and in an episode presented in *Ag.*1.15 (known also from *Hell.* 3.4.12 and already described above, par. 2), Agesilaus succeeded in controlling his wrath and therefore, attacking Tissaphernes where he did not expect, subdued many cities and obtained great quantities of booty. These examples show that on the one side anger could be well grounded, but, on other side, that, if restrained, it could generate good outcomes. Besides, it is clear that alleged positive figures as Cyrus the Great and Agesilaus (and to some extent also Clearchus) are able to control (or to use successfully) anger.

This initial survey shows that the framework coming from the other works of Xenophon does not modify the results achieved by the inquiry into *Hellenica* but rather basically confirms its conclusions: anger is experienced both by individuals and groups (the only significant example of community is *Mem.* 1.1.18) and is considered as something bad, which wise men (such as Cyrus or Agesilaus) are able to retain, but which sometimes could be well grounded and produce a favourable outcome. Four more passages provide further and most remarkable confirmation, also because they come from four different works: as we shall see, they contribute in allowing us to extend, at least to some degree and with obvious differences between historical and non-historical frameworks, the results of the survey about *Hellenica* to the *corpus* of Xenophon's works and therefore they suggest that Xenophon's idea about ὀργή was quite consistent.

1) *Constitution of the Lacedaemonians.* — The survey about *Hellenica* showed that a study of ὀργή in Xenophon is mainly a study of Spartan ὀργή in Xenophon, because, in the vast majority of the cases, we faced the anger of Spartan individuals or of the Spartans considered as a whole.[34] In other works of Xenophon we find mentions of enraged Spartans (like Clearchus and Agesilaus) as well, but to some extent the subject of Spartan anger seems less relevant. At this point, it is highly interesting to consider a passage of Xenophon's *Constitution of the Lacedaemonians* (4.6), in which the author states that young Spartans, in order to demonstrate their prowess, are allowed to combat each other διὰ τὴν ἔριν; but

---

33 About Xenophon's portrait of Clearchus see Tritle, 2004, 325–339, especially 336, and Millender, 2012, 380–400, mainly 387–88.
34 In fact, eight out of the nine passages considered in § 1 concern Spartans (the only non-Spartan passage is 4.8.6 about Pharnabazus) and the same applies to two out of the five passages considered in § 2 (the other cases relate to the Aspendians, Athenians and Argives).

when someone intervenes in order to separate them, they must stop fighting and, if they do not obey, the ephors punish them severely, because one should never yield to a sudden impulse (ὀργή) to disobey (μὴ πείθεσθαι) the laws.³⁵ This passage is extremely interesting because, generally speaking, it shows that, according to Xenophon, in Spartan culture, while ἔρις could be positive, ὀργή is negatively considered, since it clouds men's minds and prevents them from acting as they should.³⁶ The pattern of behaviour emerging from *Lac.Pol.* 4.6, with its praise for respecting the law and restraining instinctive emotions, not only recalls closely the issue of the ideal (Spartan) leader, which is a subject absolutely central within Xenophon's literary production³⁷, but also, and most importantly, it is perfectly consistent with the results of the present survey.

2) *Cyropaedia.* — An episode from the *Cyropaedia* can further substantiate Xenphon's idea about ὀργή. In a passage of the fifth book (*Cyrop.* 5.4.35), the Assyrian defector Gadatas is talking with Cyrus and admits that in his rebellion against his king he acted without reflecting upon the consequences of his actions: in fact, being wronged by the Assyrian king, he became angry and therefore he was not able to make a safe choice; he was just "pregnant" with the idea of taking revenge on his king, a man depicted as enemy of gods and mankind.³⁸ Through these clear words, Gadatas admits that anger prevented him from acting rationally and making the best and safest choice. This passage is particularly remarkable because it provides exactly the idea of ἀπρονόητος ὀργή, even though the adjective does not occur.

3) *Anabasis.* — A passage in a speech from the *Anabasis* pronounced by Xenophon himself is illuminating, because it preserves his own opinion about ὀργή. This passage, therefore, is crucial for proving or disproving the result of the present survey. When the Ten Thousand arrived at Byzantium, the Spartan Anaxibius refused to give the pay to the soldiers and so they had no money and no food. In this fragile situation, Xenophon restrained the soldiers from sacking the city,

---

35 Lipka, 2002, 146; Gray, 2007, 160.
36 This recalls the subject of Spartan σωφροσύνη, about which Humble recently expressed her doubts (1999, 339–353; and 2002, 85–109).
37 On this topic, which is much investigated, only a few studies will be mentioned: Wood, 1964, 33–66; Riedinger, 1991, 227–243; Hutchinson, 2000, 180–229; Gray, 2011, 179–245; Tamiolaki, 2012, 563–589; Buxton, 2017, 323–337.
38 Καὶ τί δῆτα οὐχ οὕτως ἐνενοοῦ πρὶν ἀποστῆναι; ὅτι, ὦ Κῦρε, ἡ ψυχή μου διὰ τὸ ὑβρίσθαι καὶ ὀργίζεσθαι οὐ τὸ ἀσφαλέστατον σκοποῦσα διῆγεν, ἀλλ' αἰεὶ τοῦτο κυοῦσ', ἆρά ποτ' ἔσται ἀποτείσασθαι τὸν καὶ θεοῖς ἐχθρὸν καὶ ἀνθρώποις, ὃς διατελεῖ μισῶν, οὐκ ἤν τίς τι αὐτὸν ἀδικῇ, ἀλλ' ἐάν τινα ὑποπτεύσῃ βελτίονα αὐτοῦ εἶναι. Concerning Gadatas see Gera, 1993, 251–261, especially 257.

pronouncing these words: "That you are angry (ὀργίζεσθε), soldiers, and believe that you are treated offensively in being deceived, I do not wonder. But if we indulge our passion (ἢν τῷ θυμῷ χαριζώμεθα), if we take vengeance for this deception on the Lacedaemonians who are here and if we sack this city, which is not to be blamed in anything, consider (ἐνθυμεῖσθε) what consequences will follow" (7.1.25). Later on, Xenophon, after having invited his soldiers not to be caught up by anger and madness (μὴ πρὸς θεῶν μαινώμεθα, § 29), proposes to them to guarantee to Anaxibius that they had no intention of doing anything violent (οὐδὲν βίαιον) and that, if they were supposed to abandon the city, they would do it in obedience (§ 31). This passage is intriguing in many aspects.[39] First, the terminology has to be closely considered: we find not only ὀργίζομαι, but also μαίνομαι and θυμός, which belong to the same semantic field. Besides, these terms are connected to the adjective βίαιος, so as to suggest that irrational emotions like anger tend to lead to violence; hence ὀργή and βία are closely connected.[40] Secondly, it is significant that Xenophon calls his soldiers to reason and that he widely lists possible consequences of a violent reaction (§§ 26–28): thus, basically, the use of reason, i.e. γνώμη, is opposed to ὀργή; unfortunately the exact Thucydidean word γνώμη is not present in Xenophon's speech, but the idea certainly occurs, and it is expressed by verbs such as ἐνθυμέομαι or οἴομαι (§ 25, 28). Therefore this passage testifies, moreover through Xenophon's own words, exactly what has been established above: ὀργή is a negative emotion and, even when it may be understandable, the reaction to a wrong could provoke serious damage if decisions are taken emotionally; instead, Xenophon suggests, decisions have to be taken through a wise and well meditated reasoning, after having calculated the advantages and the disadvantages of any action.

4) *On Horsemanship.* — The conclusions reached in the present investigation can be confirmed also by a couple of passages coming from Xenophon's Περὶ ἱππικῆς. In chapter 9 the author remarks that horses' θυμός corresponds precisely to men's ὀργή (§ 2) and that a θυμοειδής horse, just like an ὀργίλος man, often causes many irreparable injuries (πολλὰ ἀνήκεστα) to himself and to his rider (§ 7): this statement shows that ὀργή is something very instinctive, which places men on the level of animals, and that it causes irreparable damage. Moreover, in chapter 6 Xenophon writes that an angry (σὺν ὀργῇ) man should never approach a horse: in fact, anger is improvident (ἀπρονόητον γὰρ ἡ ὀργή), and often it makes a man do what he must regret (πολλάκις ἐξεργάζεται ὧν μεταμέλειν ἀνάγκη, § 13). The subject of repentance is very interesting and actually it occurs in many of the

---

[39] About this passage, see e.g. Lendle, 1995, 420–422 and Flower, 2012, 151–152.
[40] Concerning βία in Xenophon, see the paper of C. Bearzot in this volume.

passages considered, meaning that often ὀργή is transitory and, when the ability to reason is regained, people realize their mistakes and regret them.[41] But what is mostly worth noting is that Xenophon's statements in chapters 6 and 9 of the Περὶ ἱππικῆς are perfectly consistent with the survey conducted on the *Hellenica*. In accordance with all the passages considered coming from various works of Xenophon, this further demonstrates the coherence of Xenophon's thought, both in the *Hellenica* and in his other works: ὀργή is an irrational and instinctive emotion, which leads (with few but significant exceptions) to negative consequences and, if not restrained, compels men to act recklessly. Moreover, also a precise lexical overlap with the passage from which the present survey started may be found: in fact, while the terms κακόν (evil) and ἁμάρτημα (mistake) occur in *Hell*. 5.3.7 but not in chapters 6 and 9 of the Περὶ ἱππικῆς, where they appear only as concepts, the adjective ἀπρονόητος is applied to ὀργή in both contexts (*Hell*. 5.3.7 and *Eq*. 6.13). This adjective,[42] through which Xenophon means that ὀργή is an improvident recklessness, seems to me the key to interpreting the notion of ὀργή in Xenophon's historical thought.

Bibliography

Ambler, W. (2008), *Xenophon, The Anabasis of Cyrus*, Ithaca/London.
Azoulay, V. (2004), *Xénophon et les grâces du pouvoir. De la charis au charisme*, Paris.
Braund, S./Most, G.W. (eds) (2004), *Ancient Anger: Perspectives from Homer to Galen*, Cambridge.
Bruno Sunseri, G. (2011), "Tucidide e la psicologia di massa: alcune considerazioni" in: *Hormos* 3, 24–35.
Buckler, J. (2003), *Aegean Greece in the Fourth Century BC*, Leiden.
Buckler, J. (2004), "The Incident at Mount Parnassus, 395 BC" in: *Xenophon and His World. Papers from a Conference Held in Liverpool in July 1999*, C. Tuplin (ed.), Stuttgart, 397–411.
Buxton, R.F. (2017), "Xenophon on Leadership: Commanders as Friends" in: *The Cambridge Companion to Xenophon*, M.A. Flower (ed.), Cambridge, 323–337.
Cairns, D./Nelis, D. (eds) (2017), *Emotions in the Classical World. Methods, Approaches, and Directions*, Stuttgart.
Cartledge, P. (1987), *Agesilaos and the Crisis of Sparta*, Baltimore.

---

[41] See e.g. the *demos* in connection with the Arginusae trial (*Hell*. 1.7.35), Clearchus after punishing his soldiers (*Anab*. 2.6.9), both with the verb μεταμέλομαι as above in *Eq*. 6.13; and also Gadatas for his rebellion to the Assyrian king (*Cyrop*. 5.4.35).

[42] It is a highly specialized adjective, as it occurs only two times in the whole of Xenophon's literary production, i.e. in the two passages considered. In four cases the adverb ἀπρονοήτως appears: three times in the *Cyropaedia* (1.4.21–22; 4.5.10) and once in the *Cynegeticus* (3.10).

Chaniotis, A. (ed.) (2012), *Unveiling Emotions. Sources and Methods for the Study of Emotions in the Greek World*, Stuttgart.
Chaniotis, A./Ducrey, P. (eds) (2013), *Unveiling Emotions II. Emotions in Greece and Rome: Texts, Images, Material Culture*, Stuttgart.
Dillery, J. (1995), *Xenophon and the History of His Times*, London.
Fantasia, U. (2003), *Tucidide, La Guerra del Peloponneso, Libro II. Testo, traduzione e commento con saggio introduttivo*, Pisa.
Ferrario, S.B. (2012), "Historical Agency and Self-Awarness in Xenophon's *Hellenica* and *Anabasis*" in: *Xenophon: Ethical Principles and Historical Enquiry*, F. Hobden/C. Tuplin (eds), Leiden/Boston, 341–376.
Ferrario, S.B. (2014), *Historical Agency and the 'Great Man' in Classical Greece*, Cambridge.
Ferrario, S.B. (2017), "Xenophon and Greek Political Thought" in: *The Cambridge Companion to Xenophon*, M.A. Flower (ed.), Cambridge, 57–83.
Flower, M.A. (2012), *Xenophon's Anabasis, or The Expedition of Cyrus*, Oxford.
Flower, M.A. (2017), "Xenophon as a Historian" in: *The Cambridge Companion to Xenophon*, M.A. Flower (ed.), Cambridge, 301–322.
Gera, D.L. (1993), *Xenophon's Cyropaedia. Style, Genre, and Literary Technique*, Oxford.
Gish, D. (2012), "Defending *Dēmokratia*: Athenian Justice and the Trial of the Arginusae Generals in Xenophon's *Hellenica*" in: *Xenophon: Ethical Principles and Historical Enquiry*, F. Hobden/C. Tuplin (eds), Leiden/Boston, 161–212.
Gray, V.J. (1989), *Character of Xenophon's Hellenica*, Baltimore.
Gray, V.J. (2007), *Xenophon on Government*, Cambridge.
Gray, V.J. (2010), "Interventions and Citations in Xenophon's *Hellenica* and *Anabasis*" in: *Oxford Readings in Classical Studies. Xenophon*, V.J. Gray (ed.), Oxford, 553–572.
Gray, V.J. (2011), *Xenophon's Mirror of Princes: Reading Reflections*, Oxford.
Hamilton, D. (1991), *Agesilaus and the Failure of Spartan Hegemony*, Ithaca.
Harris, W.V. (2001), *Restraining Rage: The Ideology of Anger Control in Classical Antiquity*, Cambridge.
Hau, L.I. (2016), *Moral History from Herodotus to Diodorus Siculus*, Edinburgh.
Higgins, W.E. (1977), *Xenophon the Athenian. The Problem of the Individual and the Society of the Polis*, Albany.
Hobden, F./Tuplin, C. (2012), "Introduction" in: *Xenophon: Ethical Principles and Historical Enquiry*, F. Hobden/C. Tuplin (eds), Leiden/Boston, 1–41.
Huart, P. (1968), *Le vocabulaire de l'analyse psychologique dans l'oeuvre de Thycydide*, Paris.
Humble, N. (1999), "*Sōphrosynē* and the Spartans in Xenophon": in: *Sparta: New Perspectives*, S. Hodkinson/A. Powell (eds), Swansea, 339–353.
Humble, N. (2002), '*Sōphrosynē* Revisited: Was It Ever a Spartan virtue?' in: A. Powell/S. Hodkinson (eds), *Sparta: Beyond the Mirage*, Swansea, 85–109.
Hunter, V.J. (1988), "Thucydides and the Sociology of the Crowd" in: *CJ* 84, 17–30.
Hutchinson, G. (2000), *Xenophon and the Art of Command*, London/Pennsylvania.
Kalimtzis, K. (2012), *Taming Anger: The Hellenic Approach to the Limitations of Reason*, London.
Konstan, D. (2004), "Aristotle on Anger and the Emotions: the Strategies of Status" in: S. Braund/G.W. Most (eds), *Ancient Anger: Perspectives from Homer to Galen*, Cambridge, 99–120.
Konstan, D. (2006), *The Emotions of the Ancient Greeks. Studies in Aristotle and Classical Literature*, Toronto/Buffalo/London.

Krentz, P. (1995), *Xenophon, Hellenika* II.3.11–IV.2.8, Warminster.
Krentz, P. (1989), *Xenophon, Hellenika* I–II.3.10, Warminster.
Lendle, O. (1995), *Kommentar zu Xenophons* Anabasis (Bücher 1–7), Darmstadt.
Lipka, M. (2002), *Xenophon's Spartan Constitution*, Berlin.
Ludwig, P.W. (2009), "Anger, Eros, and Other Political Passions in Ancient Greek Thought" in: *A Companion to Greek and Roman Political Thought*, R.K. Balot (ed.), Oxford, 294–307.
Marincola, J. (2009), *The Landmark Xenophon's* Hellenika, Strassler, R.B. (ed.), New York.
Marincola, J. (2017), "Xenophon's *Anabasis* and *Hellenica*" in: *The Cambridge Companion to Xenophon*, M.A. Flower (ed.), Cambridge, 103–118.
Millender, E. (2012), "Spartan 'Friendship' and Xenophon's Crafting of the *Anabasis*" in: *Xenophon: Ethical Principles and Historical Enquiry*, F. Hobden/C. Tuplin (eds), Leiden/Boston, 377–425.
Müri, W. (1947), "Beitrag zum Verständnis des Thukydides" in: *MH*, 4, 251–275.
Nielsen, T.H. (2002), *Arkadia and Its Poleis in the Archaic and Classical Periods*, Göttingen.
Parker, V. (2007), "Sphodrias' raid and the liberation of Thebes: a study of Ephorus and Xenophon" in: *Hermes*, 135, 13–33.
Pelling, C. (2017), "Xenophon's Authorial Voice" in: *The Cambridge Companion to Xenophon*, M.A. Flower (ed.), Cambridge, 241–262.
Pizzone, A. (2004), "Storiografia e socratismo. Il ritratto di Teleutia tra πρόνοια e τόλμη" in : *Il Peloponneso di Senofonte*, G. Daverio Rocchi/M. Cavalli (eds), Milano, 307–324.
Pownall, F. (2004), *Lessons from the Past. The Moral Use of History in Fourth-Century Prose*, Ann Arbor.
Riedinger, J.-C. (1991), *Étude sur les* Helléniques. *Xénophon et l'histoire*, Paris.
Rood, T. (2012), "The Plupast in Xenophon's *Hellenica*" in: *Time and Narrative in Ancient Historiography. The 'Plupast' from Herodotus to Appian*, J. Grethlein/C.B. Krebs (eds), Cambridge, 76–94.
Schepens, G. (2012), "Timocrates' Mission to Greece–Once Again" in: *Xenophon: Ethical Principles and Historical Enquiry*, F. Hobden/C. Tuplin (eds), Leiden/Boston, 213–241.
Sordi, M. (1950; 1951), "I caratteri dell'opera storiografica di Senofonte nelle *Elleniche*" in: *Athenaeum* 28, 1– 53; 29, 273–348.
Sordi, M. (2000), "Trasibulo tra politica e religione" in : *RFIC* 128, 182–191.
Sordi, M. (2011), "La *nautikè dynamis* in Senofonte dall'*Athenaion politeia* ai *Poroi*" in : *Historika* 1, 11–20.
Tamiolaki, M. (2012), "Virtue and Leadership in Xenophon: Ideal Leaders or Ideal Losers?" in: *Xenophon: Ethical Principles and Historical Enquiry*, F. Hobden/C. Tuplin (eds), Leiden/Boston, 563–589.
Tamiolaki, M. (2013), "Emotions and Historical Representation in Xenophon's *Hellenika*" in: *Unveiling Emotions II. Emotions in Greece and Rome: Texts, Images, Material Culture*, A. Chaniotis/P. Ducrey (eds), Stuttgart, 15–52.
Tritle, L. (2004), "Xenophon's Portrait of Clearchus: a Study in Post-Traumatic Stress Disorder" in: *Xenophon and His World. Papers from a Conference Held in Liverpool in July 1999*, C. Tuplin (ed.), Stuttgart, 325–339.
Tsamakis, A. (2006), "Leaders, Crowds, and the Power of the Image: Political Communication in Thucydides" in: *Brill's Companion to Thucydides*, A. Rengakos/A. Tsamakis (eds), Leiden/Boston 2006, 161–187.

Tuci, P.A. (2002), "La boulé nel processo agli strateghi della battaglia delle Arginuse: questioni procedurali e tentativi di manipolazione", in: *Syngraphé IV. A cura di D. Ambaglio*, Como, 51–85.

Tuci, P.A. (2004), "Clistene, Aristagora di Mileto e il demos ateniese: due tentativi di manipolazione della volontà popolare tra fine VI e inizio V secolo?" in: *RSA* 34, 233–265.

Tuci, P.A. (2010), "Carptim memoria digna perscribere. Criteri di selezione del materiale nella storiografia greca monografica e universale" in: *Dalla storiografia ellenistica alla storiografia tardoantica: aspetti, problemi, prospettive. Atti del convegno internazionale di Studi*, U. Roberto/L. Mecella Roma, 23–25 ottobre 2008, Soveria Mannelli, 59–116.

Tuplin, C. (1993), *The Failings of Empire: A Reading of Xenophon* Hellenica 2.3.11–7.5.27, Stuttgart.

Wohl, V. (2017), "Thucydides on the Political Passions" in: *The Oxford Handbook of Thucydides*, R.K. Balot/S. Forsdyke/E. Foster (eds), Oxford, 443–458.

Wood, N. (1964), "Xenophon's Theory of Leadership" in: *C&M* 25, 33–66.

Zaccarini, M. (2018), "What's Love got to do with it? Eros, Democracy, and Pericles' Rhetoric" in: *GRBS* 58, 473–489.

Zumbrunnen, J. (2017), "Thucydides and Crowds" in: *The Oxford Handbook of Thucydides*, R.K. Balot/S. Forsdyke/E. Foster (eds), Oxford, 475–489.

P.J. Rhodes
Lawlessness and Violence in Decision-Making in Xenophon's *Hellenica*

This paper seeks to show how far Xenophon's *Hellenica*[1] depicts lawful procedures in decision-making in Greek cities, how far it depicts or implies violent overriding of those procedures. Xenophon was an Athenian who perhaps served in the cavalry in the last years of the Peloponnesian War, and probably stayed in Athens as a member of the cavalry under the régime of the Thirty, in 404/3.[2] He gave a hostile account of Theramenes' role in the trial of the generals after the battle of Arginusae, and in making peace with Sparta; but in the final account of Critias' confrontation with Theramenes it is Theramenes who was represented favourably,[3] after the killing of Theramenes he used the verb *tyrannein* of the Thirty, and he also gave a positive account of the democrats under Thrasybulus and of the eventual reconciliation, which suggests that he himself may be regarded as a "moderate oligarch".[4] He then joined the mercenary army serving on Cyrus' campaign against his brother Araxerxes, and after the defeat and death of Cyrus at Cunaxa he became one of the leaders of the Greeks as they tried to return home.[5] He returned to Greece with the Spartan king Agesilaus in 394.[6] At some point he was exiled from Athens, but probably not until after he had made his dedication in the Athenian treasury at Delphi in 394; and he was settled by the Spartans on land at Scillus in the Peloponnese.[7] Eventually he was reconciled with the Athenians, to judge from the his *Poroi* and the knowledge of Athens after 355 which it displays;[8]

---

[1] This paper uses some material from the Xenophontic part of papers on "The Classical Greek Historians on Democracy" written for an internet conference organised by the Higher School of Economics, Perm, Russia, on *Historians and Power in Antiquity*, and for a seminar at Brown University. My thanks to those who invited me to write those papers and who discussed them with me, and to Dr. Kapellos for inviting me to contribute to this volume and suggesting my topic. References which do not indicate author or work are to Xenophon's *Hellenica*.

[2] In 409, 1.1.34, 2.1–11, which "suggests autopsy": *P.A. s.n.*, Cawkwell, 1979, 9; 404/3, note the focus on the cavalry in 2.4. 2–10, 24–7, with *P.A. s.n.*, Cawkwell, *loc. cit.*

[3] For the rule of the Thirty in Athens, see Wolpert, in this volume.

[4] Arginusae, below; peace, 2.2.16–23; Critias and Theramenes, 2.3.15–56; *tyrannein*, 2.4.1; Thrasybulus, 2.4.5–7, 10–22, 30–4, 42; reconciliation, 2.4.35–43; moderate oligarch, Cawkwell, *op. cit.*, 10. On Xenophon's view of what makes a good citizen see Seager, 2001, 385–397.

[5] Xen.*An.*, esp. 1.8.15, 2.5.37, 41, 3.1.4–47.

[6] Xen.*An.* 5.3.6.

[7] Not exiled earlier, Xen.*An.* 5.3.5 with *Hell.* 4.3.21: see Badian, 2004, 41; Scillus, *An.* 5.3.7.

[8] Badian, 2004, 42.

but he seems not to have returned to live there: it may be true that his exile was revoked on the proposal of Eubulus (though hardly that it had also been imposed on a proposal of Eubulus, as the text mentioning Eubulus alleges), and that he died in Corinth.[9] That is the background against which we must see his accounts of decision-making in Athens and elsewhere.

Athens

Xenophon was not given to commenting on forms of government, except to remark on "tyrannies".[10] However, although he cannot have been present at political meetings which he reports, except presumably at Athens down to the end of the fifth century, he does on various occasions give more details of what happened at meetings in Athens than Herodotus or Thucydides did.[11]

Thus the proceedings against the generals after the battle of Arginusae are narrated in considerable detail.[12] Six of the eight generals involved in the battle returned to Athens. One was charged on another matter and in connection with his generalship, and was imprisoned; and after the others had reported to the council they too were imprisoned and the matter was referred to the assembly. At a first meeting of the assembly Theramenes and others accused the generals, and they each replied briefly, but were not allowed a *logos* in accordance with the law (οὐ γὰρ προυτέθη σφίσι λόγος κατὰ τὸν νόμον: that has commonly been taken to mean that they were not allowed the full speech which the law would have allowed; Ostwald argued instead that in accordance with the law they were not allowed a full speech; but I think the usual interpretation is more likely).[13] As darkness was

---

[9] Exile imposed and revoked, Istrus *FGrH* 334 F 32 *ap*. Diog. Laert. 2.59; death at Corinth, Diog. Laert. 2.56, 58 (but certainly not as early as 360/59).

[10] He does not refer to the Thirty as the Thirty Tyrants (that fashion seems to have been started by Ephorus: cf. Krentz, 1982, 16 n. 2), but he does twice use *tyrannein* of them: 2.3.48, 2.4.1). He uses *tyrannos* and *tyrannein* also in connection with the pro-Argive régime at Corinth in the late 390's (4.4.6); with the rulers imposed on Thebes by Sparta in 382 (5.4.1, 9, 13); with Euphron of Sicyon in the 360's (7.1.46, 7.3.7, 8, 10); and with Jason and his successors in Pherai (6.4.32 [Jason], 34–35 [Polyphron]).

[11] Exceptionally, Thucydides gives a detailed account of the institution of the Four Hundred in Athens in 411: Thuc. 8.63.3–70.

[12] 1.7.

[13] 1.7.5: usual interpretation e.g. Loeb and Budé translations; alternative Ostwald, 1986, 438; but I should be surprised if there was a law which prescribed that in some circumstances men could not make a speech.

approaching, it was decided that the council should present a *probouleuma* on how the generals were to be tried to a subsequent meeting of the assembly. Theramenes took advantage of the Apaturia to add to the pressure on the generals.

At the second assembly a *probouleuma* proposed by Callixenus recommended that without further debate there should be a single ballot on the generals, and if they were judged guilty they should be sentenced to death. Euryptolemus and others proposed to attack that in a *graphe paranomon*, but there was an outcry that it would be a terrible thing if anybody prevented the *demos* from doing what it wanted, and Euryptolemus and the others were intimidated into withdrawing. Some of the *prytaneis* refused to put Callixenus' motion to the vote, but they too were intimidated into withdrawing, apart from Socrates. Euryptolemus then both argued that the generals were not guilty and proposed two alternative forms of individual trial. On a first vote one of his proposals was carried; but when an objection had been raised there was a second vote and Callixenus' proposal was carried. The generals were condemned, and the six who were present were executed; later the *demos* regretted its decision and proposed that Callixenus and others should be tried for deceiving the people, but in the turmoil at the end of the war those trials were not held.

In what respects all this was illegal continues to be debated.[14] I believe that it was illegal not to allow the generals a *logos* at the first assembly, and I think it would be generally agreed that the procedure of the second assembly was illegal in holding a vote without allowing the generals a *logos*, i.e. in condemning them without a proper trial (*akritoi*).[15] Was it also illegal to hold a collective vote on all the generals accused rather than to vote on them individually? In Xenophon's account Euryptolemus is emphatic in calling for individual votes,[16] and it has generally held that the collective vote was illegal, but E.M. Harris argues that that was not illegal.[17] Some other occasions are attested in Athens when all the members of a board were tried: the *hellenotamiai*, possibly in 449/8; the Eleven, some time in the first quarter of the fourth century; the *thesmothetai*, in 344/3:[18] in none of those cases is the procedure clear, but in each of them I should say a collective vote cannot be ruled out. The corn-dealers accused in a speech by Lysias were

---

14 The less dramatic account of Diod. 13.101 has defenders of the generals prevented by *thorybos* from speaking but beyond that does not help us to decide what was illegal.
15 *Akritoi* 1.7.25, cf. other texts which make that point in other connections.
16 1.7.23, 26, 34; cf. Pl.*Ap*. 32 B, Xen.*Mem*. 1.1.18.
17 Harris, 2013, 339–343. MacDowell, 1978, 186–189, suggests that, while there is no other evidence that collective votes were illegal, they were contrary to normal practice.
18 Antiph. 5. *Herodes* 69 (possible date Tracy, 2014, 1–10 = 2016, 207–215); Isae. 4. *Nicostratus* 28; Dem. 58. *Theocrines* 27–8.

fairly certainly tried collectively, but they were metics and what was legal for them might not have been legal for citizens.[19] On the other hand, we know of occasions when colleagues were tried separately: Ergocles and Philocrates, c. 388, were tried in connection with the same episode but on different charges; but it seems that in 355 after the defeat at Embata Iphicrates, Timotheus and Menestheus were tried separately when they might have been tried collectively.[20] I incline to MacDowell's conclusion, that collective trial was not unlawful, and might occur when members of a board were accused collectively of the same offence, but it was sufficiently unusual to constitute a possible ground for objection when it was used. Beyond that, Xenophon mentions intimidations, in reaction to Euryptolemus' proposal of a *graphe paranomon*, and against the *prytaneis* when they were reluctant to put a dubious proposal to the vote, and an objection to the vote by which a proposal of Euryptolemus was passed.

On the rise and fall of the Thirty, Xenophon's chronology, in which the Spartan garrison arrived early and the oligarchs started misbehaving before they eliminated Theramenes, is probably correct: he champions Theramenes by having him oppose the extremists; *Ath. Pol.* champions him by placing most of the misbehaviour after his elimination.[21] Xenophon begins by having Lysander in Athens when the Thirty were appointed but not directly stating that he was present in and intimidated the assembly.[22] He states that they were appointed to draft laws, but delayed doing that and appointed a council and other officials; their initial condemnation of *sykophantai* was not unpopular, but they soon aimed at treating the city however they wished.[23] Xenophon then paints a picture of degeneration, involving clashes between Critias and Theramenes and further references to the Thirty's acting however they wished;[24] a list of the comparatively privileged Three Thousand was created and men not on that list were disarmed; the council which the Thirty originally hoped would condemn Theramenes was intimidated by armed thugs.[25]

---

19 Lys. 22. *Corn-Dealers* (metics § 5).
20 Lys. 28. *Ergocles*, 29. *Philocrates*; Isoc. 15. *Antid.* 129 and other texts (Timotheus condemned but the others acquitted: contr. Diod. 16.21.4).
21 Cf. Rhodes, 1981, 419–422. See also Wolpert in this volume.
22 2.2.23–2.3.3: Lysander's involvement *Ath. Pol.* 34.3, Diod. 14.3.2–7.
23 2.3.11–13. This is matched in the other sources; probably, as in Diod. 14.4.1, they were formally instructed both to draft new laws about the constitution and in the meantime to act as an interim government (Rhodes, 1981, 434–435).
24 See Pownall in this volume.
25 2.3.13–56; acting however they wished 21, 23; disarming 20; council intimidated 23, 50, 55.

After the elimination of Theramenes the Thirty felt that they could *tyrannein* fearlessly.²⁶ An *ad hoc* meeting of hoplites and cavalry was induced to condemn the Eleusinians, to involve them in the collective guilt and to give the Thirty a place they could flee to.²⁷ Despite his own oligarchic sympathies, and indeed his probable presence among the cavalry during the oligarchy, Xenophon paints a picture of illegality piled on illegality, in the face of repeated objections from Theramenes. Thrasybulus and the restored democracy of 403 are represented as virtuous, accepting the reconciliation and the amnesty — except that, with the excuse that the oligarchs at Eleusis were hiring mercenaries, they treacherously killed the oligarchs' generals, but then persuaded the remainder to join in the reconciliation.²⁸

While Thucydides was normally silent about the council of five hundred,²⁹ Xenophon several times mentioned its role in decision-making. Thus for the condemnation of the generals after the battle of Arginusae the council decided to arrest the generals and send them to the assembly for trial; the generals produced a letter which they had sent to the council and assembly; the assembly instructed the council to bring a *probouleuma* to a subsequent meeting; Callixenus attacked the generals in the council and it did produce a *probouleuma* for the trial; in spite of objections, eventually the council's proposal was carried.

The democratic council is mentioned also in connection with the peace terms in 404, and in 371 when after the battle of Leuctra without reference to the assembly it rebuffed a Theban herald.³⁰ For the council's rebuffing the herald there was a precedent in 479, when the Persian Mardonius sent an envoy to try to win over the Athenians, one member of the council wanted to refer the envoy and his proposals to the assembly, but the councillors and other Athenians were indignant and stoned that member to death.³¹

After the Spartans' defeat at Leuctra, in 370/69, when the Thebans invaded the Peloponnese, the Athenians were unsure how to react, and "held an assembly in accordance with a resolution (*dogma*) of the council". Envoys from Sparta and other states spoke, reminding the Athenians of times when Athens and Sparta

---

26 2.4.1.
27 2.4.8–10.
28 Reconciliation in 403, 2.4.38–43; in 401/0 (date *Ath. Pol.* 40.4), 2.4.43.
29 Cf. Hornblower, 2009, 251–264; or version in Hornblower, 1991–2008, iii. 23–31 — but Thucydides is silent about councils elsewhere too except when they played a role beyond their normal *probouleusis*, and I suspect his silences merely reflect the fact that normally it was citizen assemblies which made the final decision.
30 404, 2.2.15; 371, 6.4.20.
31 Hdt. 9.4–5, with variations in later texts. See also Harris in this volume.

had been on the same side; but more recently Athens and Sparta had been opposed, and the Athenians were at first unhappy at the thought of supporting Sparta now. But envoys from Corinth and from Phlius (Xenophon gives a short speech to the first and a substantial speech to the second) argued that now the greatest threat to Athens was from Thebes and that Athens ought to join Sparta in opposition to Thebes. "Then the Athenians deliberated, and they no longer put up with listening to those speaking against, but voted to rally round with full force" in suppport of Sparta.[32] There is no need to suppose that anything unlawful happened, but Xenophon mentions *thorybos* of approval after the Corinthian speech,[33] and probably after the second there was *thorybos* in favour of those arguing for support to Sparta and against those arguing on the other side – but *thorybos* in the assembly was an accepted fact, and should not arouse our disquiet.

As a sequel to that, in 369, a formal alliance between Athens and Sparta was made, with Sparta and its allies sending envoys to Athens to discuss the terms.[34] Xenophon's narrative begins in the assembly, with a speech by Procles of Phlius, the Phliasian envoy of the previous episode. He started and ended by referring approvingly to the council's *probouleuma*, which this time was a specific *probouleuma*, recommending an alliance by which Sparta would command on land and Athens at sea. This was received with approval by the Athenians as well as the Spartans who were present: presumably we should once more think of *thorybos*, though Xenophon does not mention that explicitly.[35] However, the Athenian Cephisodotus made a speech objecting that that arrangement would give too much power to Sparta, and proposing instead that the whole command should alternate between Sparta and Athens. "On hearing that, the Athenians were persuaded to change their minds",[36] and the assembly decided on terms which we may well consider preposterous, that the whole command should alternate every five days. The envoys present were *autokratores*,[37] so presumably they were authorised to accept and did accept the Athenian decision. Here as in the previous episode there was probably *thorybos*, and the decision finally made

---

32 6.5.33–49 (quoting 49).
33 6.5.37.
34 7.1.1–14 (*probouleuma*, 2, 11). Cf. Diod. 15.67.1: "They made an agreement about the leadership, that the Athenians should control the sea and the Spartans the land, but after that they created a joint leadership in both cities".
35 They "praised his speech strongly" (ἐπῄνεσαν ... ἰσχυρῶς τὸν λόγον αὐτοῦ: § 12).
36 7.1.14.
37 7.1.1.

seems foolish, but again Athens' procedures were working as they were intended to work.

As we have seen, the council which served during the régime of the Thirty is mentioned also: the Thirty appointed the council and the other officials as they saw fit; the council was happy to condemn sycophants; Critias expected the council to condemn Theramenes, and when it seemed likely that it would refuse he in the name of the Thirty announced the condemnation of Theramenes to the council.[38]

Sparta

For Sparta Xenophon does not give us major institutional set pieces as he does for Athens, and his most substantial set piece is connected with the acquittal of Sphodrias after his unsuccessful raid on Attica in 379/8, and the use not of violence but of personal influence to achieve that outcome.[39] The Athenians were indignant, and detailed Spartan envoys until they insisted that Sphodrias would surely be convicted. Sphodrias was recalled to stand trial (probably in the *gerousia*)[40] and failed to appear; but he was nevertheless acquitted *in absentia*. The friends of king Cleombrotus were inclined to acquit, but they were afraid that the friends of Agesilaus and "those in the middle" (τοὺς διὰ μέσου) would convict him. But Sphodrias' son Cleonymus was loved by Agesilaus' son Archidamus, Sphodrias asked Archidamus to win over Agesilaus, and Archidamus eventually tried and eventually succeeded.

Glimpses of procedure are fairly frequent. When c. 400 Agis II was succeeded by his brother Agesilaus rather than his son Leotychidas, Xenophon reports an altercation between the two claimants, the invocation of an oracle and the disputed interpretation of it (with Lysander arguing for Agesilaus), and then "the *polis*" (probably the assembly) chose Agesilaus.[41] Later he reports Lysander's attempts to control Agesilaus (cf. below), but he does not report Lysander's revolutionary plans.[42] After that he gives us a thoroughly frustrating passage, reporting the plot of Cinadon, not one of the "equals" (*homoioi*) but (presumably) one of

---

38 Appointed, 2.3.11; sycophants, 12; Theramenes, 23–55.
39 5.4.22–34. "It was judged by many that this was the most unjust judicial decision in Sparta", 5.4.24.
40 MacDowell, 1986, 139–141.
41 3.3.1–4.
42 For Lysander's revolutionary plans see Diod. 14.13 and other texts.

the "inferiors" (*hypomeiones*), and he says that when the ephors were told of it they did not even convene "what is called the little assembly" but made plans with members of the *gerousia* individually.⁴³ But the *hypomeiones* are not attested elsewhere (they perhaps were or included men who had been downgraded from the ranks of the "equals" because they could not pay their mess contributions); and the "little assembly" is not attested elsewhere. Sparta was facing what was considered to be a threat of violent revolution: clearly the ephors would have been entitled to discuss this with the *gerousia*. We cannot say how far the ephors and *gerousia* would have been entitled to act without involving the mysterious "little assembly" or the regular assembly, but planning not with the whole *gerousia* but with individual members of it suggests that they feared opposition from some of the members and did not want to give that the chance to surface: it looks as if in this emergency the ephors and *gerousia* avoided following procedures which, if not formally required, would normally have been expected, in order to prevent the revolutionaries from learning what was being planned.

For sending out Spartan military forces an expression used commonly in the *Hellenica* but nowhere else (apart from two instances in Aelius Aristides) is φρουρὰν φαίνειν, "proclaim a campaign"; often the ephors are specified as subject, and in none of the other instances do we need to suppose that it was not the ephors who did this.⁴⁴ Sparta's war against Elis began *c.* 402 when the ephors and the assembly decided to knock sense into the Eleans (*sophronisai*) and the ephors proclaimed a campaign.⁴⁵ When Sparta entered the Corinthian War in 395, this was done when "the city decided" (οὕτω δὲ γιγνωσκούσης τῆς πόλεως), and in 394 when the ephors proclaimed a campaign the *polis* ordered Aristodemus to command on behalf of his relative the young Agesipolis.⁴⁶ For the campaign against Mantinea in 385 "they" (unspecified) proclaimed a campaign, Agesilaus asked the *polis* not to give him the command because of his family connections with Mantinea, and Agesipolis led out the campaign (*phroura* again) in spite of his family connections with the other side in Mantinea.⁴⁷ For campaigning against Thebes, in 376 after Agesilaus had been taken ill "the Spartans" proclaimed a campaign

---

43 3.3.4–11 (not *homoios*, 5; *hypomeiones* mentioned, 6; little assembly, 8). For *hypomeiones* Krentz, 1995), *ad loc.*, considers demoted *homoioi* and other possible categories.
44 3.2.23, 25, 3.5.6, 4.2.9, 4.7.1*, 2*, 5.1.29*, 36*, 5.2.3*, 5.3.13, 5.4.13*, 35*, 47, 59*, 6.4.17, 6.5.10; cf. Aristid. 1. *Panath.* 266 Lenz*, 10. *Theb. Foed ii.* 29 Lenz* (both referring to fourth-century Sparta). Asterisks denote instances in which the ephors are not specified as subject.
45 3.2.23 (cf. the next year, 3.2.25). Likewise the decision to campaign in Acarnania in 389 is attributed to the ephors and the assembly, 4.6.3.
46 3.5.6; 4.2.9.
47 5.2.3.

and ordered Cleombrotus to command.⁴⁸ After Sparta's defeat at Leuctra the ephors proclaimed a campaign for specified age groups, which had not taken part in the original battle; and in 370 against Mantinea the ephors proclaimed the campaign and the *polis* ordered Agesilaus to command.⁴⁹

It appears that decisions to go to war, and within that war to send out a particular campaign, were taken by the *polis*, which I take to mean the assembly on the recommendation of the *gerousia*; the assembly also assigned commands; but the ephors had the executive task of ordering the forces out, and perhaps deciding precisely what forces should be sent on what occasion. The ephors sent orders to the navarch Samius in 402.⁵⁰ Probably they sent out non-Spartiate forces under non-royal commanders; in 398 Dercylidas in Asia Minor was sent three inspectors "from the authorities at home" (ἀπὸ τῶν οἴκοι τελῶν), and they renewed his command for another year and gave his soldiers a message from the ephors; and in 397 the ephors sent to him (perhaps to renew his command again and) to order him to move into Caria.⁵¹ However, the appointment of king Agesilaus to succeed Dercylidas in 396 (with thirty Spartiates but otherwise still a non-Spartiate army) is attributed to the persuasion of Lysander and to "the Spartans". It is in this connection that we are told that the decarchies which Lysander had imposed on the cities of the Aegean had been replaced by traditional constitutions by order of the ephors.⁵² Agesilaus in 395 received orders from "the authorities at home" to control the fleet also and to make his own appointment of a navarch.⁵³ All of this suggests that proper procedures were normally followed.

However, frequently Xenophon remarks on policy differences within Sparta, associated with individuals, and often does not indicate how these were worked out through the formal procedures. In the last years of the Peloponnesian War, when Lysander as navarch for 407/6 was succeeded by Callicratidas for 406/5,

---

48 5.4.59.
49 6.4.17; 6.5.10.
50 3.1.1. Cf. Thuc. 1.131.1, where the ephors sent a herald with a *skytale*-message to Pausanias the regent; Plut.*Lys.* 19.1–21.1, where in 404 they sent a *skytale*-message to Lysiander in Asia Minor, he returned home and gave the ephors a letter from Pharnabazus; he was afraid of the ephors but obtained their permission to visit the oracle of Zeus Ammon, and in his absence the kings discovered that he was controlling the cities through *hetaireiai* which he had established, and took steps to return power to the democrats. Plutarch represents Agesilaus II as courting the ephors rather than treating them as opponents: Plut.*Ages.* 4.3–6.
51 3.2.6; 12.
52 3.4.2–3. Contrast Plutarch's version (the kings): n. 45, above.
53 3.4.27–9.

while Lysander had had a good relationship with Cyrus and the Persians, Callicratidas objected to courting the Persians and claimed that he wanted to make peace with Athens, but declared that he had to obey the officials at home (τοῖς οἴκοι ἄρχουσι) and Lysander's "friends" tried to undermine him. He was defeated and killed at Arginusae, and it was in response to Chios that the Spartans appointed Lysander as secretary to a figurehead navarch for 405/4.[54]

In Athens in 404/3, when the democrats were beginning to fight back and the Thirty had been succeeded by the Ten, Lysander and his brother set up a blockade of Athens by land and sea, but king Pausanias was jealous of Lysander, gained the support of three of the five ephors, and led an army which joined Lysander's force, won a battle against the democrats but then encouraged both sides to negotiate with him and the ephors. The oligarchs sent a rival deputation, all the Athenians were heard by the ephors and the *ekkletoi* (apparently the members of the assembly), and a Spartan commission was sent to join Pausanias in working out a settlement.[55] In 396, when Agesilaus was sent to command Sparta's forces in Asia Minor, and was given a board of thirty Spartiates, they included Lysander, who hoped to control Agesilaus, but Agesilaus resisted that and sent Lysander on a separate mission. In 395 the thirty returned home and a new contingent of thirty was sent.[56] The conflict between Lysander and Pausanias then resurfaced: in 395 they were sent with separate forces to Boeotia to take part in the first phase of the Corinthian War; Lysander fought at Haliartus without waiting for Pausanias, and was killed; Pausanias after making a truce to withdraw was put on trial, fled into exile and was condemned to death *in absentia*.[57]

In Sparta's war against Mantinea in 385, as we noticed above, Agesilaus asked the *polis* not to give him the command because of his family connections with Mantinea, and Agesipolis led out the campaign in spite of his family connections with the other side.[58] Agesilaus was probably behind the occupation of Thebes in 382 (cf. below). After the liberation in winter 379/8 Cleombrotus, who had succeeded Agesipolis as the other king, commanded the first campaign to try to recover it, but did as little damage as possible: Xenophon reports that Agesilaus pleaded that he was too old, but in fact did not want to incur the odium of supporting tyrants.[59] Sphodrias, left as a governor in Thespiae, made his raid on

---

54 1.6.1–12; 2.1.6–7.
55 2.4.28–38. On *ekkletoi*, in § 38 and in 5.2.33, 6.3.3 [but in 6.3.3 the clause was deleted by Cobet], see Underhill, 1900, 75–76.
56 3.4.2–10; 20.
57 3.5.6–7, 17–25.
58 5.2.3.
59 5.4.13–18.

Attica (bribed by the Thebans, according to Xenophon, but more probably prompted by Cleombrotus "without the authority of the ephors", as stated by Diodorus).[60] In summer 378 Agesilaus campaigned against Thebes (because he would be a better commander, according to Xenophon, but because Cleombrotus was not eager to fight against Thebes, according to Plutarch), and again in 377.[61] But after that Agesilaus was taken ill; in 376 Cleombrotus commanded and failed to get into Boeotia, after which in response to its allies Sparta turned to an (unsuccessful) naval campaign against Athens.[62] In all of this we have a series of episodes in which kings and other leading figures do not engage in outright violence but for their own purposes fail to cooperate with one another as they ought.

Conflict with Athens continued, particularly on the west side of Greece, but in 372, when the Thebans moved into Phocis and Agesilaus was recovering, Cleombrotus was sent to defend Phocis. In 371 Athens sent envoys, and induced Thebes to send envoys, to Sparta to discuss a renewal of the King's Peace. Xenophon gives us three Athenian speeches, after which "the Spartans also voted to accept the peace". This was the occasion when the Thebans were originally included as "Thebans", but subsequently asked (in the assembly? the *gerousia*?) to be registered instead as "Boeotians", and Agesilaus refused; Plutarch writes of an altercation between Agesilaus and Epaminondas.[63] Cleombrotus from Phocis asked "the authorities at home" what he should do; a suggestion based on the need to rebuild the temple at Delphi[64] was dismissed by the assembly as nonsense; he was ordered to attack Thebes unless it would grant the independence of the Boeotian cities[65] — and the result was the battle of Leuctra, in which Cleombrotus was defeated and killed. His successor Agesipolis II died the following year, and the next king Cleomenes II reigned until 309 but has left hardly any trace in the sources.

---

60 5.4.20–33; Diod. 15.29.5–6.
61 5.4.35–57; comment on Cleombrotus, Plut.*Ages*. 26.2.
62 5.4.58–61.
63 6.3; Plut.*Ages*. 27.5–28.4. Diod. Sic. 15.38, 50.4–6, confuses the renewals of 375 and 371, but 371 must be the occasion of the altercation over Thebes.
64 On the implications of that for Spartan policy see Bearzot, 2004, 109–118.
65 6.4.1–3; response due to Agesilaus, Plut.*Ages*. 28.5–8.

Corinth and Argos

In the late 390's, when an anti-Spartan régime in some kind of union with Argos was brought into being in Corinth, Xenophon concentrates on acts of violence and tells us nothing about the formalities there.[66] Sparta's forces were based on Sicyon, the opposing forces were based on Corinth, and Corinth's land was being ravaged. "Most and the best of the Corinthians" came to desire peace, and the Argives and other enemies of Sparta were afraid that Corinth would revert to the Spartan side. (Diodorus describes the anti-Spartans as democrats, but Xenophon does not go beyond describing the pro-Spartans as "the best".) The anti-Spartans organised a massacre of their opponents; some of the opponents went up to Acrocorinth, but withdrew after receiving unfavourable omens. Some of them then went into exile. Others were persuaded that they could safely return to the city, but they saw "those acting as tyrants", and realised that boundary markers were being uprooted, their city was being called Argos,[67] and they had less power in their own city than metics [i.e. than the Argives]: they wanted to reclaim their country as Corinth and make it free, purified from assassins and subject to good legal conditions [*eunomia*]. Some of them managed to reach the Spartan army, and fighting and bloodshed continued.

What arrangements were made between Corinth and Argos, at what time(s), is hard to make out from Xenophon and our other sources, but there must have been formal decisions in both cities, and it is particularly frustrating that Xenophon gives us no details in this case. Argos had a council and an assembly in the normal Greek manner, and has left us some inscribed decrees including a few from the classical period; but from Corinth the epigraphic and literary evidence is very meagre, and although it is possible it is not certain that in the classical period there was an assembly, even with limited membership, as well as a council.[68]

The Athenian Iphicrates had been commanding a mercenary force based in Corinth. At a later stage in the Corinthian War Xenophon reports that he had put to death some of the supporters of Argos, and Argos had had him sent back to

---

66 4.4.1–13. On this episode cf. Diod. Sic. 14.86.1–3, Andoc. 3. *Peace* 18; on the union cf. Diod. 14.92.1, Andoc. 3. *Peace* 26–7, and see, for instance, Salmon, 1984, 357–362.
67 Cf. 4.5.1, 4.8.15, 34, 5.1.34, 36.
68 Rhodes with Lewis, 1997, 67–71; 72–73.

Athens, while Diodorus states that Iphicrates had intended to get control of Corinth for Athens but when he was prevented by the *demos* he resigned his command.[69]

After the King's Peace Sparta proceeded to insist on interpretations of freedom and autonomy which suited Sparta. In this case, Xenophon gives a brief report supportive of the pro-Spartan Corinthians: at first the Corinthians did not dismiss their Argive garrison; but when Agesilaus threatened them the Argives departed, the Corinthian *polis* became "itself by itself" (αὐτὴ ἐφ' αὑτῆς), the murderers and those who shared in the guilt left Corinth of their own accord, and the remaining citizens willingly received back those who had been exiled before.[70]

Later there are violent episodes known from other sources which Xenophon does not mention. He does not mention the *skytalismos* in Argos in 370/69, when demagogues incited the people against the rich, the rich planned to overthrow the democracy but were unsuccessful, and after condemning rich the *demos* turned against the demagogues.[71] For Corinth, in 366–365 Xenophon does mention attempts by Athens, in response to a speech in the Athenian assembly by one Demotion (it is striking that, though exiled from Athens, Xenophon gives for Athens information of this kind, which he does not often give for other states), to keep Corinth in alignment with Sparta and Athens. Corinth dismissed the Athenian forces in its territory, but then felt weak and isolated, hired mercenary troops, and made a treaty with Thebes which effectively marked the end of Sparta's Peloponnesian League.[72] Remarkably, however, Xenophon does not mention that the use of the mercenaries by Timophanes led to his being regarded as a tyrant, and to the involvement of his own brother Timoleon in assassinating him.[73]

---

[69] 4.8.34; Diod. 14.92.1–2 (where C.H. Oldfather in the Loeb edition and Salmon, *Wealthy Corinth*, 367, took the *demos* to be that of Athens, and the Budé translation of M. Bonnet & E.R. Bennett is ambiguous, but more probably that of Corinth is meant). Harp. ξ 2 Keaney ξενικὸν ἐν Κορίνθῳ, citing Androtion *FGrH* 324 F 48, Philoch. 328 F 150, does not mention this episode.

[70] 5.1.34. Diod. does not mention this at all.

[71] Diod. 15.58. After the renewal of the King's Peace in 375 Diod. 15.49 has a general chapter on upheavals and *staseis*, particularly in the Peloponnese, which ought probably to have been placed after Leuctra.

[72] 7.4.4–10. (Diod. 15.76.3 has a general renewal of the King's Peace at this point).

[73] Diod. 16.65.2–6 (in the context of Timoleon's being sent to Sicily in 346/5, not making it clear that this episode occurred twenty years earlier); Nep. 20. *Tim.* 1.3–6; Plut.*Tim.* 4.4–5.4.

Thebes and Boeotia

If we turn to the pro-Spartan régime imposed by Sparta on Thebes in 382,[74] Xenophon represents this as a response to rivalry within Thebes between the anti-Spartan Ismenias and the pro-Spartan Leontiades. (It was also connected with the war against Olynthus, and probably the Spartans justified their intervention by claiming that Thebes was refusing to join in enforcing the King's Peace against Olynthus.)[75] While the women were celebrating the Thesmophoria and the council was in session, Leontiades led Phoebidas and the Spartans to the Cadmea, and announced the *fait accompli* to the council and ordered the arrest of Ismenias; another polemarch was elected in place of Ismenias; Ismenias' supporters fled to Athens; Sparta decided to accept what had happened, and an *ad hoc* court of men from the Spartan alliance condemned Ismenias. Later, when Xenophon provides his striking condemnation of this act by Sparta, he refers to the Thebans who had led the Spartans to the acropolis as wanting to enslave the city to Sparta so that they themselves could be tyrants; and as he proceeds to narrate the downfall of that régime he begins with the man who was "secretary to the polemarchs around Archias". In the other cities of Boeotia, he says, *dynasteiai*, narrow cliques, had been installed.[76] It looks as if in theory what happened was that there was not formally a change of régime, but, with the Spartans in the background, Leontiades secured the appointment of a pro-Spartan board of polemarchs to continue to administer Thebes under the existing constitution; and we do not know any more about the installation and nature of the *dynasteiai* in the other cities.

While Xenophon does not exculpate the Spartans, our other sources more clearly blame the Spartans rather than their Theban collaborators. According to Diodorus, Phoebidas had instructions from Sparta to seize Thebes if possible: he did so, defeated opposing Thebans, exiled prominent men and terrorised the remainder. Plutarch in his *Agesilaus* concentrates on responsibility for the seizure, making it clear that king Agesilaus was behind Sparta's acceptance of it and likely that he had prompted it; but he adds that the government of Thebes was entrusted to Archias and Leontiades, who had helped Phoebidas, and they were in fact tyrants but in theory polemarchs. In his *Pelopidas* he begins with Sparta's suspicion of Thebes under the *hetaireia* of Ismenias and Androcleidas, which in-

---

74 5.2.25–36; Diod. 15.20.1–2; Plut.*Ages.* 23.6–24.2, *Pel.* 5.1–6.2.
75 E.g. Rhodes, 2010, 230: notice 5.2.27.
76 5.4.1–2; 46.

cluded Pelopidas, who seemed to be *phileleutheros* and *demotikos*. Archias, Leontiades and Philippus were rich and oligarchic, and they persuaded Phoebidas to seize the Cadmea, exile their opponents and give Thebes a government based on a few and subservient to Sparta. The Thebans lost their traditional constitution (*patrios politeia*), were enslaved to the group of Archias and Leontiades, and had no hope of escaping from the tyranny unless the power of Sparta was broken. (In fact Thebes, and Boeotia in general, were already mildly oligarchic before this episode, and I think Plutarch is misapplying the conventional contrast between oligarchs and democrats: I do not think Thebes and Boeotia necessarily became more narrowly oligarchic at this point, or indeed that they became democratic after their liberation in 379/8).[77]

The restoration of an anti-Spartan régime in winter 379/8 is narrated in terms of the assassination of the pro-Spartan rulers by a group of exiles who had set out from Athens.[78] We learn incidentally from narratives of later events and from inscriptions that the revived Boeotian federation had a new constitution, no longer based on the eleven regional units of the old federation, but with a federal assembly meeting in Thebes, and with its Boeotarchs all Theban, whether by law or simply *de facto* as a result of the assembly's meeting in Thebes. Xenophon says as little as possible about the federation and its leaders Pelopidas and Epaminondas; but after a series of unsuccessful attempts by Sparta to recover control he mentions that "the things of the Thebans were rekindled", and in the context of 375 that the Thebans had subdued the cities in Boeotia.[79] On the mechanisms by which the new federation was brought into being we know nothing.

When after Leuctra Theban power was extended into the Peloponnese, in 366 Epaminondas after a campaign in Achaea was approached by the "best" men and "had power to achieve" (an unusual use of ἐνδυναστεύει: he had the power to ensure that his policy was followed) that they should not be exiled and the consitutitons should not be changed, and he enrolled the Achaeans in the Theban alliance. The Arcadians and the aristocrats' opponents objected that this would hand over Achaea to Sparta, so the Thebans did not uphold Epaminondas' policy but sent governors (Xenophon uses the Spartan tern harmost) to the cities, and they joined with the masses to expel the aristocrats and establish democracies. That misfired, and the exiled aristocrats regained control and openly aligned

---
[77] Thuc. 5.38.1–3, *Hell.Oxy.* 19.2–4 Chambers. *Hell.Oxy.* 20.1–2 represents the division in Thebes as within the ranks of the "best and most notable of the citizens". See Rhodes, 2016, 59–64.
[78] 5.4.1–18; Diod. 15.25–7; Plut.*Pel.* 6.3–12.
[79] 5.4.46; 6.1.1.

their cities with Sparta.⁸⁰ What Epaminondas had done was to abstain from interfering in the cities' internal affairs; through what formalities after that the democracies were established and then the aristocracies were restored we are not told, but in each case what happened will have been some kind of revolution. This and a few other passages have been seen, probably rightly, as signs that Thebes had built up an organised body of allies to match the Peloponnesian League and the Second Athenian League;⁸¹ but that is one of many aspects of Thebes which Xenophon does not interest himself in.

Phlius

Affairs at Phlius are mentioned in the *Hellenica* at several points. *C.* 392 the Athenian Iphicrates raided the territory and killed many of those who went out to oppose him. The citizens then called in the Spartans, of whom they had previously been wary because they might restore pro-Spartan exiles, and the Spartans virtuously did nothing about the exiles and departed when the emergency was over.⁸² After the King's Peace things were very different, and Sparta was much less scrupulous in its treatment of Phlius. *C.* 384–383 the exiles approached the ephors in Sparta, they sent a threatening message to Phlius, and Phlius decreed that the exiles should be taken back and their confiscated property should be restored to them.⁸³ But after the Olynthian war had broken out the Phliasians refused to give fair treatment to the restored exiles. Further complaints were made to Sparta, the ephors proclaimed a campaign against Phlius, and Agesilaus accepted the command with enthusiasm. The Phliasians took to holding assemblies where the Spartans could see them, and some Spartans were worried about making Sparta unpopular, but Agesilaus found ways of supporting the exiles.⁸⁴ The Phliasians reduced their daily rations in order to hold out longer, and a charismatic man called Delphion prevented any suggestions of peace. In the end the food supply ran out and the Phliasians did ask for peace — from the Spartan authorities, but

---

80 7.1.41–3.
81 Cf. 7.3.11 (common *dogma* of the allies), *IG* vii 2418 = Rhodes & Osborne 57. 11, 24 (Byzantine *synedroi*), with Lewis, 1990, 71–73, against Buckler, 1980, 222–233, and Buckler, 2000, 431–436; and see also Jehne, 1999, 328–344 (Boeotian federation treated as an extension of Thebes, and external allies as an extension of the federation).
82 4.4.15.
83 5.2.8–10.
84 5.3.10–17.

Agesilaus was able to get the decision referred to himself. He made arrangements for a settlement and a new constitution, not freely adopted by Phlius but imposed by Sparta, and left a garrison in the city.[85] In the 360's, when many Peloponnesian states took advantage of Sparta's post-Leuctra weakness to break away from Sparta, Phlius remained consistently loyal.

Arcadia

One striking matter in the 360's was the formation of and later the split within the Arcadian federation. After the King's Peace Mantinea had been split into its component villages by Sparta, presumably by a tendentious announcement that that was what the terms of the treaty required, and the rich landowners were happy with that.[86] After the battle of Leuctra and the peace treaty which followed it the Mantineans, "considering themselves autonomous in all respects, all met together and decreed to make Mantinea a single city and fortify the city". That must refer to an *ad hoc* meeting which considered itself to be an assembly of the single *polis* which it brought back into existence. Sparta sent Agesilaus to protest, and "the *archontes* were not willing to convene the *demos* for him but told him to say what he needed to them". He tried to persuade them to pause in the building of their fortifications, but they replied that they could not, "since a resolution (*dogma*) had been made by the whole city that they should fortify now".[87]

Meanwhile in Tegea there was a division between men who wanted a united Arcadia with a common decision-making body (*koinon*) and those who wanted to leave the city as it was and adhere to the traditional laws. The federalists were defeated in the body of *thearoi* (we do not know the relationship of that board to the epigraphically attested Fifty and Three Hundred),[88] but they thought that if the *demos* came together they would have the advantage of numbers, and they took up arms, but were defeated in battle. They began peace talks but asked for help from Mantinea, and the upshot was that the federalists were victorious, some of their opponents were executed and many others fled to Sparta.[89] Thus far Xenophon has given us the kind of detail which he does not often give except for

---

85 5.3.21–5.
86 5.2.1–7; Diod. 15.5, 12.
87 6.5.3–5.
88 See Rhodes with Lewis, 1997, 90–92; Nielsen, 2004, 532. The body which issued a decree in the name of the *polis* is of the late fourth century (*SEG* xi 1051).
89 6.5.6–10. On federalists and city loyalists see Bearzot, 2004, 119–138.

Athens and Sparta, while making it clear that the process of creating the federation involved violence; but he then focuses on the warfare which followed, and nowhere directly states that an Arcadian federation was founded and created the new city of Megalopolis.[90]

A new phase began in 366, when Lycomedes of Mantinea persuaded the Ten Thousand in Arcadia to negotiate an alliance with the pro-Spartan Athens, and that held although Lycomedes was killed by Arcadian exiles on his return journey.[91] Further violence followed. In 365 war broke out between Elis and Arcadia, and in 364 that led to a battle in the sanctuary at Olympia. After the battle the Arcadian *archontes* began to use temple treasures to pay for their full-time soldiers, the *eparitoi*, and Mantinea led those who objected. The *archontes* summoned the Mantineans' *prostatai* (their leading men) before the Ten Thousand, and when they refused to come they condemned them *in absentia* and sent the *eparitoi* to arrest them. But support for them grew, until a resolution was passed by the *koinon* (apparently the Ten Thousand) that they should no longer use the sacred funds.

The *archontes* appealed to Thebes to send an expedition and prevent Arcadia from laconising; but "those who had the best policy for the Peloponnese" persuaded the *koinon* to send a rival deputation. There was then a truce, and a feast to celebrate it; but the anti-Spartan party started to arrest "the best men". Most of the Mantineans escaped. Mantinea insisted that nobody should be condemned without a trial, and undertook to produce before the Arcadian *koinon* all who were accused. A Theban officer who was in Tegea backed down, but in Thebes Epaminondas favoured intervening to support the anti-Spartan party.[92] That was reported to the Arcadian *koinon* (now given a passing mention) and the individual cities; the Mantineans and the others who "cared for the Peloponnese" were alarmed about Thebes, and the Mantinea campaign of 362 followed, with Mantinea and some others fighting on the Spartan side but Tegea, Megalopolis and some others fighting alongside the Thebans.[93] Here, then, despite his failure to

---

90 Diod. 15.59.1 (attributing the federation to "Lycomedes of Tegea", when Lycomedes was in fact of Mantinea), 72.4 (Megalopolis). Xenophon mentions Megalopolis only once, among the cities on the Tegean side at 7.5.5. On the constitution of the federation see *IG* v. ii 1 = Rhodes & Osborne 32.
91 7.4.2–3. Other writers report that the Theban Epaminondas, arguing against the Athenian Callistratus, failed to persuade the Arcadians to prefer Thebes and Argos: Nep. 15. *Epam.* 6.1–3, Plut. *Reg. Imp. Apophth.* 193 C–D.
92 7.4.12–40; cf. Diod. 15.77.1–4, 78.1–3, 82.1–3.
93 7.5; cf. Diod. 15.82.4–89.2 (regarding those who fought on the Theban side as "most and the strongest of the Arcadians", 84.4).

treat directly the foundation of the Arcadian federation, Xenophon does for once give the kind of institutional detail which he often fails to give except for Athens and Sparta.

Sicyon

Also for the 360's Xenophon gives us a detailed account of events in Sicyon, where political division led to violence. Sicyon had had a constitution based on "the ancient laws", but Euphron, who was already influential with the Spartans and wanted to be influential with their opponents, told them that if the rich remained in control the city would soon go over to Sparta but if there was a democracy the city would remain on their side. He called an assembly, and in the presence of the Argives and Arcadians announced that the constitution was to be on equal and fair terms (ἐπὶ τοῖς ἴσοις καὶ ὁμοίοις). He had himself and others elected generals, transferred the command of the mercenaries to his own son, cultivated and added to the mercenaries, expelled men on charges of laconism, got rid of his colleagues, and so "made everything subject to him and was clearly a tyrant".[94]

Aeneas of Stymphalus with an Arcadian army went to the acropolis, and summoned "the best" of those inside the city and those who had been exiled "without a decree (*dogma*)". Euphron fled to the harbour, was reconciled with the Spartans, and claimed (falsely, Xenophon implies) that earlier he had voted against breaking with Sparta and had set up the democracy to take revenge on those who had betrayed him. He obtained mercenaries from Athens, and with the *demos* controlled the city; but a Theban harmost controlled the acropolis. Next Euphron went to buy off the Thebans, but opponents followed him to Thebes and killed him there; they persuaded the Thebans that they had acted rightly (he was a tyrant, enslaved not merely free men but citizens, and killed, exiled and confiscated the property of not wrongdoers but whoever he chose, i.e. the best men), but in Sicyon Euphron was given an honourable burial and revered as founding hero. Xenophon ended his account with the disapproving comment, "Thus, it seems, the majority define as good men those who have benefited them".[95]

---

94 7.1.44–6; cf. Diod. 15.70.3 (369/8, in a context of 368: this first phase only, later phase not mentioned).
95 7.3 (justification for killing him § 8). Cawkwell, 1979, 381, comments, "Xenophon had watched events at Sicyon with interest and contempt for Euphron, a man who had betrayed Sparta, and whose reconversion aroused scepticism (§ 3). Xenophon was bound to condemn a

Conclusion

For Athens Xenophon gives us major set pieces: after the battle of Arginusae and for the oligarchy of 404–403, showing the violent abuse of regular procedures, and in the fourth century, showing the procedures working as they ought though sometimes leading to an unexpected result. For Sparta he does not have similar set pieces, except for the machinations behind the acquittal of Sphodrias, but he does frequently mention the working of the city's procedures. He also mentions a number of occasions when what happened was influenced by disagreements between kings or other leading individuals, but does not tell us quite as much as we might like (and he probably could) about how this worked out through the decision-making procedures. The internal affairs of other states are mentioned by Xenophon mostly when there was a change of alignment or régime, and here he is inconsistent. The union of Argos and Corinth at the end of the 390's is presented as a violent affair, without institutional detail; and violence is involved particularly in the upheavals in the Peloponnese after Leuctra, when Sparta could no longer keep régimes which it favoured in power (though we know from other sources of some violent episodes which Xenophon omits), and in the account of Euphron of Sicyon. But sometimes changes are set in their institutional context; and large areas which do not concern Xenophon's underlying interest in Sparta are omitted altogether. What he gives us depended partly, no doubt, on his access to information, and partly on how he chose to write up a particular episode.

Bibliography

Badian, E. (2004), "Xenophon the Athenian", in: *Xenophon and His World*, C.J. Tuplin (ed.), Stuttgart, 33–53.
Bearzot, C. (2004), *Federalismo e autonomia nelle Elleniche di Senofonte*, Milano.
Buckler, J. (1980), *The Theban Hegemony, 371–362 B.C.*, Harvard.
Buckler, J. (2000), "The Phantom Synedrion of the Boiotian Confederacy 378–335 B.C.", in: *Polis and Politics: Studies in Ancient Greek History Presented to M.H. Hansen*, Copenhagen, 431–436.
Cawkwell, G.L. (1979), "Introduction", in: *Xenophon, A History of My Times*, trans. R. Warner, Harmondsworth.

---

man who had carried out the revolutionary programme alluded to in § 8, to condemn also the majority who regarded him highly." On Euphron see also Harris in this volume.

Hansen, M.H./Nielsen, T.H. (eds) (2004), *An Inventory of Archaic and Classical Poleis*, Oxford.
Harris, E.M. (2013), *The Rule of Law in Action in Classical Athens*, New York.
Hornblower, S. (1991–2008), *A Commentary on Thucydides*, Oxford.
Hornblower, S. (2009), "Thucydides and the Athenian *Boulê* (Council of Five Hundred)", in: L.G. Mitchell/L. Rubinstein (eds), *Greek History and Epigraphy: Essays in Honour of P.J. Rhodes*, Swansea, 251–264.
Jehne, M. (1999), "Formen der thebanischen Hegemonialpolitik zwischen Leuktra und Chaironeia (371–338 v. Chr.)" *Klio* 81, 317–358.
Krentz, P. (1982), *The Thirty at Athens*, Ithaca.
Krentz, P. (1989), *Xenophon*, Hellenika, II. 3. 11–.2. 8, Warminster.
Lewis, D.M. (1990), "The Synedrion of the Boeotian Alliance", in: *Essays in the Topography, History and Culture of Boiotia*, A. Schachter (ed.), (*Tiresias* Supp. 3), 71–73.
MacDowell, D.M. (1978), *The Law in Classical Athens*, London.
MacDowell, D.M. (1986), *Spartan Law*, Edinburgh.
Ostwald, M. (1986), *From Popular Sovereignty to the Sovereignty of Law*, Berkeley.
Rhodes, P.J. (1981), *A Commentary on the Aristotelian* Athenaion Politeia, Oxford.
Rhodes, P.J. (2010), *A History of the Classical Greek World, 478–323 B.C.*, Chichester.
Rhodes, P.J. (2016), "Boiotian Democracy?" in: *Boiotia in the Fourth Century b.c.*, S.D. Gartland (ed.), Pennsylvania, 59–64.
Rhodes, P.J., with Lewis, D.M. (1997), *The Decrees of the Greek States*, Oxford.
Salmon, J.B. (1984), *Wealthy Corinth*, Oxford.
Seager, R.J. (2001), "Xenophon and Athenian Democratic Ideology", in: CQ^2 51, 385–397.
Tracy, S.V. (2014), "The Wrongful Execution of the Hellenotamiai (Antiphon 5. 69 71) and the Lapis Primus", in: *CP* 109, 1–10.
Tracy, S.V. (2016), *Athenian Lettering of the Fifth Century B.C.*, Berlin.
Underhill, G.E. (1900), *A Commentary with Introduction and Appendix on the* Hellenica *of Xenophon*, Oxford.

Frances Pownall
Violence and Civil Strife in Xenophon's *Hellenica*

Although he notoriously begins *in medias res*, one of Xenophon's major themes in the *Hellenica* (even if he never says so overtly) is to illustrate the rise and fall of the Spartan hegemony.[1] Not surprisingly, he offers gripping narratives of the set-piece battles at Leuctra and Mantinea, which represent the climax and the dénouement respectively of the failure of Spartan leadership, as highlighted by the concatenation of references to divine intervention in these campaigns.[2] Nevertheless, he reserves some of his most evocative and compelling narrative for episodes of civil strife, marked by egregious violence, coupled with a disregard for social and religious norms. As I shall argue, Xenophon deliberately highlights these scenes of violent *stasis* in order to illustrate one of the underlying themes of the *Hellenica*, the futility and destructiveness of internecine warfare.

The first of these episodes occurs during the first extended narrative of the *Hellenica*, Xenophon's vivid account of the rule of the Thirty (2.3.11–2.4.43),[3] which has been identified as programmatic, offering a paradigmatic model of the rise and fall of stereotypical tyrants.[4] While I do not disagree with this conclusion, especially inasmuch as one of the most common topoi of tyranny is arbitrary and excessive cruelty, it is important to examine the narrative contexts in which these acts of violence and brutality occur. Although Xenophon does downplay the ideological basis to the government of the Thirty,[5] he nevertheless takes pains to highlight the ongoing support they received from the Spartans right from the beginning, in the form of a Spartan garrison under the command of the *harmost* Callibius.[6] This Spartan garrison henceforth provided the necessary muscle for

---
1 As observed by Tuplin, 1993; cf. Dillery, 1995, esp. 179–237; Flower, 2016, 307; Buxton, 2017.
2 Cf. Pownall, 2004, 89–94 and Hau, 2016, 236–238.
3 Unless stated otherwise, all references are to Xenophon's *Hellenica* and all translations are my own.
4 So Krentz, 1982, 145 and 1995, 122; Tuplin 1993, 43–47; Dillery, 1995, 138–163; Pownall, 2016, 55–61. On the violence of the Thirty in Xenophon's narrative, see also Wolpert, in this volume.
5 See Pownall, 2012.
6 On *harmosts* as instruments of Spartan imperialism and the intense hatred they engendered among the Greek poleis, see Ruzé, 2018.

the Thirty, and Xenophon states that Callibius became complicit in the ensuing purge of their political opposition (2.3.14).[7]

In the brief introductory section in which Xenophon sets up the showpiece conflict between Critias and Theramenes that ultimately dominates his narrative of the Thirty, he states three times in quick succession that the Thirty killed many people. The first of these instances occurs at the beginning of the quarrel between the two (2.3.15), when Theramenes unsuccessfully attempted to check Critias' desire to eliminate the democratic opponents of the Thirty, for "he (i.e., Critias) was eager to kill many people" (αὐτὸς μὲν προπετὴς ἦν ἐπὶ τὸ πολλοὺς ἀποκτείνειν). During the ensuing purge of the Thirty's political opponents, Xenophon comments (2.3.17) that "many people were being killed, and unjustly too" (ἀποθνησκόντων πολλῶν καὶ ἀδίκως), which prompted further resistance from Theramenes. Once the Thirty had disarmed the population of Athens (a standard device of tyrants) with the collusion of the Spartan garrison (2.3.20), they "killed many people out of personal enmity and many for money" (πολλοὺς μὲν ἔχθρας ἕνεκα ἀπέκτεινον, πολλοὺς δὲ χρημάτων), and determined to target the metics in particular in order to continue to pay the Spartan garrison (2.3.21),[8] once again provoking the opposition of Theramenes. The verbal echoes between these passages underscore the murderous violence of the Thirty, and the repeated insistence on Theramenes' futile attempts to stem the flow sets the stage for his final confrontation with Critias.

In this extensive scene,[9] which Xenophon deliberately presents as a "trial" in which Critias "prosecutes" Theramenes (2.3.23–52),[10] violence, both actual and

---

[7] In order to emphasize the complicity of Callibius and the Spartan garrison in the violence of the Thirty right from the beginning, Xenophon deliberately deviates from the chronology of the *Ath. Pol.* (37.2), which dates the Thirty's appeal to the Spartan garrison only after the execution of Theramenes, once Thrasybulus and his forces have seized Phyle. Diodorus (14.4.30–3 with 32.6) and Justin (5.8.11 with 9.14) attempt to resolve the discrepancy with positing two appeals to Sparta. On this crux, see Krentz, 1982, 131–147 (cf. Krentz, 1995, 125–126) and Ostwald, 1986, 488–489, both of whom favour Aristotle's chronology; cf. Rhodes, 1981, 416–422; 450–451, who favours Xenophon's.

[8] The metic purge can also be explained in terms of the Spartan *xenēlasia* and the rite of passage inherent in the *krypteia*; Whitehead, 1982/83, 128–130 and Ostwald, 1986, 487.

[9] These speeches (in direct discourse) occupy what seems to be a disproportionate amount of space in Xenophon's narrative, as observed by, e.g., Krentz, 1982, 145 and Dillery, 1995, 153.

[10] And so it is also often classified by modern scholars, e.g., Gray, 1989, 94; Dillery, 1995, 155; Krentz, 1995, 129. As I have argued elsewhere (Pownall, 2018), Xenophon's presentation of the showdown scene as a trial and his use of Theramenes as a linking figure offer a retrospective reevaluation of the Arginusae trial and also foreshadow Socrates' own future trial and condemnation.

implied, underlies the speeches of both men. The scene opens with the Thirty summoning "youths whom they deemed to be the boldest" armed with concealed daggers.[11] It is at this point, in the presence of a stereotypically tyrannical bodyguard, that Critias denounces Theramenes before the Council, alleging that he is a traitor both to his fellow Athenian oligarchs and more pointedly to their Spartan supporters. He justifies the Thirty's purge by claiming euphemistically that "such things happen whenever there is a change in constitution" (2.3.24).[12] He then adds that violence is in fact a necessity in the case of political enemies, stating: "If we perceive that someone is opposed to the oligarchy, we remove him as best we can. It seems to us to be especially just that if one of us is causing harm to this regime, he should pay the penalty" (2.3.26).[13] A little later Critias states bluntly that "all changes of constitution, I suppose, bring death,"[14] but alleges that Theramenes himself, through his traitorous conduct, is responsible for both the greatest number of oligarchs killed by the people and the greatest number of democrats killed by the elite (2.3.32). Critias concludes (2.3.34) that the Spartans themselves, who possess the best constitution of all, would judge Theramenes worthy of the greatest penalty (τῆς μεγίστης τιμωρίας ἀξιωθῆναι) for his treachery. In his speech of self-defense, Theramenes emphasizes the extreme violence of the Thirty, particularly their murder of innocent people (2.3.38–43), attributing it (2.4.43) to their shameful desire for gain (αἰσχροκέρδεια) rather than any legitimate political reason, including the gratification of the Spartans (2.3.41, 45–46).

The emphasis on violence continues in the aftermath of these paired speeches. Critias' response is to bring forward the youths armed with daggers (whose threatening presence neatly frames the speeches in Xenophon's narrative) and thereby intimidate the Council, allowing him to erase Theramenes from the citizen list and condemn him to death (2.3.50–51). Xenophon then proceeds to narrate in vivid detail the dramatic scene in which Theramenes leaps to an altar and denounces (in direct speech) the injustice and impiety of the Thirty (2.3.52–53). He begins by begging the Council to receive only that which is of the utmost

---

11 καὶ παραγγείλαντες νεανίσκοις οἳ ἐδόκουν αὐτοῖς θρασύτατοι εἶναι ξιφίδια ὑπὸ μάλης ἔχοντας παραγενέσθαι. These "youths" are probably to be identified with the armed "attendants" who appear at the conclusion of this scene (2.3.54); Krentz, 1995, 129. Whitehead, 1982/83, 124 suggests that this corps was deliberately modelled on the Spartan royal guard.
12 ὅπου πολιτεῖαι μεθίστανται πανταχοῦ ταῦτα γίγνεται.
13 καὶ ἐάν τινα αἰσθανώμεθα ἐναντίον τῇ ὀλιγαρχίᾳ, ὅσον δυνάμεθα ἐκποδὼν ποιούμεθα· πολὺ δὲ μάλιστα δοκεῖ ἡμῖν δίκαιον εἶναι, εἴ τις ἡμῶν αὐτῶν λυμαίνεται ταύτῃ τῇ καταστάσει, δίκην αὐτὸν διδόναι.
14 καὶ εἰσὶ μὲν δήπου πᾶσαι μεταβολαὶ πολιτειῶν θανατηφόροι.

justice (ἱκετεύω τὰ πάντων ἐννομώτατα), that is, not to allow Critias to erase him arbitrarily from the citizen list, and continues with the striking statement (2.3.53):

> By the gods, I am not unaware of this, that this altar will not benefit me at all, but I wish to make this point also, that these men are not only most unjust toward humans but are also most impious toward the gods.[15]

After warning the Council that they are leaving themselves open to the same fate, Theramenes is dragged off to his fate, the Thirty indeed fulfilling his prediction of violating the normal rules of supplication. I have discussed elsewhere Xenophon's emphasis on the Thirty's impiety in this episode,[16] but I wonder if he is also highlighting their hypocrisy here. In spite of their declared laconophilia, the Thirty fail to adhere to one of the most basic of Spartan cultural norms, their (in)famous reputation for piety.[17]

In addition to the injustice and impiety of Theramenes' condemnation, Xenophon underlines its violence by including vivid details that are unnecessary for the strict narrative purposes of the episode (a point to which he draws our attention with one of his rare authorial intrusions into the narrative).[18] The Thirty duly order the Eleven to lead Theramenes away to his execution, and he is forcibly dragged from the altar by their leader Satyrus (2.3.54), whom Xenophon goes out of his way to characterize as "the boldest and most shameless" (τοῦ θρασυτάτου τε καὶ ἀναιδεστάτου). Theramenes does not go quietly, however, but, "as was natural" (ὥσπερ εἰκός), calls upon both gods and humans as he is being dragged away. The Council, intimidated by Critias and the Thirty, as well as the presence of the armed youths and (notably) the Spartan garrison, remain silent (2.3.55). When he continues to call out in a very loud voice (μάλα μεγάλῃ τῇ φωνῇ) as he is dragged though the agora, Satyrus attempts to threaten him into silence, to which Theramenes responds with a clever verbal riposte (2.3.56), which highlights his own bravery as well as serves to underline the violence with which he is being treated.[19] Xenophon concludes this episode by describing how at Theramenes' execution, he exhibited similar composure in the face of his imminent death by

---

15 καὶ τοῦτο μέν, ἔφη, μὰ τοὺς θεοὺς οὐκ ἀγνοῶ, ὅτι οὐδέν μοι ἀρκέσει ὅδε ὁ βωμός, ἀλλὰ βούλομαι καὶ τοῦτο ἐπιδεῖξαι, ὅτι οὗτοι οὐ μόνον εἰσὶ περὶ ἀνθρώπους ἀδικώτατοι, ἀλλὰ καὶ περὶ θεοὺς ἀσεβέστατοι.
16 Pownall, 2016, 57–61.
17 On the Spartan reputation for piety, see Parker, 1989.
18 On the significance of this, and Xenophon's other first-person comments, see Pownall, 2018, 362–363.
19 On the narrative motif of the "brave gesture" in the face of imminent death see Flory, 1978.

tossing the dregs of the hemlock and toasting Critias, as if he were playing *kottabos* (2.3.56). This quip also seems to be a dig at Critias' professed laconophilia, as the *kottabos* game and its associations with decadent and orientalizing symposia, would have been completely out of place at austere Spartan banquets.[20] Throughout his narrative of the Thirty, Xenophon is careful not only to highlight the extreme violence that is characteristic of stereotypical tyrannies (e.g., Herodotus 5.92), but also to hint at Spartan collusion in their reign of terror, culminating in the murder of Theramenes. As Martin Ostwald has observed: "It thus became clear that Athens would not be laconized without violence."[21]

After the death of Theramenes, although Xenophon does continue to highlight the tyranny and impiety of Critias and the Thirty,[22] the focus shifts to Thrasybulus and the democratic resistance, the defeat of the Thirty, and the reconciliation in Athens between the two sides. It is notable that Xenophon emphasizes the role of the Spartans, first the Spartan garrison in continuing to support the Thirty (2.4.4; 10; 28–29), and then the Spartan king Pausanias, who is credited with initiating the negotiations between the two sides and plays a major role in the reconciliation (2.4.28–39). In this section, Xenophon includes two vignettes of violence, interestingly one committed by each side. In a short but dramatic episode (2.4.26), a contingent of cavalry, which naturally as members of the elite were supporters of the Thirty, came upon some Athenians who were foraging for provisions. Lysimachus, the hipparch, cut their throats (ἀπέσφαξε), although many of them pleaded for their lives and most of the cavalry were opposed (πολλὰ λιτανεύοντας καὶ πολλῶν χαλεπῶς φερόντων ἱππέων). Xenophon draws our attention to this gratuitous act of violence and violation of the norms of supplication with his use of the brutal verb ἀπέσφαξε,[23] the identification of Lysimachus by name, and the explicit mention of the disapproval of the cavalry.[24] But, as Xenophon hints near the end of this section of his narrative, this sort of atrocity is not restricted to the Thirty and their supporters. Immediately after the Athenian democrats concluded the reconciliation agreement with the surviving supporters of the Thirty, they invited the commanders of the garrison at Eleusis to a conference and murdered them (2.4.43), in short, engaging in the same sort of treacherous brutality that had been the hallmark of the Thirty. Thus, Xenophon suggests that

---

20 On the full significance of Theramenes' sarcastic toast see Pownall, 2006.
21 Ostwald, 1986, 487.
22 As I have demonstrated in Pownall, 2012, 9–10 and 2016, 58–61.
23 Cf. Xenophon's use of this verb in reference to the Spartan execution of the Athenians sailors after Aegospotami; see Kapellos in this volume, p. 166.
24 As Krentz, 1995, 148 observes, this is the only time that the horsemen disapprove of an action of their leaders.

civil strife brings out the worst in both sides,[25] although he does reserve his more detailed and compelling narrative for the tyrannical Thirty, supported by the Spartans.

It should perhaps then come as no surprise that the next act of brutality associated with civil strife once again involves a supporter of the Spartans. Once again the narrative context is significant. Immediately following his account of the fall of the Thirty, Xenophon turns to the Spartan campaign against the Persians in Asia Minor (3.1.1–3.2.20),[26] which concludes with the apparently triumphant (but ultimately unsuccessful) truce concluded by the Spartan commander Dercylidas, whereby the Greek cities regained their autonomy from Persia in exchange for the withdrawal of the Spartan army and (tellingly) the *harmosts*. By means of a deliberate (but almost certainly false) synchronization (3.2.21: κατὰ τὸν αὐτὸν χρόνον), Xenophon juxtaposes Dercylidas' successful campaign in Asia with the distinctly less glorious Spartan war against Elis (3.2.21–31), which ultimately sets into motion a chain of events leading to the loss of control over their Peloponnesian allies and the onset of the Corinthian War (concluding with the King's Peace in which the Greeks of Asia Minor were signed back over to Persia).[27] In contrast with Dercylidas in Asia Minor, Agis' first campaign against the Eleans was unsuccessful (3.2.21–24). Agis returns to Elis the following year with more productive results (3.2.24–26). The focus of Xenophon's narrative, however, is not Agis' military achievements, but rather an episode of civil strife that occurs in Elis, when a pro-Spartan faction massacred their political opponents.

Xenophon draws our attention to this gratuitous violence by describing it with a keen eye to detail (3.2.27):

---

[25] Cf. Thucydides' juxtaposition of a war atrocity committed by the Athenians, the Mytilenean episode (3.36–50) with one committed by the Spartans, the Plataean episode (3.52–68).

[26] In this section, Xenophon does provide a vivid narration of one episode of brutality in the context of civil strife: the murder of Mania, the sub-satrap of Aeolis, by her own son-in-law (3.1.10–28). Because this egregious act of violence that subverts cultural norms involves barbarians, rather than Greeks, I do not include it in this discussion; for Xenophon's narrative purposes in narrating the Mania episode in such careful detail, see Pownall, 2016, 71–74.

[27] On the chronological impossibility of this timing, see Tuplin, 1993, 201–205 and Krentz, 1995, 171. McGilvery, 2018 suggests that "Xenophon deliberately conflated Dercylidas' campaign and the Elean War to invite his readers to contrast the spectacular successes of Spartan-led Greek armies over the Persians in Ionia with the inter-poleis conflicts on the Greek mainland which would eventually devolve into the Corinthian War." Cf. Krentz, 1995, 171. On the concentration of narratives of minor Spartan defeats involving unnecessary deaths in the period of Spartan imperialism following their victory in the Peloponnesian War, see Foster in this volume.

The faction of Xenias (who was said to measure out the silver he had inherited from his father by the bushel), wishing the city to go over to the Spartans through their actions, rushed out of a house armed with swords and began a slaughter. They killed many other people and after killing someone who looked like Thrasydaeus, the leader of the people, they thought that they had actually killed Thrasydaeus.[28]

As it turned out, however, Thrasydaeus had not been killed, but was merely sleeping off a bout of inebriation (2.3.28).[29] Those involved in the slaughter were gathered under arms in the agora, when the people learned that Thrasydaeus had not in fact died, as Xenophon rather picturesquely puts it, "his house was filled on all sides, just as the queen is by a swarm of bees."[30] There ensued a battle between the two sides, in which Thrasydaeus and his forces were victorious, and those who had begun the slaughter (οἱ ἐγχειρήσαντες ταῖς σφαγαῖς) fled to the Spartans.

Although this is a short vignette, Xenophon fleshes it out with careful attention to detail and a striking simile (reminiscent of Homeric narrative). It is notable, particularly coming so soon after Xenophon's narrative of the Thirty, that this act of brutality occurs during an episode of civil strife, and is perpetrated by supporters of the Spartans. As noted above, the episode occurs in a narrative context hinting at the failure of Spartan imperialism, and it is surely no coincidence that it is immediately followed in Xenophon's narrative by two dramatically rendered episodes detailing ongoing internal discord at Sparta: the problematic accession of Agesilaus to the Spartan throne (3.3.1–4) and the conspiracy of Cinadon (3.3.4–12).[31]

The Spartans' repeated condoning of the brutality of their supporters and their imperialistic (and even tyrannical) methods of governing their empire led inexorably to the Corinthian War,[32] an internecine conflict that pitted the most

---

28 βουλόμενοι οἱ περὶ Ξενίαν, τὸν λεγόμενον μεδίμνῳ ἀπομετρήσασθαι τὸ παρὰ τοῦ πατρὸς ἀργύριον, τὴν πόλιν δι' αὐτῶν προσχωρῆσαι τοῖς Λακεδαιμονίοις, ἐκπεσόντες ἐξ οἰκίας ξίφη ἔχοντες σφαγὰς ποιοῦσι, καὶ ἄλλους τέ τινας ἀποκτείνουσι καὶ ὅμοιόν τινα Θρασυδαίῳ ἀποκτείναντες τῷ τοῦ δήμου προστάτῃ ᾤοντο Θρασυδαῖον ἀπεκτονέναι.
29 As Krentz, 1995, 175 observes, drunkenness is not generally a positive quality for Xenophon, but on this occasion it does prevent Xenias' coup and save Thrasydaeus' life.
30 περιεπλήσθη ἡ οἰκία ἔνθεν καὶ ἔνθεν, ὥσπερ ὑπὸ ἐσμοῦ μελιττῶν ὁ ἡγεμών.
31 For an examination of how Xenophon's narrative of the Cinadon conspiracy constitutes a critique of Spartan imperialism, see Gish, 2009.
32 The Thebans denounce the Spartans for their imperialism, citing their despotic treatment of their allies and their imposition of *harmosts* (3.5.12), and explicitly equate the *harmosts* with tyrants (3.5.13): "Instead of freedom they have placed a double servitude upon them (i.e., those cities which they "liberated" from Athens), for they are tyrannized by both the harmosts and by the ten men whom Lysander placed in control of each city" (ἀντὶ γὰρ ἐλευθερίας διπλῆν αὐτοῖς

powerful cities in Greece against one another. Just as he had with his narrative of the Elean War, Xenophon juxtaposes the outbreak of the Corinthian War (3.5.1) with Agesilaus' successful campaign against the Persians in Asia (3.4.11–29).[33] Given these parallels between Xenophon's narrative of the rule of the Thirty and the Elean War, it is not surprising that his account of the Corinthian War contains another carefully-rendered scene of horrific violence occurring during an episode of civil strife.

After the opening campaigns of the Corinthian War, the conflict quickly degenerated into an inconclusive stalemate, with most of the continuing devastation falling upon the Corinthians and their territory, causing the Corinthian oligarchs to consider negotiating for peace (4.4.1). Fearing that the city would return to the control of the Spartans, the Corinthian democrats, supported by the anti-Sparta coalition in the Corinthian War, resolved to attempt a general slaughter (οὕτω δὴ σφαγὰς ἐπεχείρουν ποιεῖσθαι) of their political opponents (4.4.2). After denouncing in unusually vehement language the impiety of the conspirators for slaughtering their opponents during a religious festival (4.4.2) and for failing to respect the normal rules of sanctuary (4.4.3),[34] Xenophon proceeds to provide an equally unusually detailed and graphic narrative of the massacre (4.4.3): "Drawing their swords, they began to strike people down, one when he was in a group, another sitting, a third who was in the theatre, and even one who was presiding as a judge in dramatic competition."[35] In addition to the indiscriminate nature of their violence, the conspirators had no compunction about slaughtering their opponents who had taken refuge at the statues of the gods and the altars in the agora (a detail reminiscent of Theramenes' condemnation by the Thirty). Xenophon uses the technique of focalization to underline the impiety and gratuitous violence of the conspirators, claiming that it horrified even those by-standers who were not themselves targets (4.4.3–4).

After the massacre, an amnesty was negotiated (another parallel with the rule of the Thirty at Athens?), and some of the Corinthian oligarchs returned

---

δουλείαν παρεσχήκασιν· ὑπό τε γὰρ τῶν ἁρμοστῶν τυραννοῦνται καὶ ὑπὸ δέκα ἀνδρῶν, οὓς Λύσανδρος κατέστησεν ἐν ἑκάστῃ πόλει).

[33] Krentz, 1995, 186 aptly observes: "In his narrative of Agesilaos' first campaign, Xenophon makes the king out to be much like Derkylidas." He also draws attention to the parallels between the Spartans' motivations for declaring war in both conflicts (cf. 3.2.21 and 3.5.5): Krentz, 1995, 197.

[34] Cf. Pownall, 1998, 254–255.

[35] σπασάμενοι τὰ ξίφη ἔπαιον τὸν μέν τινα συνεστηκότα ἐν κύκλῳ, τὸν δὲ καθήμενον, τὸν δέ τινα ἐν θεάτρῳ, ἔστι δ' ὃν καὶ κριτὴν καθήμενον.

home (4.4.5). But when they perceived that the current regime was behaving tyrannically (ὁρῶντες δὲ τοὺς ἐν δυνάμει ὄντας τυραννεύοντας),[36] and that the Argives had annexed Corinth, resulting in a political union between the two poleis,[37] they decided to appeal to the Spartans for military assistance. In another lively passage, Xenophon narrates how the Spartans engaged in mass slaughter of their opponents, who were trapped beside Corinth's Long Walls (4.4.11–12):

> Some who climbed up the ladders jumped over the wall and were killed; others were shoved and struck down at the foot of the ladders and thus perished; still others were trampled by one another and suffocated.[38]

As the massacre by the Spartans continues, Xenophon graphically comments (4.4.12): "At that time, at any rate, so many fell in such a short time that people who were accustomed to seeing piles of grain, of planks, and of rocks, at that time looked upon piles of bodies."[39] The Spartans proceeded to take advantage of the civil strife in Corinth to capture the port of Lechaeum, slaughtering its Boeotian garrison in the process, an act of gratuitous violence that Xenophon renders memorable through the addition of circumstantial details (4.4.12–13): "some of them had climbed on the walls, and others onto the roofs of the ship-sheds" (οἱ μὲν ἐπὶ τῶν τειχῶν, οἱ δὲ ἐπὶ τὰ τέγη τῶν νεωσοίκων ἀναβάντες). This military success turns out to be illusory, however, for the ultimate upshot of the Spartan seizure of Lechaeum is the unexpected destruction there of the Spartan *mora* by the Athenian commander Iphicrates (5.1.11–17), one of the most devastating defeats ever suffered by the Spartan army.

Another horrific act of violence occurs during the liberation of the Theban Cadmea. During an episode of *stasis* at Thebes (5.2.25: στασιαζόντων δὲ τῶν Θηβαίων), the pro-Spartan faction led by Leontiades took advantage of the celebration of the Thesmophoria (in a parallel to the democratic coup at Corinth discussed above) to seize control of the acropolis and hand the city over to the Spartans (5.2.29). The Spartans put on trial Leontiades' political opponent Ismenias

---

36 On Xenophon's portrayal of the Corinthian democrats as tyrants, see Pownall, 2016, 62–63.
37 Fornis, 2006 argues that no actual constitutional change occurred nor did Corinth cease to be an independent state; instead this mysterious political union should be seen "as an episode more of factional turmoil" (555). As Rhodes (in this volume, p. 56) comments: "Xenophon concentrates on acts of violence and tells us nothing about the formalities there."
38 ἐνταῦθα μέντοι οἱ μὲν κατὰ τὰς κλίμακας ἀναβαίνοντες ἥλλοντο κατὰ τοῦ τείχους καὶ διεφθείροντο, οἱδὲ περὶ τὰς κλίμακας ὠθούμενοι καὶ παιόμενοι ἀπέθνησκον, οἱ δὲ καὶ καταπατούμενοι ὑπ' ἀλλήλων ἀπεπνίγοντο.
39 τότε γοῦν οὕτως ἐν ὀλίγῳ πολλοὶ ἔπεσον ὥστε εἰθισμένοι ὁρᾶν οἱ ἄνθρωποι σωροὺς σίτου, ξύλων, λίθων, τότε ἐθεάσαντο σωροὺς νεκρῶν.

and condemned him to death, in a scene reminiscent of Theramenes' trial and condemnation (5.2.35–36). Xenophon makes no overt judgement here, but it should be noticed that he comments immediately after this scene that the Spartans dispatched an army against the Olynthians "much more vigorously" (5.2.37: πολὺ προθυμότερον), a campaign that, like the dissolution of Mantinea (5.2.1–7),[40] was an overt manifestation of Spartan imperialism in explicit contravention of the autonomy clause in the King's Peace.

Xenophon condemns the seizure of the Cadmea much more overtly in a famous passage at 5.4.1:

> One could tell also of many other incidents, both Greek and barbarian, showing that the gods are not unmindful either of those who are impious or of those who commit unholy acts. Now, at any rate, I shall tell only of the events at hand. The Spartans, who had sworn to allow the cities to be autonomous, seized control of the Theban acropolis and were punished by those very people whom they had wronged, alone, even though they had never previously been defeated by anyone ever. As for those of the Theban citizens who led them onto the acropolis and wished their city to be enslaved to the Spartans so that they themselves could rule as tyrants, it took only seven of the exiles to destroy their rule.[41]

In this passage, Xenophon simultaneously denounces the Spartans for breaking the autonomy clause that they had sworn to uphold in the King's Peace and suggests that divine retribution lies behind the impending expulsion of the pro-Spartan puppet government at Thebes. He also refers analeptically to the Thirty (who are also portrayed as tyrants and Spartan collaborationists),[42] and proleptically

---

40 Interestingly, Xenophon's narrative of the Spartan campaign against Mantinea contains a marked case of the absence of political violence in circumstances of civil strife (5.2.6), perhaps because this episode offers him the opportunity to praise the *peitharchia* of the Spartans. The Spartans' superior discipline, along with their willingness to seek non-violent methods (i.e., the damming of the river running through Mantinea) to gain control of the city, allows them to end the conflict peacefully (a useful *exemplum*?).

41 Πολλὰ μὲν οὖν ἄν τις ἔχοι καὶ ἄλλα λέγειν καὶ Ἑλληνικὰ καὶ βαρβαρικά, ὡς θεοὶ οὔτε τῶν ἀσεβούντων οὔτε τῶν ἀνόσια ποιούντων ἀμελοῦσι· νῦν γε μὴν λέξω τὰ προκείμενα. Λακεδαιμόνιοί τε γὰρ οἱ ὁμόσαντες αὐτονόμους ἐάσειν τὰς πόλεις τὴν ἐν Θήβαις ἀκρόπολιν κατασχόντες ὑπ' αὐτῶν μόνων τῶν ἀδικηθέντων ἐκολάσθησαν, πρότερον οὐδ' ὑφ' ἑνὸς τῶν πώποτε ἀνθρώπων κρατηθέντες, τούς τε τῶν πολιτῶν εἰσαγαγόντας εἰς τὴν ἀκρόπολιν αὐτοὺς καὶ βουληθέντας Λακεδαιμονίοις δουλεύειν τὴν πόλιν ὥστε αὐτοὶ τυραννεῖν, τὴν τούτων ἀρχὴν ἑπτὰ μόνον τῶν φυγόντων ἤρκεσαν καταλῦσαι.

42 Pownall, 2016, 64–65 and Buxton, 2017. Hau, 2016, 237 observes that "the desire to debauch citizen women brands the polemarchs as true tyrants, unable and unwilling to keep their sexual desires under control."

to the collapse of the Spartan empire as a result of Leuctra.⁴³ It is also perhaps worth noting in this context that the subsequent military campaign led by the Spartan king Cleombrotus not only fails to recover the Theban Cadmea, but is spectacularly unsuccessful (5.4.16) and explicitly foreshadows the disastrous Spartan defeat to the Thebans at Leuctra (5.4.17).

The liberation of Thebes is one of the most colourful episodes in the *Hellenica*, for the band of seven Theban exiles disguise themselves as women and gain access to a symposium at which they assassinate the pro-Spartan rulers.⁴⁴ Although Xenophon provides a great deal of circumstantial detail, his narrative of the actual death of the Theban polemarchs is comparatively restrained, and he simply states matter-of-factly that they were killed (5.1.7). What is interesting, for our purposes, is a horrific act of violence that occurs during the aftermath, when the Theban exiles make an assault against the remaining supporters of the pro-Spartan regime. They in turn realize that they are outnumbered and request a truce (5.1.11). Xenophon provides a graphic narrative of what followed (5.4.12):

> After signing a truce and swearing the oaths, they released them on those terms. But as they were descending, the Thebans seized and killed those whom they recognized to be their political enemies... and they even seized the children of those who had been killed, whichever ones had children, and slaughtered them.⁴⁵

Not only do the Theban exiles kill their political enemies in contravention of the oaths they had sworn to allow them to withdraw unharmed, but they also massacre their children. Although Xenophon does not express condemnation explicitly, he does identify a group of Thebans subsequently killed by Cleombrotus and his Spartan troops as those who had been released, a subtle detail that neatly allows him to link crime with divine punishment.⁴⁶

Xenophon's inclusion of this scene of gratuitous violence as a coda to his narrative of the liberation of Thebes serves several functions. First of all, it allows him to draw an explicit link between the Theban exiles and the Spartans (as well as their Theban collaborators) in their impiety for breaking their oath, the very

---

43 See, e.g., Tuplin, 1993, 125–148; Dillery, 1995, 179–237; Pownall, 1998, 256–257; Hau, 2016, 236–238; Buxton, 2017; cf. Buxton, 2017, 25: "The author uses this passage to conflate the Theban junta and its Spartan sponsors in order to place their linked downfalls within a shared metahistorical framework."
44 On Xenophon's narrative of this episode see Gray, 1989, 65–70 and Pownall, 2004, 68–69.
45 καὶ σπεισάμενοι καὶ ὅρκους ὀμόσαντες ἐπὶ τούτοις ἐξέπεμπον. ἐξιόντων μέντοι, ὅσους ἐπέγνωσαν τῶν ἐχθρῶν ὄντας, συλλαμβάνοντες ἀπέκτειναν ... οἱ μέντοι Θηβαῖοι καὶ τοὺς παῖδας τῶν ἀποθανόντων, ὅσοις ἦσαν, λαβόντες ἀπέσφαξαν.
46 Cf. Pownall, 1998, 258.

offense for which Xenophon has condemned the Spartans in such vehement terms at 5.4.1. Second, his deliberate use of the graphic verb ἀποσφάζω provides a verbal echo with previous incidents of *stasis* in the *Hellenica*, where Xenophon demonstrates that acts of atrocity are not restricted to one political faction during episodes of civil strife. Finally, this scene of violence, which is gratuitous to his overall narrative, reinforces one of the dominant themes of the *Hellenica*, namely that *stasis* engenders the utter disregard for cultural and religious norms.

The Spartan defeat at Leuctra does not bring a decisive end to conflict within Greece, and the fragmentation of the Peloponnese accelerates in its wake. During this establishment of a "new order" in the Peloponnese, the Spartans attempt to prevent the reincorporation of Mantinea (6.5.4–5), symbolized by the building of a circuit wall, claiming that it would be a difficult thing to bear if this were to take place without their approval (εἰ τοῦτο ἄνευ τῆς σφετέρας γνώμης ἔσοιτο). Immediately after the Spartans' unsuccessful effort to reassert their imperialism over the Mantineans, Xenophon narrates an episode of bloody civil strife at Tegea between the faction of Proxenus and Callibius, who wished to join the Mantineans in creating an Arcadian federation, and the faction of Stasippus, who wished to maintain the ancestral constitution and remain loyal to Sparta (6.5.6; cf. 6.5.10).

Upon the defeat of their proposal by the Council, the faction of Proxenus and Callibius resorted to violence, and gathered the *demos* together openly under arms (6.5.7). Although numerically inferior, Stasippus and his faction prevailed in battle, killed Proxenus and a few with him (τὸν μὲν Πρόξενον καὶ ἄλλους ὀλίγους μετ' αὐτοῦ ἀποκτείνουσι), and routed the democrats, but did not pursue them, for as Xenophon says (6.5.7–8), "Stasippus was not the sort to wish to kill many of his fellow citizens" (καὶ γὰρ τοιοῦτος ὁ Στάσιππος ἦν οἷος μὴ βούλεσθαι πολλοὺς ἀποκτιννύναι τῶν πολιτῶν). The democrats, however, had no such scruples. They pretended to enter into negotiations for a reconciliation agreement, but only until they caught sight of the Mantinean troops approaching. Then, as Xenophon says (6.5.8–9), "some of them leaped up onto the wall and demanded that they come to help as quickly as possible, shouting at them to hurry, while others opened the gates."[47] The faction of Stasippus, meanwhile, fled the city and took refuge in the temple of Artemis (6.5.9), to no avail as it turned out, for their enemies were undeterred by the prospect of violation of religious sanctuary. In the dramatic conclusion to this episode, Xenophon narrates how the Tegean oligarchs were trapped inside the temple and stoned by their opponents:

---

47 οἱ μὲν αὐτῶν ἀναπηδῶντες ἐπὶ τὸ εἶχος ἐκέλευον βοηθεῖν τὴν ταχίστην, καὶ βοῶντες σπεύδειν διεκελεύοντο· ἄλλοι δὲ ἀνοίγουσι τὰς πύλας αὐτοῖς.

Their enemies who had pursued them climbed onto to the roof of the temple and entering into it through the ceiling began to pelt them with roof tiles. When they realized that there was no recourse, they told them to stop and said that they would come out. As soon as their enemies got them in their power, they seized them, bound them, and threw them onto a cart, and then conveyed them to Tegea. There, they along with the Mantineans condemned them to death and executed them.[48]

Although the Spartans wished to avenge the deaths of Stasippus and his followers, Agesilaus' retaliatory campaign accomplished nothing, and he was forced to withdraw without a battle (6.5.10–21).

Although this minor episode is not strictly necessary for Xenophon's narrative purposes beyond providing a motivation for the Spartans' unsuccessful campaign, he clearly takes a particular interest in it, as attested by the fullness of his account and the amount of circumstantial detail.[49] The Tegean democrats' violation of sanctuary and condemnation to death of their political enemies on trumped-up charges are features typical of civil strife in the *Hellenica*, as we have seen, and once again the narrative context is one of failed Spartan imperialism followed by an unproductive military campaign.

In each of the episodes of *stasis* that we have examined, Xenophon goes to great pains to add emotional content to the horrifically violent incidents that occur during civil strife by rendering them in vivid prose with a careful eye to detail,[50] thereby investing them with an importance that appears to belie their actual military and political significance. Furthermore, he deliberately juxtaposes these episodes of bloody *stasis* with references to Spartan imperialism, inexorably followed by unsuccessful military campaigns. It is no coincidence that Xenophon highlights Sparta's role in these episodes of *stasis* for, as Thucydides (1.19) had already observed,[51] the Spartan method of imperialism consisted of the imposition of pro-Spartan oligarchies upon the cities under their control. The extended discussion of the brutality of the civil strife in Athens during the rule of the Spartan-backed Thirty near the beginning of the *Hellenica* has rightly recognized as paradigmatic, as we have seen above. What has not been recognized be-

---

48 *οἱ δὲ μεταδιώξαντες ἐχθροὶ αὐτῶν ἀναβάντες ἐπὶ τὸν νεὼν καὶ τὴν ὀροφὴν διελόντες ἔπαιον ταῖς κεραμίσιν. οἱδὲ ἐπεὶ ἔγνωσαν τὴν ἀνάγκην, παύεσθαί τε ἐκέλευον καὶ ἐξιέναι ἔφασαν. οἱ δ' ἐναντίοι ὡς ὑποχειρίους ἔλαβον αὐτούς, δήσαντες καὶ ἀναβαλόντες ἐφ' ἅμαξαν ἀπήγαγον ἐς Τεγέαν. ἐκεῖ δὲ μετὰ τῶν Μαντινέων καταγνόντες ἀπέκτειναν.*
49 Cf. Pownall, 1998, 269–272 and Hau, 2016, 239.
50 On Xenophon's "storytelling skills" see Gray, 1989; cf. Gray, 2004.
51 Cf. Hornblower, 1995, 55 comments that this passage is "an excellent and rightly famous summing-up of Spartan imperial methods."

fore (to my knowledge) is that Xenophon's narrative of Sparta's unsuccessful minor campaigns that occur during episodes of *stasis*, scattered throughout the rest of the work, dialogue with and reinforce the themes introduced in the programmatic narrative of the Thirty.

Taken together, these passages suggest that Xenophon viewed the disorder and confusion into which Greece was plunged after the Battle of Mantinea as the natural consequence of the endemic and socially-destructive violence engendered by Sparta's ultimately futile attempts to exercise hegemony (often equated in the *Hellenica* with tyranny) on a panhellenic level. Not only does this reading more firmly anchor the apparently aporistic conclusion to the rest of the *Hellenica* (7.5.27),[52] but it suggests that Xenophon was making a subtle intertextual allusion throughout to one of the most famous passages of Thucydides' history,[53] his description of the brutality of the civil strife at Corcyra (3.81–83).[54] As it seems, both historians viewed the breakdown of normal societal restraints during episodes of *stasis* as emblematic of the internal wars that devastated the contemporary Greek world, yet another way in which Xenophon's *Hellenica* represents a continuation of Thucydides.

Bibliography

Buxton, R.F. (2017), "Modeling Hegemony through *Stasis*: Xenophon on Sparta at Thebes and Phlius" in: *ICS* 42, 21–40.
Dillery, J. (1995), *Xenophon and the History of his Times*, London/New York.
Flory, S. (1978), "Arion's Leap: Brave Gestures in Herodotus" in: *AJP* 99, 411–421.
Flower, M.A. (2016), "Xenophon as a Historian," in: *The Cambridge Companion to Xenophon*, Cambridge, M. Flower (ed.), 301–322.
Flower, M.A. (ed.) (2016), *The Cambridge Companion to Xenophon*, Cambridge.
Fornis, C. (2006), "La ficticia union política de Corinto y Argos (392–386 A.C.)" in: *Mediterraneo Antico* 9, 555–580.
Gish, D. (2009), "Spartan Justice: The Conspiracy of Kinadon in Xenophon's Hellenica" in: *Polis* 26, 339–369.
Gray, V. (1989), *The Character of Xenophon's* Hellenica, Baltimore.
Gray, V. (2004), "Xenophon and Historiography" in: *Narrators, Narratees, and Narratives in Ancient Greek Literature*, I. de Jong et al. (eds), 129–146, Leiden/Boston.

---

[52] Cf. Dillery, 1995 and Rood, 2004, who view disorder in general as a unifying theme of the *Hellenica*.
[53] Cf. Rood, 2004, who does not draw this parallel.
[54] On the significance of this passage to Thucydides' historical thought see Price, 2001; cf. Palmer, 2017.

Hau, L.I. (2016), *Moral History from Herodotus to Diodorus Siculus*, Edinburgh.
Hornblower, S. (1991), *A Commentary on Thucydides*, Vol. 1, Oxford.
Krentz, P. (1982), *The Thirty in Athens*, Ithaca/London.
Krentz, P. (1995), *Xenophon* Hellenika II.3.1–2.4.8, Warminster.
McGilvery, P. (2018), "Xenophon and the Elean War: Garbled Chronology or Deliberate Synchronism?" Abstract published on the website for the Society for Classical Studies, 149th Annual Meeting.
Ostwald, M. (1986). *From Popular Sovereignty to the Sovereignty of Law: Law, Society, and Politics in Fifth-Century Athens*, Berkeley.
Palmer, M. (2017), "*Stasis* in the War Narrative" in: *The Oxford Handbook of Thucydides*, R.K. Balot/S. Forsdyke/E. Foster (eds), 409–425, Oxford/New York.
Parker, R. (1989), "Spartan Religion," in: *Classical Sparta: Techniques Behind her Success*, A. Powell (ed.), 142–172, London.
Pownall, F. (1998), "Condemnation of the Impious in Xenophon's Hellenica" in: *HTR* 91, 251–277.
Pownall, F. (2004), *Lessons from the Past: The Moral Use of History in Fourth-Century Prose*, Ann Arbor.
Pownall, F. (2006), "Critias on the Aetiology of the Kottabos Game," in: *L'étiologie dans la pensée antique*, M. Chassignet (ed.), 17–33, Turnhout.
Pownall, F. (2012), "Critias in Xenophon's *Hellenica*" in: *SCI* 31, 1–17.
Pownall, F. (2016), "Tyrants as Impious Leaders in Xenophon's *Hellenica*" in: *Aspects of Leadership in Xenophon*, R.F. Buxton (ed.), 51–83, Newcastle upon Tyne: *Histos* Supplement 5.
Pownall, F. (2018), "Socrates' Trial and Execution in Xenophon's *Hellenica*" in: *Mouseion* 15.3, 347–368.
Price, J.J. (2001), *Thucydides and Internal War*, Cambridge.
Rhodes, P.J. (1981), *A Commentary on the Aristotelian* Athenaion Politeia, Oxford.
Rood, T. (2004), "Xenophon and Diodorus: Continuing Thucydides" in: *Xenophon and His World*, C. Tuplin (ed.), 341–395, Stuttgart.
Ruzé, F. (2018), "The Empire of the Spartans, 404–371" in: *A Companion to Sparta*, A. Powell (eds), 320–353, Wiley.
Tuplin, C. (1993) *The Failings of Empire: A Reading of Xenophon* Hellenica 2.3.11–7.5.27, Stuttgart.
Whitehead, D. (1982/83), "Sparta and the Thirty Tyrants" in: *AncSoc* 13/14, 105–130.

Edith Foster
Minor Infantry Defeats and Spartan Deaths in Xenophon's *Hellenica*

Xenophon's *Hellenica* describes violent events.[1] Notable are the atrocities of civil strife, the heavy casualty tolls of major battles, and all parties' persistent devastation of others' land and property.[2] Overall, Xenophon's account of the wars and turmoil between 411 and 362 offers little relief from disorder and deaths, particularly as he populates the intervals between major, high-casualty battles with frequent 'medium-sized slaughters' of dozens or hundreds of infantrymen. This paper will focus on the most common defeats, namely those in which Spartan and Lacedaemonian troops are killed, but it is well to note that Xenophon frequently also relates the deaths of soldiers from other cities: cf. e.g. the slaughter of Miletans by the Athenians (1.2.1–3), of Athenians at Ephesus or by Spartan peltasts (1.2.9–10 and 5.4.14), of Eleians by the Arcadians (7.4.13–14), or of Pylians by the Arcadians (7.4.26).[3]

Nevertheless: scenes in which an ambush or the Spartans' own problematic leadership lead Spartan and Lacedaemonian cohorts to a minor defeat and group death outnumber those featuring other cities by a long way and are in general impressively numerous in *Hellenica*. For instance, groups of Spartans are ambushed and die in nine main scenes that span the length of Xenophon's narrative: 2.4.4–7, 3.2.2–5, 4.1.16–19, 4.5.7–18, 4.8.33–39, 5.1.10–12, 5.4.38–40, 6.5.26–27, and 7.1.15–17. Mistakes and/or the over-confidence of a Spartan commander play a conspicuous role in some of these ambush stories; such failings are also key for further tales of defeat, in which commanders were not ambushed but allowed passions to dictate the timing or form of aggressive actions. A commander's anger, sometimes together with other failings, such as greed and cruelty, causes additional Spartan defeat and deaths at 2.4.32–33, 5.3.1–7, and 6.2.17–24. Personal ambition causes Sparta's loss at 3.5.17–20, the distractions of a love affair at 4.8.17–19. Finally, Archidamus' defeat by the Arcadians at Cromnos (7.4.20–25) perhaps results from desperation.

---

1 I thank Dr. E. Baragawanath for her comments.
2 For civil strife and violence, see Pownall in this volume.
3 On the large number of battle narratives in *Hellenica*, see Tuplin, 1989, 37.

This list of 15 passages does not comprehend all of Sparta's minor defeats in *Hellenica*.[4] However, it offers a significant sample. The initial section of this paper examines Xenophon's defeat narratives, dividing them into ambush stories and flawed leader stories. The paper then approaches two main questions. First, it asks why Xenophon chose to tell stories of minor Spartan defeats so frequently. Second, it examines the character of Xenophon's emphasis on violent death.

1 Spartans Ambushed

Xenophon sometimes does, and sometimes does not describe the consequences of a minor defeat by specifying the number of casualties.[5] When he does, the number gives group death an impressive specificity and immediacy. It is therefore noteworthy that numbers describe the consequences of *Hellenica*'s first two ambush scenes. In the first, light-armed Athenians kill 120 Laconian hoplites (2.4.4–7); in the second, light-armed Bithynian Thracians kill 185 hoplite guards of the Spartan commander Derkylidas (3.2.2–5). In both cases, hoplites have been 'borrowed' by third parties who use them for their own ends, and in both cases the vividly depicted defeat and enumerated deaths raise questions about the integrity or prudence of the Spartan leadership that 'lent' out the soldiers.[6]

---

4 Six more Spartan defeat stories will be referenced in this paper: 4.3.22–23 (ambush and death of the Polemarch Gylis), 4.4.10 (doomed sally of Pasimachus at the Battle of Lechaeum), 5.4.42–45 (death of Phoibidas), 5.4.56 (Alcetas careless from a love affair, loses Pagasae), 5.4.59 (ambush of Cleombrotus' light-armed troops at Cithaeron), 7.1.41 (careless Naucles fails to guard Oneium).

5 Of the 21 stories of minor Spartan defeats mentioned in this paper, ten feature casualty figures. Cf. 2.4.6 (120 Spartan hoplites); 3.2.5: no casualty figure provided directly, but since all 200 hoplite guards (cf. 3.2.3) are killed, less 15 who got away, the casualty figure is 185; 4.1.19 (100 soldiers with Agesilaus); 4.3.23 (18 Spartiates); 4.5.17 (250 Lacedaemonian hoplites); 4.8.38 (12 harmosts, 200 of Anaxibius' forces, and 50 Abydenian hoplites); 5.1.11: (9 Spartiates); 5.1.12 (150 Aeginetans, 200 of Gorgopus' troops); 5.4.45 (two or three Spartans, plus Phoibidas); 5.4.59 (40 Spartan light-armed troops); 7.4.25 (30 Spartiates). Other narratives name the most prominent dead and use words such as ἄλλοι for others who died (2.4.33 and 4.4.10); παμπλήθεις are killed at 4.8.19 and 5.3.6; συχνούς describes the peltasts killed at 5.4.39 (whereas the dead Spartiates are individually named); at 6.2.24 we see only that the corpses are given back; at 6.5.26 πάντες die; at 7.1.17 a heavy death toll is implied by the story of an attack on sleeping Spartans. I wish to thank Catherine Rubincam for sharing her forthcoming work on military numbers in Xenophon.

6 At 2.3.13–14 Xenophon shows that both Lysander in Sparta and especially the Spartan harmost Callibius at Athens were suborned by the Thirty to allow them to use their Spartan guards in any

In our first passage, the Spartans have given 200 hoplite guards to the Thirty Tyrants at Athens (cf. 2.3.13–14, 2.3.21). These troops, along with two divisions of Athenian cavalry, have been sent to guard against the rebels who occupied the fort at Phyle, and camp in rough country about a mile and a half from the fort (2.4.4). Unfortunately for them, the rebel leader Thrasybulus has assembled a much larger group of 700 men. Setting out from the fort at night, Thrasybulus settles his forces near the Spartan camp and waits for the moment at dawn when the Spartans are just getting up and beginning to make some noise. His forces then attack the unprepared Spartans at a run, killing some men immediately and pursuing others until they have killed 120 hoplites, along with a few cavalrymen whom they had found still in their beds.[7] They do not pursue the Spartans very far, but quickly return to the Spartan camp, set up a trophy, take any weapons and equipment they find, and retreat to Phyle. The story ends when the Athenian cavalry that comes to assist the Spartans finds no rebels remaining at the Spartan camp; they wait nearby until relatives can pick up the corpses.

The story of Thrasybulus' attack displays commonalities with many of our ambush scenes. Successful attackers outnumber their adversaries, plan their attack, wait for the critical moment,[8] and strike by surprise; the attackers are frequently light-armed troops or cavalry, not hoplites.[9] Xenophon's brief narrative

---

way they saw fit. Derkylidas had not been corrupted in this way; however, he supplied Greek guards to a rapacious force of Odrysian Thracians. Xenophon's remark that Derkylidas himself 'plundered safely' (3.2.2) shows that Derkylidas knew better than to plunder so harshly that the local people would attack him. Nevertheless, he lent the guards to a party whose behavior was almost guaranteed to provoke such attacks. Lysander and Derkylidas had both recently won substantial victories when their 'allies' request guards, and perhaps lent away a few hundred men without much forethought.

[7] The detail that they were killed in their beds adds pathos to their deaths. See *Iliad* 10: 482–490, and the deaths of the Spartan guards at Pylos (Thuc. 4.32.1, also a dawn attack); further pathos arises when Xenophon mentions that one casualty was nicknamed 'Nikostratus the handsome'.

[8] This moment is frequently dawn. See Riedinger, 1991, 231.

[9] Agents of minor Spartan defeats in *Hellenica*: 2.4.4–7: light-armed troops; 2.4.32–33: light-armed; 3.2.2–5: light-armed; 3.5.17–20: hoplites and cavalry; 4.1.16–19: cavalry; 4.3.22–23: light-armed; 4.4.10: hoplites; 4.5.7–18: light-armed; 4.8.17–19: cavalry; 4.8.33–39: light-armed; 5.1.10–12: light-armed (followed by hoplites); 5.3.1–7: cavalry, then peltasts, then hoplites; 5.4.38–40: cavalry; 5.4.42–45: hoplites; 5.4.56: not stated; 5.4.59: light-armed; 6.2.17–24: not stated, probably light-armed; 6.5.26–27: light-armed; 7.1.15–17: not stated; perhaps hoplites; 7.1.41: hoplites; 7.4.20–25: hoplites. Thus, light-armed troops are the main agent of defeat in 9/21 defeats, cavalry are the main agents in 4/21 defeats, and hoplites the main agents of 4/21 defeats; in three cases Xenophon does not state the armament of the attackers precisely, but from the

contrasts the leaderless, outnumbered, and surprised Spartans with the rebels, who have a named leader, more men, and the advantage of surprise. The surviving Spartans' flight from the scene is opposed to the rebels' tactical withdrawal, the victor's trophy to the Spartan corpses.[10] He thus illustrates the utterly contrasting situations of victory and defeat.

Perhaps even crueller than this scene is the somewhat longer story of the deaths of Dercylidas' guards in Bithynian Thrace, since Xenophon shows that these hoplites tried but failed to defend themselves. In this story, Dercylidas has lent 200 hoplite guards to the Odrysian Thracians, who have come to join him at his camp in Bithynian Thrace. The Odrysians set their camp a few miles away from Dercylidas' fortifications. Leaving the Greek guards to watch over it, they plunder the area with their force of 200 cavalry and 300 light-armed men and quickly fill it with prisoners and booty for the Greeks to confine and protect.

The Odrysians' profitable attacks were guaranteed to generate a response, especially once the plundered Bithynians perceive 'how many [Odrysians] had gone out and how many [i.e. few] Greek guards they had left behind' (3.2.3).[11] The Bithynians raise all their peltasts and cavalry and attack the Greek hoplites at dawn. Once again, therefore, we find ourselves reading the story of a dawn attack in which hoplites are surprised and substantially outnumbered by light-armed troops. Xenophon describes their defeat in vivid detail:

> ἐπειδὴ δ'ἐγγὺς ἐγένοντο, οἱ μὲν ἔβαλλον, οἱ δ'ἠκόντιζον εἰς αὐτούς. οἱ δ'ἐπεὶ ἐτιτρώσκοντο μὲν καὶ ἀπέθνησκον, ἐποίουν δ'οὐδὲν κατειργμένοι ἐν τῷ σταυρώματι ὡς ἀνδρομήκει ὄντι, διασπάσαντες τὸ αὐτῶν ὀχύρωμα ἐφέροντο εἰς αὐτούς· [4] οἱ δὲ ᾗ μὲν ἐκθέοιεν ὑπεχώρουν, καὶ ῥᾳδίως ἀπέφευγον πελτασταὶ ὁπλίτας, ἔνθεν δὲ καὶ ἔνθεν ἠκόντιζον, καὶ πολλοὺς αὐτῶν ἐφ'ἑκάστῃ ἐκδρομῇ κατέβαλλον· τέλος δὲ ὥσπερ ἐν αὐλίῳ σηκασθέντες κατηκοντίσθησαν.
> 3.2.3-4

> And when [the Bithynians] came close, some hurled spears at [the guards] and others javelins. And since the [guards] were wounded and dying, but unable to fight back because they were confined by the palisade (which was about the height of a man), they tore apart their fortification and began to rush against them. [4] But the [Bithynians] retreated wherever the [guards] ran out, and since they were peltasts, they easily escaped the hoplites, and they

---

movements described we might attribute one more defeat to light-armed soldiers and one more to hoplite attack.

10 Cf. Lateiner, 1977, on ending battle narratives with references to trophies.
11 Other ambush stories also exhibit the dangers of over-confident plundering. The Spartan king Agesilaus, the great plunderer of *Hellenica*, is normally successful at extricating his men after plundering. Nevertheless, he suffers two minor defeats to cavalry attacks (cf. 4.1.17–19, and 5.4.39–40). For Agesilaus, see Riedinger, 1991, 210 and Tuplin, 1993, 72–73. Not without sarcasm, Riedinger, 1991, argues that *Hellenica* describes the 'Golden Age' of Spartan plundering (209).

kept throwing javelins from this side and that and struck down many of [the guards] each time they ran out; in the end [the guards] were javelined down as if shut up in a sheepfold.

Xenophon's story of the guards' futile defensive efforts and final entrapment displays a horrible death, nor does Xenophon spare his reader the knowledge that the men's corpses were subsequently plundered (a fact that usually goes unmentioned): alerted by men who had escaped early in the battle, soldiers from Dercylidas' camp arrive to help, but find only the 'naked corpses' of the stripped guards (3.2.5).

Xenophon finishes his accounts of the ambushes at Phyle and in Bithynia by explaining the fate of the hoplites' corpses, sealing the outcome of the battle. His accounts demonstrate the cruelty of the on-going wars and in particular the vulnerability of heavy-armed hoplites to light-armed attacks. They foreshadow the longest and fullest description of a successful light-armed attack on Spartan hoplites, the so-called 'disaster at Lechaeum' near Corinth, in which 250 Spartan and allied hoplites are killed.[12]

The narrative of the Lechaeum 'disaster' is unusually long and complex.[13] It begins with reports of post-disaster reactions, one of which is the bifurcated reaction of the Spartans to this defeat: Xenophon writes that whereas the main part of the Spartan army, 'unaccustomed to such disasters', mourned greatly, the relatives of the dead 'went around as if radiant with victory, glorying in their domestic disaster' (4.5.10). While the army perceives a catastrophe, therefore, the relatives seem to draw a personal victory from the deaths of their fathers, sons, or brothers in this defeat.

This divided Spartan response to the battle deaths is the immediate setting for Xenophon's explanation that 600 Lacedaemonian hoplites and two divisions of cavalry had been accompanying the citizens of Amyclai homeward to celebrate the Hyacinthia festival. When the polemarch commanding the force was a few miles from Sicyon, he sent his cavalry support onward with the Amyclaians and turned back toward Lechaeum, his base, with the 600 hoplites (4.5.12). Splitting his forces in this way was his crucial error, the cause of which was over-confi-

---

12 Cf. also the story of the similarly fatal light-armed ambush of the polemarch Gylis and 17 other Spartiates after the battle of Coronea (4.3.22–23).
13 The story of the Spartan 'disaster' at Lechaeum both responds to the previous story of the defeat of the Argives at Lechaeum (4.4.9–12) and also includes an important religious element; neither can be discussed here. In terms of length, we might compare the story of this Spartan disaster to other battles: of the preceding stories of Sparta's much larger hoplite victories, only the story of the Battle of Nemea (4.2.9–23) is as long.

dence: he knew that the nearby Corinthians would certainly see him and that Corinth was stocked with domestic and allied light-armed troops and hoplites (4.5.12). But because of the Corinthians' previous defeats, one of which was a resounding defeat at Lechaeum itself, he was contemptuously over-confident (κατεφρόνουν) that they would not attack (4.5.12).[14]

In contrast to their Spartan opponent, the Athenian commanders inside Corinth, Callias and Iphicrates, think things through and decide that an attack is safe (4.5.13). Callias stations his hoplites close to Corinth, and Iphicrates attacks with the peltasts, causing the same immediate woundings and deaths as the light-armed attack in Bithynia;[15] as in Bithynia, the hoplites' efforts to respond are useless, and they are also frustratingly repetitive: despite the continuous casualties, the polemarch (who remains nameless) sends out successive waves of hoplites to pursue the light-armed attackers. Since the peltasts have been instructed to shoot at the hoplites from a distance, the hoplites can never catch up to them and they die from javelin fire with each attempt. The cavalry, once it comes, is equally useless (as Xenophon explicitly remarks, 4.5.16), failing to use its advantage of speed to kill some of the peltasts and scare the rest away.

The result is a battle account that begins with deaths and in which the Spartans continuously run out to further deaths, whereas their light-armed enemies become more numerous and more confident (4.5.15).[16] Thucydides' detailed narrative of the victory of Athenian light-armed troops over heavy-armed Spartans on the island of Sphacteria (Thuc. 4.32–36) seems to be Xenophon's main paradigm;[17] his explanations of the battle closely agree with Thucydides' analysis of how and why light-armed forces can harm hoplites.[18] But Xenophon's account is

---

[14] Xenophon has also prepared us for the Spartans' over-confidence in face of peltasts, showing at 4.4.16–18 that a single victory had made them contemptuous of peltasts and also of their allies' fear of peltasts. In fact, when peltasts fight in *Hellenica* they are nearly always victorious (Riedinger, 1991, 225).

[15] 3.2.3 (Bithynia): ἐπειδὴ δ'ἐγγὺς ἐγένοντο, οἱ μὲν ἔβαλλον, οἱ δ'ἠκόντιζον εἰς αὐτούς. οἱ δ'ἐπεὶ ἐτιτρώσκοντο μὲν καὶ ἀπέθνησκον...; 4.5.14 (Lechaeum): οἱ δὲ Λακεδαιμόνιοι ἐπεὶ ἠκοντίζοντο καὶ ὁ μέν τις ἐτέτρωτο, ὁ δὲ καὶ ἐπεπτώκει...

[16] Xenophon's analysis of the potential of light-armed troops was of great contemporary interest during the 4th century. On the increasingly tactical use of light-armed troops in the 4th century, see especially Konijnendijk, 2018, 95–126.

[17] See also Thucydides' account of Demosthenes' defeat by Aetolian light-armed troops at Thuc. 3.96.3–98.

[18] Cf. Thucydides' summation of the peltast advantage at 3.93.3: καὶ ὅτε μὲν ἐπίοι τὸ τῶν Ἀθηναίων στρατόπεδον, ὑπεχώρουν, ἀναχωροῦσι δὲ ἐπέκειντο ['and when the Athenian force would advance, they withdrew, but they attacked [the Athenians] when they were withdrawing'] and at 4.32.4: φεύγοντές τε γὰρ ἐκράτουν καὶ ἀναχωροῦσιν ἐπέκειντο ['for the [light-armed troops]

distinctively different: Thucydides stretches out the Sphacteria battle, offering vivid descriptions of the difficulties of the battlefield (e.g. the ash, dust and inability to see, the noise and inability to hear, the inadequacy of armour, the fatigue and mental stress, the thirst and hot sun; cf. Thuc. 4.33-35). Moreover, while Thucydides also describes the hoplites' futile pursuits of the light-armed troops (4.34.1), he stresses that the overwhelmingly numerous light-armed forces finally encircled the hoplites, rendering them helpless (4.34.3). Xenophon on the other hand focusses on the hoplites' increasingly unsuccessful attacks, punishing a bad strategy by showing how each attack captures no peltasts and how each inevitable hoplite retreat ends in further deaths.[19] The contrast between Thucydides and Xenophon is helpful for perceiving Xenophon's focus on Spartan deaths and their causes, to the exclusion of many other factors.

In the end, the Spartans fall into complete disorder; in addition to showing the violent deaths of 250 men, Xenophon tells the story of a humiliating failure, since the hoplites ultimately flee in any possible direction (4.5.17). This outcome was partly due to the fact that the Spartan commander had not learned to respond to the light-armed attacks that had been causing Spartan defeats for 35 years and thus suggests Spartan rigidity.[20]

---

won control by fleeing and attacked those who were withdrawing']. Cf. e.g. Xenophon at 4.5.15: ὡς δὲ ἐδίωκον, ᾕρουν τε οὐδένα ἐξ ἀκοντίου βολῆς ὁπλῖται ὄντες πελταστάς· καὶ γὰρ ἀναχωρεῖν αὐτοὺς ἐκέλευε, πρὶν τοὺς ὁπλίτας ὁμοῦ γίγνεσθαι· ἐπεὶ δὲ ἀνεχώρουν ... ἀναστρέφοντες οἱ περὶ τὸν Ἰφικράτην, ὅ τε ἐκ τοῦ ἐναντίου πάλιν ἠκόντιζον καὶ ἄλλοι ἐκπλαγίου παραθέοντες εἰς τὰ γυμνά. [But when [the Spartans] pursued, they caught no one, since they were hoplites pursuing peltasts [who kept] a javelin's cast away; for [Iphicrates] had given orders to the peltasts to withdraw before the hoplites got near them. But when [the Spartans] retreated... those around Iphicrates turned back, and some again threw javelins upon the Lacedaemonians from the front, and others who were running alongside threw from the flanks at their exposed body parts.] Cf. also 3.2.4.

19 καὶ εὐθὺς μὲν ἐπὶ τῇ πρώτῃ διώξει κατηκόντιζον ἐννέα ἢ δέκα αὐτῶν...[16] ἐπεὶ δὲ κακῶς ἔπασχον, πάλιν ἐκέλευσεν ὁ πολέμαρχος... ἀναχωροῦντες δὲ ἔτι πλείους αὐτῶν ἢ τὸ πρῶτον ἔπεσον. ἤδη δὲ τῶν βελτίστων ἀπολωλότων, οἱ ἱππεῖς αὐτοῖς παραγίγνονται ... ποιοῦντες δὲ καὶ πάσχοντες τὰ ὅμοια τούτοις καὶ αὖθις, αὐτοὶ μὲν ἀεὶ ἐλάττους τε καὶ μαλακώτεροι ἐγίγνοντο... (4.5.15-16). And immediately in their first pursuit the peltasts javelined down nine or ten hoplites... [16] And since [the first group of hoplites] was suffering badly, the polemarch renewed the order... But as these [older men] were withdrawing, even more of them fell than of the first group. And now, when the best men had already been killed, the cavalry joined them ... and doing and suffering things similar to this again and again, the Lacedaemonians themselves were becoming successively fewer and less confident...

20 The battle on Sphacteria occurred in 425, the ambush at Phyle in 403, the ambush in Bithynia in 399, and the disaster at Lechaeum in 390. On the Spartans' inability to adapt, see Humble, 2006. This inability was not a given. Two Spartan commanders of the Peloponnesian War,

Xenophon's bewildering number of ambush stories, only a few of which I have here described,[21] fall into didactic groups: for instance, two or more narratives illustrate the vulnerability of hoplites to light-armed attack, exhibit the dangers of plundering, or criticize bad decisions.[22] All ambush stories demonstrate the power of surprise attacks and display the Spartans and their allies reduced to total helplessness; finally, ambushes result in heavy casualties, which Xenophon persistently emphasizes.

2 Spartan Leaders Defeated

The ambush stories thus offer a kind of military education, but also touch on a critique of Spartan leadership. As the wars of *Hellenica* wear on, they begin to be accompanied by defeat stories that showcase greater psychological complexity and expose the failings of more prominent Spartan leaders.[23] Two such accounts occur in the last section of Book Four, namely the stories of the deaths of Thibron (4.8.18–19) and Anaxibius (4.8.34–39).

Like the story of the slaughter in Bithynia, Thibron's story illustrates the dangers of plundering. Thibron had been sent to Asia Minor in 391 when the Spartans perceived that the current satrap, Struthas, was on Athens' side. Having arrived, Thibron plunders Persian royal territory.[24] As time goes on, Struthas observes how 'carelessly and in what disorder' Thibron conducts his operations, and decides to attack. At the moment of the attack, sometime after breakfast, Thibron happens (4.8.18) to be in his tent with his lover, Thersander, who was an excellent flute player, according to Xenophon, and as a Laconizer also laid claim to war

---

Brasidas and Gylippus, show greater flexibility, including in their response to light-armed attacks; see especially Brasidas at Thuc. 4.127.2.

21 For others, see above n. 4, and especially the vivid story of the clever and energetic Spartan commander Gorgopus, whom the Athenians ambush on the island of Aegina, killing him, other Spartiates, 150 Aeginetans, and at least 200 of his free rowers (5.1.10–12).
22 Conspicuous in this last regard are the stories of the defeat of Ischolaus (6.5.26) and of an unnamed commander at Mt. Oneon (7.15–17). The stories are united by the fact that each commander makes a mistake that allows enemy forces to cross into the Peloponnesus, and because in each story Xenophon explicitly criticizes that error. There is a third story in this set, since the 'careless' (7.1.41) guard of the Spartan Naucles and Athenian Timomachus allows the Thebans again to pass Oneon a few years later, in 366 or 365.
23 Cf. Rood, 2017, 270: '*Hellenica* more frequently displays ethical concerns toward the end.'
24 This was the very behaviour with which Agesilaus had alienated Struthas in the first place (8.4.17), so that Thibron in some sense pays for Agesilaus' habitual wasting, as well as his own.

strength (ἀλκή).²⁵ Although this is an attack in broad daylight, Xenophon depicts no fighting: only death, flight, and ironic survival:

> ὁ δὲ Στρούθας, ἰδὼν ἀτάκτως τε βοηθοῦντας καὶ ὀλίγους τοὺς πρώτους, ἐπιφαίνεται πολλούς τε ἔχων καὶ συντεταγμένους ἱππέας. καὶ Θίβρωνα μὲν καὶ Θέρσανδρον πρώτους ἀπέκτειναν· ἐπεὶ δ' οὗτοι ἔπεσον, ἐτρέψαντο καὶ τὸ ἄλλο στράτευμα, καὶ διώκοντες παμπλήθεις κατέβαλον...
>
> And Struthas, seeing that they were coming out to defend in a disorganized way and that those leading were few, appeared with a numerous and well-organized cavalry force. And they killed Thibron and Thersander first, and when these fell, they routed the rest of the army, and pursuing them they threw down very many... (4.8.19)

Some of Thibron's soldiers are saved to friendly cities, and more are saved because of Thibron's disorganization: as frequently, he had led out his sally without announcing it (4.8.19), so that many men had not participated in the battle.²⁶ Their lucky survival arises from the same disorganization that was responsible for the deaths of their compatriots.

Anaxibius, who had politicked his way into a command on the Hellespont (4.8.32), also dies partly because of careless contempt for the enemy; in addition, he fails to heed the warnings of his sacrifices.²⁷ Unfortunately for him, his experienced enemy, Iphicrates, again has a large force of peltasts (4.8.34, cf. 4.5.9–18).

Like Thibron's story, Anaxibius' story begins with the plundering that gives his attacker time to watch and make his plans: Iphicrates perceives Anaxibius' aims, anticipates what route he will take, and then sets up his ambush. Iphicrates also uses his naval forces as a decoy, commanding them to sail in such a way that it looks as if he has gone out to collect money (4.8.35). Anaxibius then acts just as Iphicrates wants him to: he proceeds carelessly through country he thinks is friendly, especially since he hears that Iphicrates has sailed out to collect money. Iphicrates patiently bides his time and suddenly attacks when the Spartans are most vulnerable.

The story ends with a dramatization of Anaxibius' perceptions and speech: once attacked, he sees that there is no hope. His army is stretched out long, and his allies, who are in steep country, cannot help him soon enough; he also sees that everyone around him is stricken with shock. As a result, he gives a speech in

---

25 For another Spartan who is ambushed when distracted by a love affair, see Alcetas (5.4.57).
26 See Christenson, 2017, 382–383, on Xenophon's admiration for military competence, and his view that leaders need both competence and courage.
27 Cf. Pownall, 1998, 264.

which he declares 'that it is noble for him to die on the spot' and advises the others to flee to safety (4.8.38). He then dies fighting, as do his lover and 12 harmosts from the surrounding cities, but his men also fall as they are trying to flee. About 200 of Anaxibius' men die (4.8.39). The casualty figure again spotlights the harm to Sparta, but also to the men themselves, particularly as the deaths are entirely unnecessary.

Anaxibius' story is largely a standard ambush story. Iphicrates plans, lays his trap, bides his time, attacks, and kills his over-confident opponent. The addition is Anaxibius' dubious speech. Having carelessly led his men into fatal trouble, Anaxibius makes no attempt at all to organize and defend, but falls back, when it is too late, on the appearances of heroism and Spartan military tradition, mouthing slogans about how it is noble for him to die in his position.[28] He then dies a death which appears to be noble, but which in reality harms his city and dooms his men (and through Xenophon, his lasting reputation). Thus, the avoidable deaths and defeats of both Thibron and Anaxibius are surrounded with specious 'Spartanness'; Thibron's lover claims Spartan virtues in an ill-disciplined camp; Anaxibius after carelessness and impiety.[29]

In preparation for perhaps the most harmful Spartan leader of all, King Cleombrotus, whom Xenophon makes responsible for Sparta's defeat and the deaths of 1,000 men at the Battle of Leuctra, Spartan leaders are represented as continuing to grow worse toward the end of the war.[30] I will offer two more examples of Xenophon's minor defeat stories: Anger causes the death of Teleutias (5.3.1–6) anger, cruelty, and avarice that of Mnasippus (6.2.20–24).[31]

---

28 Tuplin, 1993, 78 calls it a 'smug little speech'.
29 On these claims to 'Spartan' virtues, compare Loraux, 1977, 110, who makes a strong argument that the aim of the Spartan *ethos* of the 'beautiful battlefield death' was victory and the preservation of the largest possible number of soldiers and therefore the state as a whole. Anaxibius' claim of Spartan virtue *after* he has betrayed this essential aim of preserving Spartan forces therefore rings false. On the idea that the Spartan *ethos*, properly understood, aims at preserving the army and the state, cf. Xen. *Lac.Pol.* 9.1–2, with Tyrtaeus 8.11–14, both analysed by Loraux *ad loc. cit.*
30 See Tuplin, 1993, on Xenophon's bad Spartan leaders, who are 'examples of what not to do' (164), and Riedinger, 1991, who argues that the accumulating stories of bad leaders expose the psychology of imprudence (240).
31 On *orge* in *Hellenica*, see Tuci in this volume.

Teleutias is not the first leader whose anger causes Spartan casualties in *Hellenica*. For instance, irritation had also caused the Spartan king Pausanias to issue hasty and imprudent commands.[32] However, Xenophon gives Teleutias' behavior a lengthier and more dramatic treatment, contrasting it not only to that of his calmer opponents, but also to that of his calmer allies. For instance, he prefaces his account of Teleutias' ill-fated attack on Olynthus with the story of the allied Thessalian leader Derdas, who ambushes the Olynthian cavalry. Like Teleutias, Derdas sees the Olynthian cavalry in the field; unlike him, he does not get irritated, but rather bides his time (ἡσυχίαν τε εἶχε 5.3.1), keeping his troops in readiness until he sees his chance to attack the enemy cavalry when it is disorganized. He then pursues them right up to the walls of Olynthus, killing 80 of them (5.3.1–2).[33]

Teleutias, by contrast, allows himself to be provoked (ἀγανακτήσας τῇ τόλμῃ αὐτῶν 5.3.3), when the Olynthian cavalry calmly (ἥσυχοι... ἡσυχῇ 5.3.3) parades out of Olynthus and crosses the river, heading in his direction. He therefore orders his peltasts to attack at a run. The Olynthian cavalry calmly (ἥσυχοι 5.3.4) crosses back over the river and Teleutias' peltasts energetically follow, thinking that the cavalry is retreating. But now the peltasts are between the cavalry and the river. The horsemen turn and attack, killing about a hundred of them. Teleutias gets angry again (ὀργισθείς 5.3.5) when he sees this, and swiftly (ταχύ) leads his hoplites forward, telling them 'to pursue the peltasts and the cavalry, and not to let them go' (5.3.5). In following this order, his hoplites advance too close to the city walls, come under fire, and are compelled to retreat in disorder (τεθορυβημένως 5.3.5).[34] At this opportunity, the Olynthians send out their cavalry, peltasts, and finally their hoplites against the disorganized Greek phalanx (τεταραγμένῃ τῇ φάλαγγι 5.3.6). The expected result ensues: Teleutias dies and

---

[32] Cf. 2.4.31–33, where King Pausanias had become irritated at Athenian light-armed troops from Peiraeus. Like Teleutias later, he ordered his men to attack as quickly as they could, sending his cavalry and the fastest hoplites ahead of the main army. These killed 30 of the Athenian light-armed troops and chased the rest to Peiraeus' theatre, where, however, all the light-armed and hoplite rebels happened to be arming (2.4.33). The rebels threw everything they had at the Spartans (ἠκόντιζον, ἔβαλλον, ἐτόξευον, ἐσφενδόνων), many of whom were wounded (2.4.33); in their retreat several Spartiates died.
[33] Teleutias' imprudence at Olynthus is also contrasted to his own previous prudence, even in preparing for this very expedition; cf. 5.1.20; 5.2.38–39. Xenophon had earlier warmly praised his achievements; cf. 5.1.24.
[34] Likewise, at the Battle of Haliartus (3.5.18–20), Lysander pressed forward to the walls of the town too quickly, resulting in defeat, his own death, and the deaths of some of his men.

his forces flee to friendly cities, as the enemy follows 'killing men' (5.3.6). Xenophon gives no numbers, but remarks that the Olynthians killed 'that very part of the army which was useful' (ὅπερ ὄφελος ἦν 5.3.6). Thus, although he does not provide a casualty figure as he did, for instance, for Anaxibius, he nevertheless stresses the harm to Sparta from Teleutias' actions.[35]

As mentioned, an even worse Spartan commander, Mnasippus, displays anger, brutality, and avarice before leading his men to their deaths on the island of Corcyra. Mnasippus, who has been appointed commander of a large Spartan force of 60 ships (6.2.3) and about 1,500 mercenaries (6.2.5), is commanded to attack Corcyra. He does so, blockading the harbour and besieging the city from the land, so that the inhabitants can bring in nothing. He also wastes the land, including very wealthy estates, and makes a lot of profit (6.2.5–7). In this position of superiority Mnasippus treats the Corcyraeans with extraordinary cruelty and stops paying his mercenaries, even though he has plenty of money (3.2.15–16). Not surprisingly, then, the Corcyraeans watching the Spartans from the city are able to observe that the mercenaries on guard have grown lax and disorganized; they make a sally from the city, kill some of Mnasippus' men and take some others prisoner (6.2.17).

Like the other commanders who led men into Sparta's disasters, Mnasippus is a fighter. He suits up, his hoplites suit up, and he tells the company commanders to lead out the mercenaries. Reminded that unpaid mercenaries will not willingly obey, he strikes his officers with his staff and spear, earning general hatred (6.2.19).[36] He himself (αὐτός-6.2.20) then routs the enemy with his hoplites and chases them to the city gates, where the Corcyraeans regroup, shooting at him from the monuments.[37] The Spartans perceive that they are vulnerable and try to wheel their phalanx to create a stronger formation, but the intensity of the Corcyraean attack breaks the manoeuvre (6.2.22). Mnasippus now becomes isolated from and unable to help the rest; he and 'a very few' (7.2.23) men at the front become the objects of ever more numerous Corcyraeans. Once they kill him, all the Corcyraeans together pursue the Spartan forces and might have overrun the Spar-

---

35 Xenophon follows this story with an authorial reflection on harmful and improvident anger (5.3.7), and then immediately shows that the Spartans are raising another very large force to send to Olynthus 'in order to quench the pride of the victors' (ὅπως τό τε φρόνημα τῶν νενικηκότων καταοβεσθείη 5.3.8). The anger Teleutias has demonstrated is therefore not uncharacteristic of the Spartan state as a whole.
36 Cf. Harris in this volume.
37 I.e. from tombs and other memorials erected outside the city.

tan camp if they had not turned aside to capture the Spartan camp followers. Xenophon does not supply casualty figures but says only that the Corcyraeans set up a trophy and gave back the corpses under a truce (7.2.24).

Xenophon devotes detailed attention to the defeats of Teleutias and Mnasippus, showing the stages of battles that begin when Teleutias and Mnasippus allow attacks on guards or light-armed troops to drag them into actions for which they are unprepared. Their trigger reactions do not rescue these forces and cause ever further losses, up to and including the loss of strategically valuable Corcyra. Their arrogant indignation at being challenged (in Mnasippus' case, by anyone, to anything that he does) is at the root of this disastrous military response. By contrast, in the stories of Thibron, Anaxibius, Teleutias, and Mnasippus Sparta's enemies show forethought and calm. The virtues necessary to winning battles seem have passed over, in Xenophon's view, to Sparta's opponents.[38]

3 Conclusion: Spartan Death in Minor Defeats

Xenophon has used his numerous stories of minor Spartan military defeats to expose the weaknesses of Spartan tactics and especially of Spartan leadership. It is therefore interesting to note that 14 from 21 of these defeat stories cluster in Books 3 through 5 of *Hellenica*, which narrate the period after Sparta had defeated Athens in the Peloponnesian War and during which the Spartans were at the height of their power. The deaths of Thibron and Anaxibius, for example, occur shortly before the declaration of the 'King's Peace' (5.1.31), a moment at which the Spartans feel that their power is particularly secure (5.1.35–36).

Our defeat stories therefore run parallel to Xenophon's account of Sparta's post-war attacks on Persia and bloody victories over other Greeks in the Corinthian War. Xenophon's accounts of Spartan victories in Greece had particularly emphasized Spartan violence: his description of the battle of the River Nemea shows that the Spartans killed 'many' Athenians, Corinthians, Argives, and Boeotians in turn, whereas they themselves lost only eight men (4.2.21–22, with 4.3.1); likewise, he writes that the Spartans killed many Thebans at the battle of Coronea (4.3.19), and finally, that they killed large number of Argives at the battle of Lechaeum: 'At that time,' he writes, 'so many [Argives] fell in a short time as

---

38 This is also the case with the detailed presentation of Archidamus' defeat at Cromnos (7.4.21–25, where the Arcadians remain calm under attack, but Archidamus disintegrates into disorganization. Cf. Riedinger, 1991, 240.

people are accustomed to see heaps of grain, wood, or stones; at that time they were seeing heaps of corpses' (4.4.12).[39] The repetitive defeat stories relate to Xenophon's accounts of these stunning hoplite successes, since the focus on Spartan death in the defeat stories answers the focus on Spartan killing in the narratives of their hoplite victories.

This idea — that the defeat stories create a counterpoint to Xenophon's portrayal of Spartan aggressions and successes — may help to explain why there are so many of the same kind of story and also why they focus to such an extent on violent death. But there is more to be said about Xenophon's representation of death in these stories, since the presentation offers a criticism of not only of Spartan practices in respect to war, but also of Sparta's beliefs.

As we have seen, both the ambush stories and the bad leader stories showcase Spartan deaths. On the one hand, Xenophon emphasizes death as both the immediate result and main outcome of surprise attacks. On the other hand, the bad leader stories climax with the death of a leader and some number of his men.

Both types of defeat story therefore develop similarly gruesome themes, and not surprisingly Xenophon casts the stories in rather severe language, representing the fatalities through the repetition of a small number of verbs that describe the ever repeating killing and dying,[40] and using casualty figures (cf. note 4) to add pathetic precision.[41] Although Xenophon elsewhere offers elaborately rhetorical death scenes,[42] the minor defeat stories display few literary figures.[43]

---

39 On these battles and Xenophon's emphasis on Spartan killing of other Greeks, see Foster, forthcoming.
40 A word study of the 21 passages discussed in this paper reveals the limited vocabulary of killing and death. Five verbs clearly indicate killing: ἀποκτείνω (ten times), καταβάλλω (five times), κατακοντίζω, ἀποκτιννύω, and ἀπολύω (each once). Verbs that clearly indicated dying are more frequent, but not more diverse: ἀποθνῄσκω (twenty times), πίπτω (five times), ἀπολύομαι, and συνθνῄσκω (each once). Cf. Pownall, in this volume, on Xenophon's use of σφάζειν in scenes of violent civil strife; Xenophon does not use this verb at all to describe these battle scenes.
Six of the passages use verbs for killing only and no verbs for dying (2.4.4–7, 4.1.16–19, 4.8.17–19, 5.4.38–40, 5.4.59, 6.2.17–24). Six passages use verbs for dying only, and none for killing (3.5.17–20, 4.4.10, 4.8.33–39, 5.1.10–12, 5.4.42–45, 6.5.26–27). Six of the passages use both killing and dying verbs (2.4.32–33, 3.2.2–5, 4.3.22–23, 4.5.7–18, 5.3.1–7, 7.4.20–25). Three (shorter) passages use neither (5.4.56, 7.1.15–17, 7.1.41), but rather state that there were casualties or that a military objective was attacked and captured. All passages necessarily use verbs to indicate attacking, some of which might also be interpreted as verbs of killing.
41 Cf. Hornblower, 2011, 163 and *passim*.
42 See especially 4.5.11–12.
43 Cf. 'like sheep in a sheepfold' (3.2.4), which is the only simile.

Xenophon employed these sparse rhetorical tools to vivid effect. For instance, of our dead leaders, only two, particularly problematic, leaders were the direct objects of the verb 'to kill' (ἀποκτείνω): Struthas kills the careless and disorganized Thibron in a daylight attack on his camp (4.8.17–19), and the Corcyraeans kill the cruel and greedy Mnasippus (6.2.17–24). In these cases, Xenophon represented an enemy's achievement, namely the victorious killing of the Spartan commander, and the story remains narrator focalized to the end.

All other named leaders of our minor defeat stories (that is: Gylis, Teleutias, Lysander, Pasimachus, Anaxibius, Gorgopus, Phoibidas, Ischolaus, and numerous Spartiates) 'die' or 'are slain': that is, Xenophon used some form of the verb ἀποθνῄσκω at the climax of the story. In this manner of narrating death, the specific killers disappear and the leaders themselves become the subjects of the verbs (e.g. 'then Ischolaus died'... 6.5.26). The leader becomes a casualty, and Xenophon frequently draws special attention to the death or deaths as events in their own right through the use of the historical present tense: the deaths of Gylis, Teleutias, Pasimachus, Anaxibius, Ischolaus, and the Spartiates who fought and died under Pausanias (2.4.33) are emphasized in this way.[44] The sense that the death of a Spartan leader is an event surely reflects the Spartan point of view, from which vantage point each leader's death signals and represents the military defeat itself.[45] These deaths are not, therefore, placed at the very end of the defeat stories, but at the climax of the story, with the flight and deaths of the men following.

Xenophon's strategies for employing verbs of killing and dying help to shape our perception of the character of Spartan losses: while all of the defeat stories support (and partly create) his presentation of Sparta's worsening man-power shortage,[46] those in which Spartans are transformed into war losses more heavily emphasize Sparta's gradual bleeding of men. In addition, through their undecorated ubiquity (no death is brought forward as special through a more detailed

---

44 Xenophon emphasizes the use of ἀποθνῄσκω with the historical present tense seven times in our passages (2.4.33, 2.4.34, 4.3.23, 4.4.10, 4.8.39, 5.3.6, 6.5.26), but otherwise uses the HP only for verbs that indicate an attack. Except for at 2.4.34 (where Xenophon uses the HP to mark the deaths of 150 Athenians killed by Pausanias' forces at Peiraeus), all instances of ἀποθνῄσκω in the HP in our passages mark the deaths of Spartiates. Thucydides had also occasionally used this technique: cf. e.g. 5.10.9 (death of Cleon at Amphipolis), 6.101.6 (death of Lamachus in Sicily). See Lallot, Rijksbaron, et al., 2011.

45 This seems particularly likely to be the case in that Xenophon's first readers were mostly Athenians, for whom the Spartan view of events would stand out more clearly.

46 Explicit remarks on *oliganthropia* are found at 6.5.28 and 7.5.10. On the importance of this manpower shortage for Spartan warfare, cf. van Wees, 2004, 83–85.

description) Xenophon's reports of Spartan deaths support his critique of the Spartan ideal of the 'beautiful death' in battle.⁴⁷ In our defeat stories, the Spartans and their allies die fighting bravely, but this helps Sparta not at all: because they are preceded by bad organizational and military errors, both the dubiously heroic deaths of Spartan leaders, and the brave but doomed efforts of their subordinates are wasted.

Xenophon seemed to problematize the *ethos* of 'the beautiful battlefield death' when he showed the response of the Spartan families after the 'disaster' at Lechaeum. The families of those who died at Lechaeum rejoiced because their sons and brothers were now heroes who had died fighting for Sparta (4.5.10), whereas the survivors would be met with accusations of cowardice (4.5.14). But their sons and brothers died, as Xenophon showed, from random javelins that could not distinguish cowards from the brave (cf. Thuc. 4.40.2) and because the Spartan officer who commanded them was both over-confident and not well instructed in what to do. The narrative of the battle surely shows that the deaths of these men were a disaster for Sparta not only because of the loss of life, but because of what the defeat revealed about Spartan warfare. Moreover, Xenophon went out of his way to show that the deaths at Lechaeum were not beautiful, but humiliating and pitiable. When the Spartan army mourns this defeat (4.5.10), they seem to recognize the character of the events in a way more similar to Xenophon's view. In contrast, the Spartan families were rejoicing at what was in fact a disaster for the city.

This hint that the social context had become problematic, i.e. that the families were calling all those who had died in battle brave men, all those who survived cowards, and weighing no other circumstance, supports Xenophon's main demonstration of what we might call 'the beautiful death problem'. *Hellenica* repeatedly displays Spartan commanders who applied the honour code to death in battle, but to no other kind of military or moral decision. Anaxibius' last-second resort to Spartan ideals therefore rang hollow, as was discussed above. Thibron, Teleutias, and Mnasippus no doubt also fought bravely in their last hour. However, in Xenophon's descriptions, the 'beautiful deaths' of such leaders were not gifts of virtue to the city (Thuc. 2.43.1), but rather offered a speciously heroic exit for corrupt and incompetent leaders, who were taking their men, and therefore Sparta's defensive capacity, with them when they died.⁴⁸ The idea that men could

---

47 On the 'beautiful death', see Detienne, 1968, Loraux, 1977, Vernant, 1982; on death in battle Boedeker, 2003, Griffin, 1980, Holmes, 2007, van Wees, 2004, and other sources listed in the bibliography.
48 Cf. n. 29.

make up for any previous bad actions by dying in battle for the city (cf. Thuc. 2.42.3), was therefore harming Sparta as much as anything else, since it partly underlay the carelessness of her leaders and therefore contributed to the frequency of her defeats.[49]

Xenophon's minor defeat stories do change over the course of *Hellenica*. Whereas the initial stories show hoplite vulnerability to light-armed attacks, subsequent stories focus more prominently on the harm done by bad leaders and the final stories reveal the paralysing effects of post-Leuctra demoralization. Nevertheless, main themes emerged. The minor defeat stories show Spartans dying in ambushes planned by their enemies or because they themselves made unplanned attacks; either way, the enemy had the intellectual and tactical advantage. They emphasize the unnecessary deaths of Spartans and allied soldiers. They show that the top leadership of Sparta (e.g. Thibron, Anaxibius, Teleutias, Mnasippus) had ceased to take war seriously, and that their deaths were more inevitable than heroic. In terms of Xenophon's representation of warfare, the stories emphasize the terrible brutality of the continuous intercine warfare in Greece, disturbing with demonstrations of weakness and violent death especially the narrative that describes Sparta's glory period after winning the Peloponnesian War, a period in which the Spartans believed that they were consolidating their power.

Bibliography

Baragwanath, E. (2012), "A Noble Alliance: Herodotus, Thucydides, and Xenophon's Procles" in: *Thucydides and Herodotus*, E. Foster/D. Lateiner (eds), Oxford, 316–345.

Bichler, R. (2016), "Probleme und Grenzen der Rekonstruktion von Ereignissen am Beispiel Antiker Schlachtenbeschreibungen" in: *Historiographie-Ethnographie-Utopie*, Wiesbaden, 43–65.

Boedeker, D. (2003) "Pedestrian Fatalities: The Prosaics of Death in Herodotus" in: *Herodotus and his World*, P. Derow/R. Parker (eds), Oxford, 17–36.

Bosworth, B. (2009), "Thucydides and the Unheroic Dead" in: *Art in Athens during the Peloponnesian War*, O. Palagia (ed.), Cambridge, 168–187.

---

[49] Cf. also Herodotus' Aristodemus, whose motivation for dying was to vindicate himself, rather than help the city, with the result that Aristodemus' contemporaries considered his death only dubiously heroic. I owe this observation to Emily Baragwanath, who also observed that Xenophon's focus on the Spartans' deaths follows Herodotus' Solon's admonition 'to look to the end in everything' (Hdt. 1.32.5–9): the Spartans' would-be noble deaths expose a core problem of their lives.

Burke, K. (1969), *A Rhetoric of Motives*, California.
Christenson, P. (2017), "Xenophon's Views on Sparta" in: *The Cambridge Companion to Xenophon*, M. Flower (ed.), Cambridge, 376–399.
Crowley, J. (2012), *The Psychology of the Athenian Hoplite: The Culture of Combat in Classical Athens*, Cambridge.
Detienne, M. (1968), "La Phalange. Problèmes et controverses" in : *Problèmes de la guerre en Grèce ancienne*, J.-P. Vernant (ed.), Paris, 119–42.
Dillery, J. (2017), "Xenophon: The Small Works" in: *The Cambridge Companion to Xenophon*, M. Flower (ed.), Cambridge, 195–219.
Fenik, B.C. (1968), *Typical Battle Scenes in the Iliad*, Wiesbaden.
Foster, E. (2017), "Campaign and Battle Narratives in Thucydides" in: *The Oxford Handbook of Thucydides*, R. Balot/S. Forsdyke/E. Foster (eds), Oxford, 301–315.
Foster, E. (forthcoming), "The Paradoxical Battle Narratives of Xenophon's Hellenica" in: *Representations of Warfare in the Ancient World*, R. Bruzzone/D. Sells (eds).
Griffin, J. (1980), *Homer on Life and Death*, Oxford.
Hau, L. (2015), *Moral History from Herodotus to Diodorus*, Edinburgh.
Holmes, B. (2007), "The *Iliad's* Economy of Pain" in: *TAPA* 137, 45–84.
Hornblower, S. (2011), *Thucydidean Themes*, Oxford.
Humble, N. (2006), "Why the Spartans Fight So Well, Even If They Are In Disorder – Xenophon's View" in: *Sparta and War*, S. Hodkinson/A. Powell (eds), Wales, 219–233.
Kapellos, A. (2011), "Xenophon *Hell.* 2.2.23" in: *PP* 66, 132–138.
Lateiner, D. (1977), "Heralds and Corpses in Thucydides" in: *CW* 71/2, 96–106.
Lallot, J./Rijksbaron, A./Jacquinod, B./Buijs, M. (eds) (2011), *The Historical Present in Thucydides/Le présent historique chez Thucydide*, Leiden.
Loraux, N. (1982), "Mourir devant Troie, tomber pour Athènes: de la gloire du héros à l'idée de la cité" in : *La Mort, les morts dans les sociétés anciennes*, G. Gnoli/J.-P.Vernant (eds), Cambridge, 27–45.
Loraux, N. (1989), "La 'Belle Mort' Spartiate" in: *Les Expériences de Tirésias: Le féminin et l'homme grec*, Paris, 77–92. (First published in *Ktèma* in 1977.)
Marincola, J. (2017) "Xenophon's *Anabasis* and *Hellenika*" in: *The Cambridge Companion to Xenophon*, M. Flower (ed.), Cambridge, 103–118.
Nicolai, R. (2006), "Thucydides Continued" in: *Brill's Companion to Thucydides*, A. Rengakos/A. Tsakmakis (eds), Leiden/Boston, 693–719.
Paul, G.M. (1989), "Two Battles in Thucydides" in: *Echos du Monde Classique/ Classical Views* xxxi, n.s. 6, 307– 312.
Pownall, F. (2016), "Tyrants as Impious Leaders in Xenophon's Hellenica" in: *Aspects of Leadership in Xenophon*, *Histos* Supplement 5, Richard Fernando Buxton, Newcastle upon Tyne, 51–83.
Riedinger, J.-C. (1991), *Étude sur les Helléniques de Xénophon et l'histoire*, Paris.
Romilly, J. (2012), *The Mind of Thucydides*. Edited by H. Rawlings/J. Rusten (eds), Ithaca.
Rood, T. (2004), "Xenophon and Diodorus: Continuing Thucydides" in: *Xenophon and His World*, Papers from a Conference held in Liverpool in July 1999, C.J. Tuplin (ed.), Stuttgart, 341–396.
Rood, T. (2017), "Xenophon's Narrative Style" in: *The Cambridge Companion to Xenophon*, M. Flower (ed.), Cambridge, 263–278.
Roisman, J. (2003), "The Rhetoric of Courage in the Athenian Orators" in: *Andreia: Studies in Manliness and Courage in Classical Antiquity*, R.M. Rosen/I. Sluiter (eds), Leiden, 127–143.

Tuplin, C.J. (1989), "Military Engagement in Xenophon's Hellenica" in: *Past Perpectives: Studies in Greek and Roman Historical Writing*, I.S. Moxon/J.D. Smart/A.J. Woodman (eds), 37–66.

Tuplin, C.J. (1993), *The Failings of Empire: A Reading of Xenophon* Hellenica 2.3.11–7.5.27, Stuttgart.

Tuplin, C.J. (2004), *Xenophon and His World*, Papers from a Conference held in Liverpool in July 1999, (ed.), Stuttgart.

Underhill, G.E. (1900), *A Commentary with Introduction and Appendix on the* Hellenica *of Xenophon*, Oxford.

Van Wees, H. (2004), *Greek warfare: Myths and Realities*, London.

Vernant, J.P. (1982), "La belle mort et le cadavre outragé" in: *La Mort, les morts dans les sociétés anciennes*, G. Gnoli/J.P. Vernant (eds), Cambridge, 45–76.

Edward Harris
Violence and the State in Xenophon: A Study of Three Passages

According to modern political theory, a community must have three basic features to qualify as a "state."[1] First, a state must have clearly marked geographical borders, which indicate the limits of its jurisdiction. Inside these borders, the state has power over all those who are within its territory. If the army of another community crosses this border under arms without the state's permission, this is considered an act of war (e.g. Thuc. 2.12.1–2). Second, a state makes a strict distinction between its members who are considered citizens and those who are not members and are considered resident aliens or foreigners. Third and most important for the topic of this essay, a state makes a distinction between private individuals and officials.[2] Only officials have the power to carry out the laws of the state and have "a monopoly of legitimate force within defined borders" to use the famous phrase of Max Weber.[3] Private citizens may have the right to use force in a few unusual circumstances, but these are exceptions to the general rule that private citizens should not resort to violence to resolve their disputes or to enforce their rights.[4]

This essay explores the use of violence within the community in three passages from the works of Xenophon. The first part starts with a passage from the *Anabasis* (5.7.24–30), in which soldiers attempt to stone individuals as a means of punishment, and examines attitudes toward spontaneous violence by private individuals within the community. The second part examines another passage in the *Anabasis* (5.8.1–26) and studies the use and abuse of violence by public officials in the Greek *polis*. The third and final part starts with the rule and murder of Euphron of Sicyon in Xenophon's *Hellenica* and looks at the use of violence by private individuals against those accused of tyranny. The overall aim of the essay

---

[1] This discussion draws on my analysis in Harris, 2013, 22–59. For the three main features of a state see Hansen, 1998, 37–40.
[2] For the distinction between *archontes* (officials) and *idiotai* (private citizens) see Rubinstein, 1998.
[3] Weber, 1972, 822. The views of Riess, 2012, 391 and *passim* that there was a "partial ritualization of violent interaction" in Classical Athens is not convincing. In almost none of the passages adduced by Riess do the authors use the language of ritual to describe violence. Riess, 2012, 72–76 also uncritically follows the view of Forsdyke about informal justice, but see the criticisms of this view on Part I of this chapter.
[4] For the exceptions in Athenian law see Harris, 2013, 50–58.

is to show that Xenophon's attitudes toward violence within the community are very much in line with general Greek attitudes of his time. He was not more radical or more conservative than his contemporaries in this regard.

1

> But I would not feel so all alone
> Everybody must get stoned.
>
> Bob Dylan

When the Ten Thousand reached the territory of the Cerasuntians, discipline was starting to break down. In a speech to the army, Xenophon warns the soldiers about the dangers of insubordination (5.7.27–30). He says that if anyone can appoint himself general and urge his companions to stone people, the army's commanders will be incapable of commanding their troops. To illustrate his point, he reminds them of two recent incidents. First, he mentions how the soldiers assaulted Zelarchus, the market official, because they thought he was mistreating them.[5] Zelarchus appears to have escaped, but Xenophon observes that their spontaneous violence was counter-productive. If he was guilty, they lost their chance to exact a penalty from him. If he was innocent, he was afraid that he would have been put to death unjustly without a trial. His words effectively illustrate the drawbacks of "popular" justice: such punishment can strike the innocent as well as the guilty and undermine confidence in fairness. Xenophon also reminds the soldiers that their spontaneous violence against the Cerasuntian ambassadors, which resulted in three being stoned to death, has made it impossible for the army to enter the territory of Cerasus.

Xenophon makes it clear in this passage that spontaneous violence by crowds is not an alternative form of justice, but simply a form of lynching, which may result in harsh injustice and undermines the law and order needed for military discipline and social peace. One cannot find any discussion of this passage in a chapter of a recent book by S. Forsdyke about "Street Theater and Popular Justice in Ancient Greece."[6] Forsdyke claims that there existed alongside the official forms a punishment a popular form of punishment and that "the Greeks

---

5 On this incident see O'Connor, 2016.
6 Forsdyke, 2012, 144–170.

made much more flexible use of the various modes of social control than is recognized by modern scholarship."⁷ Forsdyke goes so far as to assert that "the classical Athenians (for example) showed no hesitation in punishing particular individuals through informal, yet highly public, forms of popular justice."⁸

Forsdyke pays no attention to the passage from Xenophon's *Anabasis* and its implications, and most of the evidence she discusses pertains to punishment allowed by the laws of the state. For instance, she notes that *moichoi* could be humiliated by the husbands and fathers of women who were seduced.⁹ This was however not a form of punishment that lay outside the laws, but one that was permitted by the laws of Athens (Lys. 1.49).¹⁰ As Canevaro has shown, this form of punishment was accepted by the formal institutions of the state; it was not a form of popular justice that lay outside the jurisdiction of the courts.¹¹ In fact, the practice of locking up a seducer was one that the laws of Athens recognized and regulated against abuse ([Dem.] 59.66). If someone unjustly claimed that a person was a *moichos* and locked him up, the victim could bring a public charge against him. The existence of this statute shows both that the laws sanctioned the practice and also that they recognized that such a use of violence by a private individual could be abused by the unscrupulous.¹²

Forsdyke claims that this humiliation would have taken place in public, but presents no evidence to support this assertion. She next observes that a law of Athens made it possible for a court to sentence a convicted criminal to confinement in the stocks for five days (Dem. 24.114). It is true that this is a form of public humiliation, but it is certainly not a type of informal justice that lay outside the formal legal system. The defendant in this case was brought to court in normal way, convicted after a formal trial and placed in the stocks by public officials (probably the Eleven). Forsdyke compares the practice at Lepreum of leading seducers around the city for three days and making women who were seduced

---

7 Forsdyke, 2012, 145.
8 Forsdyke, 2012, 145. Forsdyke here confuses two meanings of the term "public" which can refer to public activies taking place in the context of the formal institutions of the state or to activities that take place in the open where they can be witnessed by large numbers of people. This confusion between the two senses of the term undermines much of her analysis.
9 Forsdyke, 2102, 147–8 repeatedly mistranslates the term *moichos* as "adulterer" but the term clearly covered those who seduced unmarried women as [Dem.] 59.66–70 makes clear. See Harris, 2013, 120 with references to earlier treatments.
10 *Pace* Cohen this is the law cited by Euphiletus at Lys. 1.28. See Carey, 1995.
11 For excellent criticisms of Forsdyke's claim that the punishment of *moichoi* was a type of informal justice see Canevaro, 2017, 53–55.
12 See Harris, 2013, 55–57.

stand for eleven days in a diaphanous tunic with no belt; the seducers were bound and led around the city for three days (Aristotle fragments 611–642 [Rose]).[13] She also mentions the punishment of women who were seduced at Cyme and made to stand in the marketplace and to ride around on a donkey (Plutarch *Moralia* 291f–292A). In her paraphrase of the evidence from Aristotle (fragments 611–42 [Rose]), however, she omits some crucial details, which reveal that these were not informal, popular forms of justice. The full text of these passages indicate that these people were also deprived of their civic rights (*atimon* in Plutarch; *atimousi* in Aristotle), which shows that these practices were not informal social customs, but legally mandated punishments. These are not forms of popular justice that lay outside the formal institutions of the courts, but punishments enforced by the formal institutions of the state.

One incident on which Forsdyke lays much emphasis is the stoning of Lycides in 479 BCE (Hdt. 9.4.1–5.3). After the Persians occupied Athens for a second time, Mardonius sent Myrichides, a man from the Hellespont, to ask the Athenian on Salamis to join them in an alliance against the other Greeks. After Myrichides presented this proposal in the Council, Lycides, one of the members of the Council, replied that it was better to accept this proposal and to place it before the Assembly. Herodotus is uncertain whether he did this because he had been bribed or because he actually thought that this was the best advice. The Athenians inside the Council and those outside considered this shocking, surrounded him and stoned him to death. Herodotus adds that they sent Myrichides away unharmed. The news of the event spread, and when the women learned about it, they encouraged each other, went to the house of Lycides on their own initiative, and stoned his wife and children to death.

Before drawing any general conclusions about this incident, one must bear several points in mind. First, the incident did not take place in normal circumstances. The Athenians had retreated to Salamis and were not in control of Attica. The enemy was camped around Athens, right across a narrow channel of water. Herodotus does not comment on the events, but he has clearly singled out an unusual and isolated event because it was extraordinary. The incident certainly has no parallel in the history of the democracy in the fifth and fourth centuries BCE. The stoning of the innocent wife and her children was fortunately not repeated as far as our sources indicate. Forsdyke attempts to downplay the "Modern horror at this ghastly violence against an innocent woman and her children" and criticizes Rosivach rather unfairly for calling the incident random "mob vio-

---

[13] Forsdyke, 2012, 144.

lence." She defends by claiming that "Rituals of popular justice follow established forms and tend to target particular individuals. They do not involve widespread violence and destruction."[14] This is a rather strange defense of what happened. First, one would like to know what these "established forms" are? Can Forsdyke name any similar incidents in Athenian history either before or after this incident? As Rosivach rightly observes, "None of our ancient sources, for example makes the general statement that stoning was at any time an ordinary form of execution at Athens, and similarly, while individuals may have been stoned in archaic Athens, there is no convincing evidence that later tradition remembered any specific stoning earlier than that of Lycides in 479."[15] Second, it may be true that the incident did not involve "widespread violence and destruction" but that does not justify the killing of a man without trial and an innocent woman and her children. This is like playing down the atrocities of the Holocaust by saying, "Well, it could have been worse. The Nazis could have killed ten million Jews instead of six million." The small scale of the atrocity in no way diminishes its horror. But what is interesting is that when Lycurgus (*Leoc.* 122) referred to the incident in 331 BCE, he subtly changed key details.[16] First, he cites a decree passed about the punishment of a man who proposed betraying the city (he does not give a name).[17] Second, Lycurgus does not express the doubts of Herodotus about the man's motives and states unequivocally that he was attempting to betray the city (*prodidonai*). Third and most significant, he omits the story about the women of Athens murdering his wife and children. What is clear from Lycurgus' version is that the spontaneous violence and the killing of the wife and children were considered to be embarrassing details, which had to be edited out when presenting the story to an Athenian audience.[18] In short, there is no reason to think that the Athenians were following any "established forms" in this atrocity, which was clearly an exceptional case in a time of extraodinary stress. One should not generalize on the basis of one such incident.

---

14 Fordsdyke, 2012, 157.
15 Rosivach, 1987, 236.
16 For the date of the speech see Harris, 2013, 233, note 54, refuting Engels, 2009, 113.
17 Cf. Rosivach, 1987, 238: "we can account for Lycurgus' version by assuming that the very rarity of stoning at Athens made stoning too significant to be forgotten, while its lawlessness and repulsiveness were offensive enough to Athens' self-image that the stoning was subsequently reinterpreted as a legal act."
18 Demosthenes (18.204) gives a briefer version, calls the man Kyrsilos and places the incident before the battle of Salamis. He includes the stoning of his wife by the women, but omits the killing of the children, which would also suggest that the found this part of the story abhorrent.

In fact, it is Xenophon (*Hell.* 1.2.13) who informs us about the only other known case of execution by stoning in Athens. A cousin of the famous Alcibiades who was also called Alcibiades fled with him after being condemned for parodying the Mysteries. He was serving on a Syracusan ship when he was captured by the Athenians at Ephesus. The Athenian general Thrasyllus sent the other prisoners to Athens but had Alcibiades executed by stoning on the spot. As Rosivach rightly notes, "the stoning was not a spontaneous act of mob violence but the communal execution of an order of a commanding general."[19] One might add that Alcibiades had already been condemned to death in an Athenian court; Thrasyllus was merely carrying out the sentence of the court. In both the case of Lycides and Alcibiades, a crowd of average Athenians executed an offender. In the first case there are two versions, and the later version is clearly an attempt to clean up embarrassing details about mob violence. In the latter case, the violence was not spontaneous but the execution of a formal sentence at the order of a general. There is no reason to believe that spontaneous violence against someone who violated communal norms was a regular occurrence or was regarded as an acceptable alternative to the justice of the courts.

Forsdyke also claims that "the razing of houses was primarily a form of popular justice, despite its occasional incorporation in formal law."[20] This seriously misrepresents the evidence for the practice. In a useful article, Connor has collected eleven passages in the ancient sources about razing of the house, but not all the evidence is of equal value. The story of the punishment of Hesiod's murderers belongs in the realm of myth (Plutarch *Moralia* 162b–c), and the story from Nicolaus of Damascus (*FGrHist* 90 F 60) about Cypselus mistakenly has Cypselus as the son of Periander (compare Hdt. 5.92). In the Locrian law dated to the last quarter of the sixth century BCE, however, the penalty of destroying the house is a legal punishment for proposing a division of land (Meiggs and Lewis 1969: no. 13). Isocrates (16.26) reports that the Peisistratids hated the Alcmeonids so much that they razed their houses and dug up their graves. This is hardly popular justice, but the outrageous behavior of tyrants. According to a scholion on Aristophanes *Lysistrata* 273 the Athenians razed the houses of the Athenians in Eleusis who collaborated with King Cleomenes in 506 BCE and confiscated their property. This was clearly an official act, not spontaneous popular violence. According to Herodotus (6.72) the Spartans convicted King Leotychidas of accepting bribes and razed his house after he fled into exile. This also appears to have been done as a result of a vote of the Assembly. Diodorus (12.78.5) reports that the Argives

---

[19] Rosivach, 1987, 246.
[20] Forsdyke, 2012, 159.

confiscated the property of their commanders in 419 BCE and razed their houses. The language of the passage again suggests an official decision. According to Craterus (*FGrHist* 342 F17), the Athenians voted to confiscate the property of the oligarch Phrynichus and to raze his house. Once more the language indicates a formal vote in the Assembly. A document found in the life of Antiphon ([Plutarch] *Mor.* 834A) contains a decree condemning Antiphon and Archeptolemus, but this purports to be an official document of a judicial decision. The final passage comes from Plutarch's *Life of Timoleon* (22.1–3) and recounts how Timoleon made a proclamation that all Syracusans who wished should demolish the houses and memorials of the tyrants. In this case too the decision to demolish a house is made by an official and is not the spontaneous initiative of a crowd. *Pace* Forsdyke none of these passages can be used as evidence to demonstrate the existence of informal methods of "popular justice."

Forsdyke makes much use of comparative evidence from the Medieval and Early Modern periods for popular forms of protest that might involve violence, especially against the wealthy.[21] In each case, however, the societies in which these practices occurred did not have political or legal institutions that granted access to craftsmen and peasants. These classes used informal practices like the *charivari* to express their grievances because the formal institutions that governed them gave them only limited opportunities to protest against injustice. This was not true for the citizens of Athenian democracy, who could vote in the Assembly and try cases in the courts. Xenophon (*Mem.* 3.7.6) informs us that the Assembly was filled with fullers, leather-workers, joiners, smiths, farmers and merchants. Six thousand Athenians served as judges each year, and this number must have included many outside the elite. The average Athenian craftsman or farmer did not have to resort to informal means of social control to achieve justice. The formal institutions of the Assembly, Council and courts provided him access and made such an alternative system unnecessary. As is also evident from the evidence examined above, the Athenians knew that the use of violence by private individuals could be abused for personal vendettas and that spontaneous violence deprived people of the right to a trial, one of the basic rights of Athenian democracy. As Cinzia Bearzot perceptively observes in her essay about the people of Phlius in this volume: "In *Hell.* 5.3.13 the Spartans acknowledge that the Phliasians hostile to the exiles have behaved arrogantly (ὑβρίζειν) and therefore they mobilize in favour of the latter. In this case *bia* and *hybris* materialize above all in the deprivation of political and civil rights, which denies the equal status of

---

21 Forsdyke, 2012 *passim*. For the "popular" nature of Athenian political and legal institutions see Canevaro, 2017.

citizens."[22] When Xenophon condemns the violence of the crowd during the March of the Ten Thousand, he is expressing widely held views about the use of physical force.

2

After Xenophon gave his speech to the soldiers about the need for discipline, it was agreed that those responsible for the violence should be tried and that in the future no one be allowed to initiate such lawlessness (*anomia*). The generals would make the accusations, and the *lochagoi* would serve as judges (*An.* 5.8.1).[23] They then proposed that the generals be tried for their past conduct. Philesius and Xanthicles were condemned to pay damages of twenty *mnai* for not guarding the cargoes of the merchants, and Sophaenetus to a fine of ten *mnai* for failing to do his duty in his assigned office (*An.* 5.8.1). Accusations were also brought against Xenophon for beating several men and for striking them in a humiliating way (*hybrizontos*). Xenophon invited the first man to state where he had struck him. The soldier replied that it was when they were perishing from cold when the snow was very deep (*An.* 5.8.2–3). Xenophon then asked the soldier why he was struck, if it was over a boyfriend or when they were drunk. After the soldier admitted that this was not the case, Xenophon asked him what his position was, and he replied that he was selected by his mess-mates to serve as a muleteer (*An.* 5.8.5). Xenophon then remembered the man and explained why he had beaten him. Xenophon had ordered that all the baggage be given to others to carry and ordered the muleteer to carry a sick man who could not keep up when the enemy were pursuing them. When Xenophon saw him later, he was digging a hole to bury the man. But the sick man lifted his leg, and everyone shouted that he was still alive. The muleteer said that the man might be as alive as he wished, but refused to carry him farther. At this point Xenophon struck him because the muleteer seemed to know that he was still alive. The muleteer objected that the man died later anyway. Xenophon said that all men are going to die, but that was no reason to bury him alive (*An.* 5.8.6–11). At this point the soldiers who were listening shouted that Xenophon did not hit him enough times.

---

22 See Bearzot, p. 16 in this volume.
23 Note how the language of the resolution follows the standard formula about laws applying "in the future" (τοῦ ... λοιποῦ). See Harris, 2006, 425–429.

Xenophon then delivered a speech about hitting soldiers for their own benefit (*An.* 5.8.13–26). He recalls other cases when he struck soldiers for lack of discipline (*An.* 5.8.13: *ataxias*). Had he not done so, they would have all been slaughtered by the enemy. In other cases he struck men who refused to get up in cold weather, which helped them to survive (*An.* 5.8.14–17), but he never struck anyone to humiliate them but only for their own benefit (*An.* 5.8.18–19). He observes that when he hit these men, the soldiers did not object and come to the victim's aid (*An.* 5.8.21) and criticizes them for not remembering how his actions saved lives and his praise and rewards for individuals (*An.* 5.8.25).

The incident is very valuable for the light it sheds on Greek attitudes about the use of physical force by officials. Xenophon is accused of using force to insult a man, but defends himself by stating that he was justified in beating both the muleteer and others. The passage shows that generals and other officials did not have the absolute right to use force in any circumstances, but makes a strict distinction between the use of force for the public good and the use of force to humiliate someone and to treat him in a way inconsistent with the dignity he deserves. To keep officials accountable, the army institutes legal procedures and allows those who feel as if they have been mistreated to bring an accusation. In this case the Ten Thousand are implementing a key feature of the rule of law, namely, that all officials should be accountable, a principle widely recognized throughout the Greek world.[24]

In a recent essay, S. Hornblower has studied the use of the *bakteria* by Spartan officials and the use of the *skeptron* to enforce discipline. He draws attention first to an incident recounted by Thucydides (8.84.2–3) in which the Spartan commander Astyochus lifted his stick (*bakteria*) against Dorieus who was speaking up for his sailors who were complaining about not being paid. When the sailors saw this, they rushed at Astyochus who fled to an altar. Hornblower claims that the Spartans "Say it with sticks" and claims that the use of "the stick or *bakteria* of a Spartan officer, and particularly the servile symbolism which came with it, were more than free Greeks could stomach." This would give the impression that in other Greek communities officials were not allowed to use such instruments against those who were disorderly, whether they were citizens, foreigners or slaves and that the Spartans were unusual in using physical violence in this way. There is much evidence against Hornblower's view. It may be that officials in other Greek communities did not use the *bakteria* or *skeptron* to enforce disci-

---

24 See Fröhlich, 2004.

pline, but they certainly had the right to use physical force as Xenophon did during the march of the Ten Thousand and to beat the disorderly with *rhabdoi*, a term which is often translated as "stick."

Perhaps the most famous use of this form of discipline occurred in 420 BCE. The Spartans had been barred from participating in the Olympic Games that year because the Eleans claimed that they had attacked the fortress of Phyrkos during the truce for the games. The Spartans claimed that they had not yet received the announcement of the truce, but the Eleans replied that it did not matter because the attack occurred during the period of the truce (Thuc. 5.49.1–5). The Eleans offered a compromise solution, but when the Spartan refused this, the Eleans imposed a fine and barred them from the sanctuary (Thuc. 5.50.1–2). Lichas, the son of Arcesilaus, a Spartan, entered a chariot in the games. When his chariot won, it was announced as belonging to the Boeotian people, but when Arcesilaus went to crown the charioteer, he was beaten by the *rhabdophoroi* (Thuc. 5.50.4. Cf. Xen.*Hell*. 3.2.21). No one objected to this use of force because it was perfectly legal for the officials at the games to beat those who were disorderly.

There is much evidence for officials using *rabdoi* and similar objects for maintaining order at athletic competitions or in the gymnasium. The famous inscription from Beroia about the gymnasium dated to the second century BCE mentions flogging as a punishment several times.[25] In the first case the law orders: "let the gymnasiarch beat anyone with a whip who is disobedient" (lines B 8–10). In the second, the gymnasiarch is to flog boys who do not obey and *paidogogoi* who are not free (lines B 21–23). In the third, the gymnasiarch is to beat those who cheat in the games (lines B 69–70). In the fourth, the gymnasiarch is also to beat those who do wrong (lines B 97–99). In a valuable essay on flogging athletes, Crowther and Frass draw attention to a fragment of a law from Olympia dated to the late sixth century, which instructs a judge to punish a wrestler who breaks a finger by striking (*paion*) the offender anywhere except the head.[26] The *Etymologicum Magnum* (s.v. *alytarches*) states that the *alytarches* was responsible for maintaining order at the Olympic games and that in other places the term used is *rhabdophoros* or *mastigophoros*, which indicates that such officials were found throughout the Greek world.

The image of the official maintaining order at the games was often used in oratory and other literature. According to Plutarch (*Them*. 11.2–3), when Eurybiades, the Spartan commander of the Greek fleet at Salamis, wished to sail to the Isthmus, Themistocles objected. Eurybiades replied that they beat (ῥαπίζουσι)

---

25 For the text see Gauthier and Hatzopoulos, 1993.
26 Crowther and Frass, 1998, 59.

those who start too soon at the games. To which Themistocles retorted that those who start too late never win. In Plato's *Protagoras* (338a. Cf. Pollux 3.153) Hippias urges the company to appoint a *rabdouchos* to keep order in the contest between Socrates and Protagoras, a passage which shows that the practice of using such officials in contests was widespread. Aristophanes uses the image of the *rabdouchos* when he says that comic poets who praise themselves should be beaten (Ar.*Pax* 734–735).

Officials carrying *rhabdoi* were often assigned the task of keeping order at festivals. In a decree from the deme of Paiania dated to the early fifth century BCE the *hieropoioi* are given the power to carry the *rhabdos* and to use it as they order (*IG* i³ 250, lines 9–11; *LSS* 18, lines 9–11). In the well-known law from Andania about the Mysteries there are several rules about officials using physical force to maintain order (*IG* V 1 1390, *LSCG* no.65).[27] One section about those who are disorderly commands: "When the sacrifices and the Mysteries are celebrated, everyone must keep religious silence and obey orders. The sacred men must scourge anyone disobeying or conducting himself indecently toward the gods and ban him from the Mysteries" (trans. Gawlinski) (lines 39–41). The next section has equally strict orders given to the *rhabdophoroi*: "There are to be twenty *rhabdophoroi* appointed from the sacred men, and they just obey those carrying out the Mysteries and take care that everything is done decorously and orderly by those attending, just as those appointed over them order. They must scourge those disobeying or conducting themselves indecently. If one of the *rhabdophoroi* does not do as is written, or if he commits some other wrong or does something to the detriment of the Mysteries, having been judged in the presence of the sacred men, if found guilty, he is not to participate in the Mysteries" (trans. Gawlinski) (lines 41–45). And toward the end of the inscription the *rhabdophoroi* are commanded to scourge anyone whom the Ten order them to scourge (lines 165–167). What is striking is that the officials are instructed to scourge anyone disobeying, not just slaves. In an inscription from Korope about the oracle of Apollo, the generals and the *nomophylakes* are to select three *rhabdouchoi* who are not younger than thirty and are to have the power to stop anyone who is disorderly (*LSAG* no. 83, lines 23–26). There is a list of several *rhabdophoroi* from Lebadeia in the first century BCE (IG VIII 3078).

The Athenians also had officials who used whips to maintain order in the marketplace. When Dikaiopolis sets up his market in Aristophanes' *Acharnians* (723–24), he appoints three straps (*himantes*) as *agoranomoi*. When a sycophant

---

[27] For commentary on the inscription see Gawlinski, 2012.

attempts to denounce a Megarian in the market, Dikaiopolis summons his *agoranomoi* to keep him out (*Ach.* 968. Cf. Plato *Leg.* 936c). In the Assembly the herald and the *prytaneis* in the fifth century BCE might order the Scythian archers to remove physically those whom they considered disorderly (Ar.*Ach.* 54–58; *Eq.* 665; *Eccl.* 143, 258–259). They also appear to have carried whips (Ar.*Th.* 933–934).

Even though the use of the *bakteria* to maintain discipline may have been a Spartan habit, the use of physical force by public officials to keep order was found throughout Greece. Spartan officials were in no way unusual. When the sailors grew angry at Astyochus for threatening Dorieus (Thuc. 8.84.2–3), it was not because they thought such a use of violence was insulting for a free man as Hornblower believes, but because they thought that Astyochus' reaction was not justified in this case. All Doreius was doing was to support the reasonable claims of the sailors to be paid. Dorieus was not being disorderly. There is a similar incident reported by Xenophon in the *Hellenica* (6.2.15–19). During his siege of Corcyra in 373/2 BCE, Mnesippus thought that he was about to take the city and grew overconfident. He dismissed some of his mercenaries and fell into arrears with the pay of the rest. The people in the city saw that the Spartan positions were not well guarded and made a sortie, capturing some and killing others. Mnasippus took some hoplites and ordered the captains and senior officers to lead the mercenaries. Some of the captains objected that it was hard to maintain discipline when their men were not receiving their supplies. At this point, Mnasippus struck one of the officers with his *bakteria* and another with the butt end of his spear (*styraki*). This lowered the morale of the troops, who started to hate him. Here too what offended the troops was Mnasippus' insensitive response to their reasonable demands. In other circumstances such a use of physical force would have been justified if used to maintain discipline. What was offensive about the Spartan general Pausanias was not his use of force, but his excessive and unnecessary use of force (Th. 1.95.1; Plutarch *Arist.* 23.1–3).[28] When King Cleomenes used his *skeptron* to strike any Spartan he met, this was considered a sign of madness (Hdt. 6.75.1). On the other hand, Xenophon did not find it inappropriate during the march of the Ten Thousand for Clearchus to use a stick to beat anyone whom he caught shirking (*An.* 2.3.11). In fact, he lists this among the qualities that made Clearchus a good leader.

Spartan officials were not the only ones to be criticized for excessive use of force. In the speech *Against Androtion* (Dem. 22) the accuser Diodorus charges the defendant with abusing the powers of his office when collecting arrears to the

---

28 Hornblower, 2000, 77, note 15 gets the reference to Plutarch *Aristides* wrong (23.1–3, not 11).

eisphora.²⁹ Diodorus admits that it was necessary to collect the money owed to the Treasury, but insists that Androtion should have carried out his task in accordance with the laws and for the benefit of the Athenians. Instead he invaded the houses of private citizens with the Eleven. This forced poor citizens to go up to the roof to escape to their neighbor's house or to hide under the bed as a way of avoiding being dragged off to prison. To make the situation worse, he had citizens arrested in front of their wives (Dem. 22.51–53). He contrasts the actions of Androtion with those of Satyrus, who was able to collect thirty-four talents to provide for naval equipment without making any enemies or causing any complaints (Dem. 22.63). Had he confined himself to collecting money, Androtion would have been beyond reproach, but he insulted Athenian citizens (Dem. 22.59–62).

In another speech in the demosthenic corpus ([Dem.] 47.52–61), a trierarch recounts his efforts to recover naval equipment. A law of Periander gave trierarchs the power to collect such equipment from those who had not returned it. Sometime in the 360s one trierarch was instructed to collect equipment from Demochares and Theophemus. The trierarch started by confronting the two men and requesting that they comply, but they refused. He then summoned each man to court and won a judgment against each man. Demochares returned the equipment in his possession, but Theophemus did not. The trierarch then reported the latter's refusal to the Council, which passed a decree instructing him to recover the equipment in any way possible. This measure appears to have given trierarch the power to distrain on the property of Theophemus if he continued to disobey. The trierarch then took a public slave and went to the house of Theophemus. A slave woman answered the door but said that Theophemus was out. After his return, the trierarch once more asked for the equipment, which met with yet another refusal. At this point the trierarch asked Theophemus to accompany him to the men in charge of the fleet and the Council or to return the equipment. If Theophemus continued to be obstinate, he would seize some of his property as payment. When the trierarch seized the slave woman, Theophemus intervened and stopped him from dragging her away. There were two versions about what happened next. According to the trierarch, Theophemus struck him when he went to seize other property. The trierarch then went to the Council and later brought suit against Theophemus and won a judgment against him. But Theophemus also brought a suit against the trierarch for assault on the grounds that he struck first and won a judgment.

---

29 The date of Androtion's assignment is debated. Harding, 1976, 193, note 54 places it during his service in the Council in 356/5; Moscati Castelnuovo, 1980, 254–257 places it in the 370s. On the speech in general see Harris, 2008, 167–196.

What this incident reveals is that officials in Athens had to be very careful about the use of force. One should note the restraint of the trierarch at each step, and his care in justifying each of his actions.[30] He only resorts to force after Theophemus continues to resist and after all other options have been exhausted. On the other hand, the case against the trierarch shows that Theophemus thought that the trierarch had used excessive or unnecessary force just as the muleteer thought that Xenophon had gone too far in his use of force during the march of the Ten Thousand. The possibility that officials might use force without legal justification was a potential problem in both Athens and Sparta and no doubt in other Greek communities as well.

There is a famous passage in *Against Androtion* about the difference between free men and slaves: "the bodies of slaves are subject to punishment for their crimes, but free men can keep theirs safe from harm even in the worst disasters" (Dem. 22.55). It is true that in many laws and decrees a difference is made between penalties for free men, who are subject to fines, and those for slaves, who are punished with a number of lashes, normally fifty.[31] Yet as the evidence for the use of force by officials reveals, the contrast is too simplistic. When inflicting penalties for an offense, officials would make free men pay fines to the Treasury, but when attempting to maintain order in public spaces, officials could also use physical force to compel free persons to obey their commands. One must above all place the statement in *Against Androtion* in context: the accuser is attempting to cast the defendant's actions in the worst possible light and to accuse him of treating free men like slaves, the classic mark of abusive behavior (*hybris*). To blacken the character of Androtion, he does not mention that officials had the power to use physical force if necessary to maintain order when free men were disorderly in some circumstances.

Just as in other communities, Spartan officials were supposed to use physical violence with restraint, for the public benefit and not for the purpose of insulting free men or without justification. The views about the use of force by officials implicit in Xenophon's account of his beating a soldier during the March of the Ten Thousand were followed widely in the Greek world; they were not unusual in any way and do not represent a Spartan approach to the conduct of officials.[32]

---

[30] For an analysis of the incident see Harris, 2013, 49–50.
[31] E.g., *SEG* 26:72, lines 14–16. See Hunter, 1994, 154–184. Hunter does not discuss the use of force by public officials against free persons, which undermines much of her analysis. Hornblower, 2000 relies heavily on Hunter's work.
[32] In general, Hornblower, 2000 does not distinguish between the legitimate and the illegitimate use of force by officials.

3

In his *Hellenica* Xenophon is the only Greek historian to give an account of the political career of Euphron of Sicyon. In the early 360s Euphron told the Argives and the Arcadians that if the wealthiest families of Sicyon retained control, the city would join with Sparta. On the other hand, if there were a democratic government, it would remain faithful to the Arcadians and Argives. He then invited them to a meeting of the people and declared that the constitution would henceforth be on the basis of the same and equal rights (ἐπὶ τοῖς ἴσοις καὶ ὁμοίοις). Following the change in government, he asked the people to choose generals, and Euphron was elected along with Hippodamus, Cleander, Acrisius, and Lysander.[33] He next removed Lysimenes from the command of the mercenary troops and placed his son Adeas in the post. To secure the loyalty of the regular troops and the mercenaries, he distributed much money from public and sacred funds. He also made use of property confiscated from those exiled for pro-Spartan leanings. Finally, he put some of his colleagues in office to death by treachery and exiled others. In this way he gained control of everything and was clearly a tyrant (σαφῶς τύραννος ἦν). He gained allies abroad partly by money, partly by sending troops. As many scholars have noted, Xenophon is not sympathetic to Euphron partly because of his hostility to the upper classes, partly on account of Euphron's anti-Spartan policies. What is nevertheless clear is that Euphron did not seize power by force in the same way as other tyrants did. Despite his hostility, Xenophon states that Euphron was elected general with four others and ruled through a constitutional office. Euphron convinces the people change the form of government from an aristocracy, in which wealthy men had considerable power, to a democracy. Xenophon does not indicate what legal means he used to drive his opponents into exile, but later states that they were banished without a legal decision (7.3.1: *aneu dogmatos*). Although Xenophon mentions mercenaries, these are used to help allies and not to gain power. Euphron later commanded these mercenaries in an expedition with the Theban governor at Sicyon to help the people of Pellene against the army of Phlius (Xen.*Hell.* 7.2.11–15).

The description of his rule by Diodorus (15.70.3) is much briefer. He states that Euphron made an attempt to set up tyranny with the help of the Argives but does not mention the change of government or his election to officer. After gaining power, he exiled forty wealthy Sicyonians and confiscated their property.

---

[33] For the tendency of the Greek *polis* to appoint boards of generals and for the reasons behind the practice see Harris, 2010 and Harris, 2015.

With this money he assembled a force of mercenaries and ruled over the city. Xenophon's account is not sympathetic, but the account of Diodorus is even more hostile and draws on the stereotype of the tyrant who gains power through a coup d'état and uses mercenaries to gain control of the city.[34]

What is interesting for the topic of violence in Xenophon is the murder of Euphron. When Aeneas of Stymphalos summoned the most powerful men to the Acropolis and sent for those who had been sent into exile illegally (Xen.*Hell.* 7.3.2), Euphron panicked and started to communicate with the Spartans, claiming that he had voted against leaving the Spartan alliance and that he had set up a democracy to take revenge on his opponents who were hostile to Sparta. He then handed the harbor to the Spartans (Xen.*Hell.* 7.3.2–3). Soon after this, he reversed himself, gathered mercenaries from Athens, and seized power with the help of the people. Seeing that he could not gain control without Theban support, he collected some money and started out for Thebes with the intention of persuading them to drive out the wealthy. When the former exiles saw what he was doing, they assassinated him on the Acropolis of Thebes when Theban officials and the Council were meeting there (Xen.*Hell.* 7.3.4–5).

The officials brought a charge of murder against the assassins before the Council. They accused them of taking matters into their own hands in front of the members of the Council who alone had the power to decide who should be put to death and who should not. They warned that if the murderers were not punished, no one would dare to visit Thebes in the future if anyone can kill someone before he explains his reasons for coming there. Such men lack all respect for religion, justice, the law, and the interests of the city (Xen.*Hell.* 7.3.6). This speech echoes many of the themes found in the speech of Xenophon examined in the first part of this paper. The murderers have usurped the state's monopoly of deadly force, in this case, the right to execute offenders. This is a dangerous precedent and must be punished harshly.

All the other assassins denied that they had committed the murder except one who defended himself with strong arguments (Xen.*Hell.* 7.3.7–11). He cited the precedent of the Theban execution of the polemarchs Archias and Hypates who were acting like tyrants and keeping the city enslaved to the Spartans (Xen.*Hell.* 5.4.1–9). Euphron was a tyrant for several reasons: first, he had stolen gold and silver from temples; second, he was on good terms with the Spartans; third, he had given pledges to the Thebans, then turned the harbor over to the Spartans; and fourth, he had put to death or sent into exile innocent men. Next he sided with the Athenians, the enemies of Thebes, and was about to bribe the

---

34 On the stereotype of tyranny see Harris, 2018.

Thebans. Even though he came to Thebes on his own accord, he did so to cause more harm and was both a traitor and a tyrant. Finally, he pointed out that exiles from the cities of the alliance should be subject to extradition. But he returned without any decision of the allies and thus deserves to be put to death.

The Thebans acquitted the man and decided that Euphron had received the punishment he deserved. But the citizens of Sicyon considered him a brave man. They brought him back, buried him in the marketplace and honored him as the founder of the city. Xenophon comments that most men consider those who have brought them benefits to be good men (Xen.*Hell.* 7.3.12). In this case, Xenophon presents us with an exception to the rule that only public officials have the power to use deadly violence. The accusers argue that the murderers have set a bad example and must be punished. The defendant however argues that the use of force was justified on several grounds but mainly because Euphron was a tyrant and a traitor. He and his companions therefore had the right to act on behalf of the community. The contrast with Xenophon's condemnation of the violence to the *agoranomoi* is very significant: Xenophon argued that it was not clear whether the market officials had wronged them or not. In this case, however, the killer argues that the guilt of Euphron was clear, and the members of the Theban council agreed. The exception to the general rule that only officials can execute wrongdoers is justified on the grounds that Euphron's actions were generally agreed to be unjust and detrimental to the people of Sicyon and Thebes.

In a recent book David Teegarden has claimed that laws about killing tyrants were a tool used by democrats to defend their form of government against subversion.[35] According to Teegarden, the challenge faced by democrats in protecting their regime was a "coordination problem." Though united in their defense of tyranny, they might be isolated and unable to organize opposition to a seizure of power by a tyrant or a group of oligarchs. The use of violence against usurpers would then help them to unify their forces. Teegarden claims that the right to kill a tyrant originated in the decree of Demophantus, which he mistakenly believes was enacted in 410 BCE after the overthrow of the Five Thousand.[36] Finally, Teegarden argues that the existence of this law enabled the men of Phyle to rally forces and to overthrow the government of the Thirty in 403 BCE. This incident

---

[35] Teegarden, 2014.
[36] The document at Andoc. 1.96–98 is not an authentic document, and the decree of Demophantus was enacted after the fall of the Thirty. See Lycurgus *Against Leocrates* 124–126 and Harris, 2013/2014. The case against the authenticity of this document is now accepted by many scholars.

from Xenophon's history of Greece provides several reasons for calling Teegarden's views into question. The Athenians certainly had no coordination problem in this case.

Above all, the story of Euphron demonstrates that the ideology of killing a tyrant without bringing him to trial was not invented by democrats. In fact, the hostility to tyrants long preceded the year 411 BCE and even Cleisthenes' reforms of 508 BCE. Herodotus (5.71) reports that when Cylon gathered a band of followers and attempted to seize the Acropolis and set up a tyranny, he was not able to succeed and sat as a suppliant at the statue (probably of Athena). The *prytaneis* of the *naukrariai* invited him to rise with the promise that they would not put him and his followers to death, but they were killed anyway, and the blame fell on the Alcmeonidai. When explaining the "pollution of the Alcmeonidai," Thucydides (1.126.2–11) gives a more detailed account, but agrees with Herodotus about Cylon's attempt to set up a tyranny, about the popular opposition to his action, and the murder of his followers who had supplicated and been promised safety. Thucydides differs on some details such as the identity of the officials (the nine archons vs. *prytaneis* of the *naukrariai*) who were in charge.[37] Roughly a generation later, one sees the same hostility to tyrants in Solon's poetry of Solon who was archon in the year 594/3 BCE. Solon (fr. 32 [West]) declares:

> If I spared the land of my country,
> and did not grasp after tyranny and violence, which
> would have defiled and dishonored my reputation,
> I am not ashamed. Thus I think that my fame will surpass that of all men.

One should note the association of tyranny with violence in this passage. In another passage, Solon (fr. 9 [West]) associates the rule of one man (*monarchou*) with slavery for the people.

> From a cloud come the might of snow and hail,
>   Thunder from shining lightning,
> by powerful men a city is destroyed, and into the slavery
>   of a single man the people falls through its folly.
> Once you raise a man up too high, it is not easy to restrain
>   him later; right now you might heed this advice.

Like other early lawgivers, Solon also enacted several statutes to prevent the rise of tyranny: 1) he forbid officials to hold office for more than one year, 2) he made

---

[37] On supplication in general see Naiden, 2006, especially 105–129 on the significance of raising suppliants.

officials accountable and laid down penalties for those who did not follow the law, 3) he entrusted various functions not to a single official but to boards of magistrates, 4) he placed entrenchment clauses in laws to prevent any individual from altering laws for his personal benefit.[38] There was also a law passed before the Peisistratid tyranny, which provided that "anyone who rises up to establish a tyranny or who aids and abets a tyranny shall be *atimos*, both he and his family" ([Arist.]*Ath.Pol.* 16.10). The author of the *Constitution of the Athenians* calls the laws in this period about tyranny "mild," but Hansen, following a view of Hignett, claims that the author misinterpreted the meaning of *atimos* in the law and did not realize that in this period it meant outlawry, that is, exile or banishment.[39] Rhodes uncritically accepts this view.[40] In a recent essay, however, C. Joyce has shown that *atimia* in this period only meant loss of rights.[41] The right to kill a tyrant without incurring pollution was only enacted later after the overthrow of the Thirty (Lycurgus *Leoc.* 124–126). Just the same, the law shows that the hostility to tyranny was well established in the early sixth century, long before Cleisthenes' reforms. After the Peisistratid tyrants were driven out by Cleomenes, the Athenians honored Aristogeiton and Harmodius with statues in the agora, the only Athenians to receive this honor in the fifth century.[42]

The Corinthians abolished tyranny not long after Solon's legislation and established constitutional government. When Cleomenes attempted to invade Attica and place Hippias back in power, the Corinthian Socles reminded the Spartan king and the other Peloponnesians about the horrors of tyranny (Hdt. 5.90–93). And opposition to tyranny lay at the heart of the Greek resistance to the Persian king Xerxes and helped to unite the Greeks as an ideology.

The opposition to tyranny was originally rooted not in a belief in democracy, the rule of the people, as opposed to other forms of government because this attitiude is well attested long before the reforms of Cleisthenes and before the term *demokratia* was coined in the late fifth century BCE.[43] In the poems of Solon and elsewhere, tyranny is the opposite of the rule of law (*eunomia*). As Canevaro and I have shown, the rule of law was an ideal shared widely throughout the Greek world.[44] This ideal contained many features such as equality before the law, the

---

[38] See Harris, 2006, 17–25.
[39] See Hansen, 1976, 75 and Hignett, 1958, 161.
[40] Rhodes, 1981, 222.
[41] Joyce, 2018, who decisively refutes the view of Dmitriev, 2015 that *atimia* could bring death or exile even in the fourth and third centuries BCE.
[42] On these statues see recently Azoulay, 2014.
[43] For the context in which the terms *demokratia* and *oligarchia* were coined see Harris, 2016.
[44] Harris, 2006, 3–28; Canevaro, 2017.

accountability of officials, trial before impartial judges, the right of defendants to know the charges before the trial, the principle that there should be no punishment without law, the prohibition of *ex post facto* laws, and the accessibility of statutes and legal procedure.[45]

The career of Euphron as recounted by Xenophon shows that opposition to tyranny could be used both by the proponents of constitutional regimes opposed to democracy and by the advocates of democracy. What made Euphron a tyrant was not the way in which he seized power but the way he exercised power. Xenophon makes it clear that Euphron convinced his fellow citizens to change the constitution and that he was elected as general. It only became apparent that he was a tyrant when he started to drive his opponents into exile without a trial and confiscate their property, to take control of sacred funds, and to appoint his son to command the mercenaries. What made Euphron a tyrant was his violation of the rights of individual citizens, his violation of rules about sacred property and his personal control over mercenary troops. Even though Xenophon respected the principle that only the officials of the state should have the right to use deadly force, he also recognized that in the case of tyranny there was an exception to this general rule. On the other hand, there is a certain consistency in his views: for Xenophon the only justification for the use of violence was for the sake of justice and the benefit of individuals and the community. The killing of a tyrant was not only a way to protect democracy; it was mainly a way to restore the rule of law when it was threatened.

Bibliography

Azoulay, V. (2014), *Les tyrannicides d'Athènes. Vie et mort de deux statues*, Paris.
Canevaro, M. (2017), "The Popular Culture of the Athenian Institutions: 'Authorized' Popular Culture and 'Unauthorized' Elite" in: Grigg (2017) 39–65.
Canevaro, M. (2017), "The Rule of Law as the Measure of Political Legitimacy in the Greek City States" in: *Hague Journal of the Rule of Law* 9, 211–236.
Cartledge, P./Millett, P./von Reden, S. (eds) (1998), *Kosmos: Essays in Order, Conflict and Community in Classical Athens*, Cambridge.
Connor, R. (1985), "The Razing of the House in Greek Society" in: *TAPA* 115, 79–102.
Crowther, N.B./Frass, M. (1998), "Flogging as a Punishment in the Ancient Games" in: *Nikephoros* 11, 51–82.
Dmitriev, S. (2015), "Athenian *atimia* and legislation against tyranny and subversion," in: *CQ* 65, 35–50.

---

45 See Harris, 2013, 3–20.

Forsdyke, S. (2012). *Slaves Tell Tales and Other Episodes in the Politics of Popular Culture in Ancient Greece*, Princeton.
Gauthier, P./Hatzopoulos, M. (1993), *La loi gymnasiarque de Beroia*, Athens/Paris.
Gawlinski, L.C. (2012), *The Sacred Law of Andania*, Berlin.
Grig, L. (ed.) (2017), *Popular Culture in the Ancient World*, Cambridge.
Hansen, M.H. (1976), *Apagoge, Endeixis, and Ephegesis against Kakourgoi, Atimoi, and Pheugontes*, Odense.
Hansen, M.H. (1998), *Polis and City-State: An Ancient Concept and its Modern Equivalent*, Copenhagen.
Harding, P. (1976), "Androtion's Political Career" in: *Historia* 25, 186–200.
Harris, E.M. (2010), "The Rule of Law and Military Organization" in: *Symposion 2009*, G.Thür (ed.), Vienna, 405–418.
Harris, E.M. (2013–2014), "The Document at Andocides 1.96–98" in: *Tekmeria* 12, 121–153.
Harris, E.M. (2013), *The Rule of Law in Action in Democratic Athens*, Oxford.
Harris, E.M. (2015), "Military Organization and One-Man Rule in the Greek *Polis*" in: *Ktema* 40, 83–91.
Harris, E.M. (2016), "The Flawed Origins of Ancient Greek Democracy" in: *Nous, Polis, Nomos*, A. Havlíček/C. Horn/J. Jinek (eds), St. Augustin, 43–55.
Harris, E.M. (2018), "The Stereotype of Tyranny and the Tyranny of Stereotypes: Demosthenes on Philip II of Macedon" in: *Festschrift for M. Hatzopoulos*, P. Paschidis (ed.), Athens, 1–12.
Havlíček, A./Horn, Ch./Jinek, J. (eds) (2016), *Nous, Polis, Nomos. Festschrift Francisco L. Lisi*, St. Augustin.
Hignett, C. (1958), *A History of the Athenian Constitution*, Oxford.
Hunter, V.J. (1994), *Policing Athens: Social Control in the Attic Lawsuits, 420–320 B.C.*, Princeton.
Hornblower, S. (2000), "Sticks, Stones, and Spartans: The Sociology of Spartan Violence" in: *War and Violence in Ancient Greece*, H. Van Wees (ed.), London, 57–82.
Joyce, C. (2018), "*Atimia* and Outlawry in Archaic and Classical Greece," in: *Polis* 35, 33–60.
Lewis, S. (2004), "Καὶ σαφῶς τύραννος ἦν: Xenophon's Account of Euphron of Sicyon" in: *JHS* 124, 65–74.
Moscati Castelnuovo, L. (1980), "La carriera politica dell'Attidografo Androzione" in: *Acme* 33, 251–278.
O'Connor, S. (2016), "The *Agoranomoi* at Cotyora (Xen. *An*. 5.7.21–29): Cerasuntians or Cyreans?" in: *CQ* 66, 84–99.
Riess, W. (2012), *Performing Intepresonal Violence: court, curse and comedy in fourth-century bce Athens*, Berlin/Boston.
Rhodes, P.J. (1981), *A Commentary on the Aristotelian* Athenaion Politeia, Oxford.
Rosivach, V.J. (1987), "Execution by Stoning in Athens" in: *CA* 6, 232–248.
Rubinstein, L. (1998), "The Athenian political perception of the idiotes" in: *Kosmos: Essays in Order, Conflict and Community in Classical Athens*, P.A. Cartledge/P.C. Millett/S. von Reden (eds), Cambridge, 125–43.
Teegarden, D. (2014), *Death to Tyrants! Ancient Greek Democracy and the Struggle Against Tyranny*, Princeton.
Van Wees, H. (ed.) (2000), *War and Violence in Ancient Greece*, London.
Weber, M. (1972), *Wirtschaft und Gesellschaft*, Tübingen.

Nathan Crick
The Rhetoric of Violence in Xenophon's *Anabasis*

> To substitute violence for power can bring victory, but the price is very high; for is not only paid by the vanquished, it is also paid by the victor in terms of his own power.
>
> Hannah Arendt, *On Violence*, 53

> When Xenophon saw what was going on, fearing that the army might start looting and that irreparable damage might be done both to the city and to the interests of himself and the soldiers, he ran forward and rushed inside the gates with the crowd.
>
> Xenophon, *Anabasis* (7.1.18)

The dramatic opening scene of Book 7 of the *Anabasis* places the tension identified by Hannah Arendt between violence and power at the center of the action. In the words of Michael A. Flower, this book "opens with one of the most dramatic scenes in all of Greek historical writing (7.1.12–31), a miniature gem that can stand comparison to anything written by Herodotus or Thucydides" (151). The army of 10,000 Greek mercenaries—now reduced to 7,000—is at this point nearing the end of their long journey into and back out of Persia in their failed attempt to help Prince Cyrus overthrow his brother and take the Persian throne. The original generals all massacred, Xenophon has taken charge of the army. But now fortune seems to have smiled on the army at last. Xenophon has reached the Spartan city of Byzantium and has befriended its Spartan governor Cleander, who has promised to lead the army back into Greece while Xenophon departs for home on his own. Yet unfavorable omens have spooked Cleander. Growing uneasy with the army's presence inside the city walls, Cleander and the Spartan admiral Anaxibius under false pretexts convince Xenophon to lead the army outside the city. Sensing betrayal, the soldiers break ranks and frantically turn back to the city, only to have the gates barred. They fly into a rage: "The soldiers hammered at the gates, saying they were being treated extremely unfairly, and were being pushed outside into enemy country, and they threatened to break the gates down unless people inside opened them voluntarily" (7.1.16). When this did not happen, some of the remaining soldiers inside "hacked through the bar with axes and threw the gate open; and then they all rushed in" (7.1.17). It was at this point that Xenophon identified his rhetorical situation and acted not so much to save the city but to salvage his power.

Particularly remarkable about Xenophon's action is its rhetorical character. As Flower observes, Xenophon uses "his rhetorical skills to calm them and to bring them to their senses by pointing out the terrible consequences that would follow if they gratify their anger by punishing the Spartans who are present and plundering the blameless Greek city" (151). How Xenophon accomplishes this feat is a masterpiece in persuasion. Once he enters the city, he encounters pure chaos. The people of the city are fleeing the marketplace, taking refuge in their homes or dragging their ships into the sea while their leaders retreat to the citadel. Meanwhile, soldiers rush up to Xenophon with an opportunity: "Now is your chance, Xenophon, to become a great man. You have a city, you have triremes, you have money, you have an army in us. Now, if you wanted to, you could do good to us and we could make you great" (7.1.21). Xenophon agrees to the proposition and gives the command to fall in and have the soldiers arrange themselves in their detachments, presumably preparing them for a full assault on the city. Yet Xenophon has interpreted the meaning of greatness in a different way. For the soldiers, to be great meant to take charge in violently sacking the city; for Xenophon, to be great meant to preserve the honor, discipline, and power of his army. Consequently, once the soldiers are calmed down, he seizes the moment to speak, warning them against violence: "For heaven's sake let us not go off our heads and die in dishonor, fighting against our own native cities and our own friends and kinsmen, all of whom are in the cities that would be making war on us" (7.1.29). Better to suffer injustice than to gratify one's impulses at the expense of long-term gains. The soldiers are persuaded. They secure promises of aid from Anaxibius and peacefully leave the city in search of plunder elsewhere.

This episode captures perfectly the complex relationship among rhetoric, violence, and power that appears in Xenophon's work. This relationship, of course, was theorized quite explicitly in Xenophon's *Memorabilia*, when in his recounting of conversations with Socrates on the topic, Xenophon gives his own view on the matter. For him, violence is the irrational application of physical force to unwilling bodies, whereas rhetoric involves the rational persuasion of free men. Consequently, violence and rhetoric not only operate by opposite means but also obtain opposite effects, as "violence involves enmity and danger, whereas persuasion produces the same results without danger and in a friendly spirit; for the victims of violence feel they have been deprived, and are resentful, while those who have yielded to persuasion are appreciative of having received a kindness" (*Memorabilia* 1.2.10). Moreover, the nature of these effects have a direct bearing on the nature of power, which refers in Xenophon to the capacity of an individual to make others follow one's will without the need for organized coercion. As he argues, "anyone who ventures to use violence will also need not a few accomplices, while the man who can persuade will need none, because he will be sure of his power to persuade even if he is single-handed" (1.2.11). This sort of power is clearly on display in Xenophon's speech to his troops in Byzantium; through a single rhetorical performance, he cools their raging souls and transforms them from a chaotic band of looters into a disciplined and virtuous fighting force who feel kindness toward their leader. His rhetoric has used reason to more carefully direct violence in such a way that attains their desired ends without sacrificing their power.

Yet the *Anabasis* is a rich text not only because it seems to confirm his sentiments expressed in the *Memorabilia*, but also because it complicates its simple dichotomy. For Xenophon shows himself fully prepared to use force to attain his aims when convenient and often uses rhetoric to justify past acts of violence or to threaten future violence if his expectations of "justice" are not met. Violence, in fact, is present in almost everything Xenophon does or says in some way, although often implicit and subtle. What I wish to explore in this essay, therefore, is how rhetoric and power relate to one another in different rhetorical situations as narrated by Xenophon in the *Anabasis*. Through this exercise I hope to both reveal the subtlety of Xenophon's rhetoric and to clarify the overall relationship among rhetoric, violence, and power in rhetorical performance as it continues in the present.

1 Violence, Power, and Rhetoric

> From its mythic origins to its resurgence in the late 20th century, rhetoric has always formed itself in an intimate relation with violence. On the one hand, rhetoric's origin is in its difference from violence, its renunciation of it, its being an alternative to violence, its providing a discursive means to resolve conflicts that would otherwise become violent. Rhetoric is the great other to violence. On the other hand, rhetoric has been widely suspected of being mostly nothing other than violence and domination and trickery disguised, violence masquerading as reason and language, but every bit as coercive and domineering as an armed interlocutor.
>
> James Crosswhite, *Deep Rhetoric*, 134

In his work on *Deep Rhetoric*, James Crosswhite follows in the tradition of Xenophon and Arendt by tackling the difficult question of the relationship between rhetoric and violence. In the above epigraph Crosswhite eloquently establishes the dialectical tension between rhetoric and violence that so often permeated the work of the Greek classics like the *Anabasis*. For him, "the question is whether and to what extent violence constitutes the political-rhetorical order, permeates rhetoric, inhabits our social engagements, determines our reason decisions, and forms our individual and social identities" (162). As we have seen Xenophon already articulate, one of the common philosophical threads, particularly within the Socratic tradition, was the celebration of rational speech as what Crosswhite calls the "great other" to violence. To persuade another person through *logos* is to appeal to the highest of the human faculties—reason—that makes us something other than brutes and that casts aside the need for violent force. Yet we also see Xenophon, as in his negotiations with Anaxibius, clearly exerting rhetorical force by referring to past and future violence which bolster his words through precedent and coercion. Without an army behind him capable of sacking the city, Xenophon would be treated no better than a stranger or a slave. His triumph of rational discourse amounts to little more than a raised fist.

For Crosswhite, we must bridge the gap between rhetoric and violence without simply collapsing one into the other. On the one hand, "to deny the differences between real physical violence and the contest of ideas in language would be not only madness but also a kind of evil" (135). In line with the Socratic tradition, to dissolve the difference between rhetoric and violence is to allow violence to run amok: "Hannah Arendt wrote valiantly in this vein, distinguished sharply between power and violence, and strongly promoted a public, agonistic rhetoric, as well as a kind of thinking that was an inner performance of it, as a way of fighting back the violence" (135). On the other hand, to maintain a firm and absolute distinction between the two would be to ignore the fact "that there is violence in language and sociology that cannot be fully eradicated without eradicating language and sociology themselves" (135). Violence must therefore be defined in broader terms. For him, violence "describes any force that is exerted without complete assent and participation — physically, emotionally, symbolically, in any way at all — on a person or group or on the things which are valuable to them, or on the cultural and linguistic symbols and physical habitats out of which they come to understand what is valuable to them and what is not" (162). Violence thus integrates an element of symbolic meaning that rationalizes physical force that forces another population endure something against its will because of the threat of violence behind it.

Yet Arendt's original conceptual structure remains important to understand the nature of these subtle relations. To begin, it is important to note that, for Arendt, the primary tension is not necessarily between rhetoric and violence but between power and violence. Violence she defined as the magnification of physical strength through the use of technologies that have an instrumental character. Violence is the means of directly overcoming the opposition of nature through channeling and magnifying force, and as such is a way in which "which man measures himself against the overwhelming forces of the elements in which through the cunning invention of tools he knows how to multiply far beyond its natural measure" (*Human* 140). Importantly, Arendt associates violence not only with overcoming human opponents but also with the fabrication process of breaking and remaking physical material to achieve an end. Violence can thus destroy but it can also build, as a hammer might do violence to stones in order to fit them together into a wall. For her, "this element of violation and violence is present in all fabrication, and *homo faber*, the creator of the human artifice, has always been a destroyer of nature" (138). What Arendt means by a "destroyer of nature" is that violence replaces naturally created things with man-made things fabricated according to mental blueprints and ideal forms. Violence is thus essential to what she calls our "Promethean revolt" by which we "erect a man-made world only after destroying part of God-created nature" (139). Through violence we force recalcitrant matter to conform to the ideals of our minds, even if those ideals require the destruction of human life.

In the *Anabasis*, we find acts of pure violence perfectly demonstrated in chapter 2 of Book 5, when the army goes on a plundering expedition in the country of the Drilae. Encountering a city with considerable booty, Xenophon gave the order for "the herald to proclaim that those who wanted to plunder had permission to go in" (5.2.18). The city was quickly overrun, but enemy soldiers managed to secure themselves inside of a citadel. Determining that the enemy's position was absolutely impregnable, Xenophon gave the order to retreat—only to then be attacked from the citadel and have their retreat barred by great pieces of timber thrown from the roofs of nearby houses. Able neither to attack nor retreat, Xenophon felt trapped until he saw one of the houses on the right of the citadel catch fire, and "gave the order to set fire to the houses on the left as well" (5.2.25). When the enemy had fled, "Xenophon then ordered all those who are out of range of the missiles to carry wood onto the space between them and the enemy," thus allowing them to safely retreat (5.2.25). By the end of the attack, "the whole city was burned to the ground — houses, towers, palisade and everything else except the citadel" (5.2.27). The Greeks then marched away, taking their booty with them. I call these acts manifestations of pure violence because they are done without any consent whatsoever from either the natural or human material being acted upon. The enemy soldiers continually fight against the Greeks, while the town itself is burned to the ground—all to achieve a single strategic end of acquiring booty.

The plunder of the city also highlights two important characteristics of violence identified by Arendt, namely its instrumental quality and its element of arbitrariness. Violence always contains an element of arbitrariness because it is impossible to ever determine, with absolute precision, a sequence of a chain of consequences. There is always something in nature that violates our expectations. She writes that "violence harbors within itself an additional element of arbitrariness: nowhere does Fortuna, good or ill luck, play a more faithful role in human affairs than on the battlefield" (*Violence* 4). Xenophon in fact acknowledges violence's arbitrary nature in his narration of the plunder of the city, when he says that "still doubtful what to do next, some god showed them a way of saving themselves. One of the houses on the right, through someone or other's action, suddenly caught fire" (5.2.24). The second characteristic of violence is its instrumental quality that always operates in the category of means and ends: "Violence, being instrumental by nature, is rational to the extent that it is effective in reaching the end that must justify it" (Arendt, *Violence* 79). However, because of the element of arbitrariness, its effectiveness as an instrument is always severely restricted. Consequently, for her, "since when we act we never know with any certainty the eventual consequences of what we are doing, violence can remain rational only if it pursues short-term goals" (79). In this case, Xenophon was wise to cut his losses and flee the city rather than persist in trying to take the citadel, for perhaps Fortuna might not be so friendly next time.

When we turn our attention to power, we find its nature is quite different than violence; it deals explicitly with the relations of human beings to one another as mediated through speech and symbols, not through physical force. Power, for Arendt, "corresponds to the human ability not just to act but to act in concert" (*Violence* 44). Unlike violence, power is not instrumental. Power simply refers to the capacity to act together based on a common understanding grounded in a sense of cooperation and trust. This capacity for collective action is an intrinsic good, not something justified by its outcomes or results. That is why, for her, power is also the essence of politics. As she explains, "what makes man a political being is his faculty of action; it enables him to get together with his peers, to act in concert, and to reach out for goals and enterprises that would never enter his mind, let alone the desires of his heart, had he not been given this gift — to embark on something new" (82). Power thus makes its appearance the moment a feeling of solidarity is achieved between individuals formally separate from one another. As she explains, "while strength is the natural quality of an individual seen in isolation, power springs up between men when they act together and vanishes the moment they disperse" (*Human* 200). For instance, when Xenophon describes the moment he decides to take the initiative after the assassination of the other generals in Book 3 and commit himself to victory in the face of considerable odds, he feels the thrill of power in his closing appeal to the remaining generals: "Quite likely there are others who feel the same as I do. Well then, in heaven's name, let us not wait for other people to come to us and call upon us to do great deeds. Let us instead be the first to summon the rest to the path of honour"

(3.1.24). What he calls "honour" is not an instrumental end, but a virtue that is a product of power itself, namely the praise of those with whom you are acting in concert. Violence thus stands in opposition to power because it does not operate according to the same logic. Similar to what Xenophon expressed in the *Memorabilia*, violence achieves goals because it forces its subjects to obey, even against their own will; but power as a lasting capacity for collective action is produced only through the voluntary actions of a group who feel, at some level, that sense of kindness and fellowship that makes such action possible.

This difference between violence and power is captured in the distinction between legitimacy and justification. Arendt writes: "Power springs up whenever people get together and act in concert, but it derives its legitimacy from the initial getting together rather than from any action that then may follow. Legitimacy, when challenged, bases itself on an appeal to the past, but justification relates to an end that lies in the future. Violence can be justifiable, but it will never be legitimate" (*Violence* 52). In other words, violence is always justified by what it produces based on the assumption of reliable causes and effects. Consequently, violence is most justifiable in the realm of purely physical nature that operates according to the laws of physics. When it enters the arbitrary realm of human choice and action, violence tends to lose its justification because it cannot promise outcomes; indeed, it often produces the opposite results. Power, by contrast, needs no justification. Power does not come into being to promise results but is itself a result; the capacity to act in concert is therefore self-justifying. However, power maintains itself through a shared feeling of legitimacy based on promises and relationships formed in the past that are still trusted to be active in the present as a binding agent between actors. This still-active sense of promise that solidifies a group grants legitimacy to power and at its most confident becomes channeled by select representatives as authority, which for Arendt represents "unquestioning recognition by those who were asked to obey; neither coercion nor persuasion is needed" (45). One has thus reached the pinnacle of power when authority becomes absolute and when orders are obeyed not because they guarantee results but because they wield legitimacy that is acquired from the promises of the past.

For our purposes, rhetoric can thus take the place of power within this dialectic because it is through rhetoric that power is constituted in the political realm, a realm that Arendt associates with the action of speech. For her, nothing showed the opposition between violence and power more starkly than the fact that pure violence can be done in silence, while power can exist only within the realm of speech which produces a common understanding. As she explains, "it is because of this silence that violence is a marginal phenomenon in the political realm; for man, to the extent that he is a political being, is endowed with the power of speech" (*Revolution* 9). Consequently, for her, "in so far as violence plays a predominant role in wars and revolutions, both occur outside the political realm, strictly speaking, in spite of their enormous role in recorded history" (*Revolution* 9). What Arendt wanted to preserve was that sense of freedom to appear before others in a public realm and begin something new through an act of persuasive speech. The Greek *polis*, as she understood it, was the place

> where free men assembled and conversed, and by doing so centered what was truly 'political'— that is, what belonged to the *polis* and was therefore denied to all barbarians and other unfree people—on this world of coming together, being together, speaking about something with one another; and they saw this entire arena under the sign of divine *Peitho*, the power to persuade and influence, which reigned among equals and determined all things without force or coercion. War, and the brute force it entailed, was, on the other hand, entirely excluded from what was truly political, which arose and had its validity among the citizens of the polis.
>
> (*Politics* 164)

Rhetoric thus represented, at its height, the free political speech of a free people capable of persuading and influencing one another according to their own principles and enabled by their lasting promises. For instance, when Xenophon wishes to calm his troops in Byzantium, he makes an appeal to legitimacy: "My advice to you is that, since you are Greek yourselves, you should try to get justice by obeying the leaders of the Greeks" (7.1.30). This is nothing more than an appeal to authority granted on the basis of their collective identification as Greeks. The result is an increase in their power, their capacity to act in concert as a unit, which would have been dispersed and wasted in a disorganized looting of the city, each man for himself.

As noble as this sounds, Arendt was also very clear that this form of justice applied only to a sliver of the population at any one time in these cultures. Political freedom and equality under the law only applied to free men, in which "to be free meant both not to be subject to the necessity of life or to the command of another *and* not to be in command oneself. It meant neither to rule nor to be ruled" (*Human* 32). In other words, freedom was in actuality reserved only for the patriarchs of households sufficiently large and well organized to take care of life's necessities in the private sphere. Freedom for these men was thus found in the political sphere in which they met other "free" men on a relatively equal playing field in which there power was negotiated purely through rhetorical means. By contrast, within the household, life was organized hierarchically according to clear social stratifications kept in order in large part through the threat of violence. As she explains, the Greeks took for granted "that freedom is exclusively located in the political realm, that necessity is primarily a pre-political phenomenon, characteristic of the private household organization, and that force and violence are justified in the sphere because they are only means to master necessity — for instance, by ruling over slaves — and to become free" (*Human* 31). Under these conditions, justice, if it had any meaning at all, simply referred to the maintenance of an orderly household in which every individual does their duty within the social position allotted to them and not exceeding it. This sense of hierarchy within the social order, enforced by the ever present sense of violence against those who would exceed their position, is what Crosswhite refers to as "a social violence in which one's own reasoning is overcome through coercive communication" (144). It is that sense in which one censors one's own thought and speech to conform to the order of things—such as when Xenophon warns his troops against "self-made generals" who exceed their authority and threaten to dissolve the discipline of the fighting unit (5.7.29).

Therefore, Arendt was perfectly aware that violence and power were never so far apart in actual life. Her effort to separate them was in order to isolate their unique features in order to facilitate ethical judgment. But she was well aware that there is nothing "more common than the combination of violence and power, nothing less frequent than to find them in their pure and therefore extreme form" (*Violence* 52). She simply wanted to clarify their different logics so that in complex situations, the function of each could be discerned more precisely. For instance, the conclusion of the crisis in Byzantium is a message to Anaxibius that read as follows: "We have entered the city with no intention of taking violent action. What we want is to obtain some practical help from you. If we receive none, we shall at least make it clear that we are leaving the city because we obey your orders, not because of a trick" (7.1.31). The end result is that they find a guide named Coiratadas to lead them out of the city and receive promises from Anaxibius to send a report back to the Sparta praising the soldiers for their virtues to ensure a welcome homecoming. Clearly, this result was due primarily from the not-so-subtle threat of violence if practical help was not forthcoming, and not because Anaxibius had been persuaded of their good intentions. Indeed, his true motives soon become clear, when "as soon as they had left the city Anaxibius had the gates shut and issued a proclamation that any soldier found inside the walls would be sold as a slave" (7.1.36). As so often occurs when rhetoric and violence work together, there is always some mixture of consent and resistance.

Because rhetoric and violence so often occur together, it is important to attend to this genre of speech genres in order to discern its contours and characteristics. By a rhetoric of violence in a general sense, I mean symbolic action which acquires a significant part of its persuasive force by direct or indirect reference to acts of violence, past, present, or future. A rhetoric of violence is thus distinct from pure rhetoric on the one hand, which elicits voluntary and rational assent in a relative state of equality, and pure violence on the other hand, which uses mute force to directly attain its end by treating others as irrational objects. A rhetoric of violence thus appeals alternately, and not always coherently, to both legitimation and justification to achieve its persuasive intent. A speaker may draw on legitimation to solicit voluntary assent based on shared principles and identifications but then appeal to justification when violence must be wheeled in to ensure compliance or eliminate resistance altogether. But as I shall argue in the next section, the most central characteristic of the rhetoric of violence is its appeal to justice as a motivational tactic that combines both legitimation and justification and channels power by distinguishing between those deserving of a place in the world and those condemned to the desert.

2 Rhetoric and Justice

> As for the people of Cotyora, who you say are your subjects, if we have taken anything of theirs, it is their own fault. They did not act towards us like friends. They shut their gates to us, and neither let us inside their city nor gave us a chance of buying food outside their walls...As for your charge that some of us have made their way in by force and quartered there, these are the facts. We asked them to receive our sick into their houses, and when they did not open their gates, we went inside at a place where the nature of the ground made it possible to do so. Otherwise we have committed no act of violence...The rest of us, as you see, camp in the open air and in our formations, ready, if we are treated well, to make a good return for it, and to defend ourselves if we are treated badly.
>
> (*Anabasis* 5.5.19–21)

Xenophon's rhetoric of violence is on full display in his negotiations with the ambassadors from Sinope, the city to whom Cotyora paid tribute as a colony. The Greek army had arrived at the coastal city of the Black Sea, injured and hungry after eight days marching through the country. There they had decided to stay for 45 days, sacrificing to the gods, organizing processions, and holding athletic sports. They also had taken supplies from the settlements of the "people of Cotyora, since they would not give the Greeks facilities for buying food and would not even take the sick man inside their walls" (5.5.6). Meanwhile, word came to Sinope that the land was being ravaged; ambassadors were sent from Sinope warning Xenophon to either set things right or face a military alliance against them. Xenophon's response was a masterpiece in the rhetoric of violence. First, Xenophon establishes the legitimacy of his power by reference to their common Greek heritage, later explaining that he "relied in the first place on the claims of their common Greek nationality for a considerate attitude and for the best possible advice" (5.6.2). Second, he justifies prior acts of violence by explaining that "when we come to a place where we are given no opportunities to buy food, then, whether it is a native country or Greek country, we take our own supplies and do this not out of wanton aggression, but from necessity" (5.5.16). Lastly, he cloaks the entire act within the context of justice, arguing that it is the people of Cotyora, and not the marauding army of mercenaries who showed up on their doorstep, who are responsible for the acts of violence done to them. In violating the norm of friendship which is expected between Greeks, they have brought punishment upon themselves. It is, in fact, Xenophon's mercenaries who deserve an apology—which they subsequently receive, along with "gifts of friendship" (5.5.25).

What is important to discern in this episode is the functional definition of justice that is at work here, for this will provide the last and most essential component of the rhetoric of violence. In his discussion of the *Anabasis* and the *Hellenica*, John Marincola writes that "it is very clear that Xenophon has an overt interest in justice, in the sense of right action, fair dealing, and the observance of appropriate reciprocity toward individuals, estates, and, of course, the gods" (114). While this is true in a general sense, it is less clear in what, exactly, that interest in justice consists. Marincola only points to one example that involves Xenophon himself in the *Anabasis*, his speech to Seuthes, an uncertain ally and minor king of Thrace, in which he contrasts the noble life with one that simply is concerned only with the accumulation of money: "I, Seuthes, on the other hand, consider that there are no nobler and more brilliant possessions that a man, and particularly a man who holds power, can have than honor and fair dealing and generosity. A man who has these is rich in the possession of many friends and rich in the fact that many others want to become friends of his" (7.7.41). As Socrates might say, this is a wonderful praise of justice, but it does not tell us the nature of justice itself. After all, in an earlier speech to his troops when considering to ally with Seuthes, he expressed a very different opinion: "This is what I think: so long as you keep together in your present great force, you are sure both of respect and of finding supplies. One of the results of power is the ability to take what belongs to the weaker" (7.3.5). Where is a principle of justice that can reconcile these attitudes which seem on their face to be contradictory?

Once again, we can turn to Arendt for a clue. For her, justice is not a transcendent ideal or universal right that belongs to everyone and guarantees equality; justice is a distributive principle developed and enforced by a specific people who occupy a specific world. Justice determines in practice what we mean by terms like "equality", "fairness", or "right." For instance, "equality, in contrast to all that is involved in mere existence, is not given us, but is the result of human organization in so far as it is guided by the principle of justice. We are not born equal; we become equal as members of a group on the strength of our decision to guarantee ourselves mutually equal rights" (*Totalitarianism* 301). The problem is that we often forget the essential relationship between justice and what is, in essence, power—in this case the power to act together as a group based on a shared commitment to certain principles. And there is a reason for this forgetting, particularly in the Judeo-Christian world: "We are so accustomed to understanding law and justice in terms of the 10 Commandments, as precepts and prohibitions whose sole purpose is to demand obedience, that we easily forget the spatial character of laws. All laws first created space in which they are valid, and this space is the world in which we can move about in freedom. What lies outside this world is without law and, even more precisely, without world; as far as human community is concerned, it is a desert" (*Politics*, 189–90). What Arendt is referring to here, of course, is first the Greek *polis* and later the Roman empire, both of which guaranteed a level of justice for its citizens within their borders and guaranteed, at least for its elite, the freedom of action and the equality of treatment in the political sphere. For her, the political institutions did not somehow recognize and protect a pre-existing sense of justice existing in a Platonic form; they constituted a sense of justice that that was designed to regulate how each part of a common whole was to be treated in accordance with every other part.

This understanding of justice being rooted within the specific borders of a common world accounts for the seeming contradiction in Xenophon's position. On the one hand, when Xenophon confronts populations clearly outside the boundaries of his Greek world, he treats those people as nothing more than desert dwellers to whom justice does not apply. In this world, the only code is that to the stronger go the spoils. This ethic is quite clear throughout the *Anabasis*, as the Greeks casually plunder any foreign city without a second thought, such as when Xenophon closes chapter 3 of book 7, with the offhand comment that after carrying out maneuvers, "about one thousand slaves, two thousand oxen and ten thousand other cattle were taken" (7.3.48). Rhetorically, the audience for this sort of rhetoric is not the plundered but the plunderer; it is to convince those who enslave, kill, or steal from perceived desert dwellers that they are acting not only from necessity but from a transcendent justice by which, as Xenophon said, the powerful have every right to take what they want from the weaker.

On the other hand, Xenophon speaks very differently when he is clearly within the boundaries of a common world. The purest case of such a rhetoric occurs in chapter 8 of Book 5, when Xenophon must defend himself in public against some of his men who had alleged "they had been beaten by him" and "had acted in an overbearing manner" (5.8.1). One specific accuser was a soldier

Xenophon had struck after refusing to carry a wounded soldier from the battlefield, choosing instead to bury him alive. When the soldier protested that the wounded man died all the same, Xenophon retorted: "No doubt we shall all die. Is that any reason why we should all be buried alive?" (5.8.11). With regards to other acts of violence, Xenophon then provided a broader defense of his actions: "I admit, soldiers, that I have struck men in cases where there has been lack of discipline — the sort of people who were quite content to have their lives saved by you marching in formation and fighting when it was called for, but who left the ranks themselves and ran ahead and wanted to get more of their fair share of booty. If we had all behaved like this, we should all have been wiped out" (5.8.13). Comparing this to how doctors use knives and hot irons for the good of their patients, Xenophon justifies his violent discipline on the basis of power, which is to say to maintain the capacity to act in concert as a collective fighting unit. Moreover, he appeals to justice into other ways, appealing to their shared sense of how injured men should be treated as well as the right proportion of booty that should be allotted to each soldier according to their status within the social hierarchy. In this case, rhetoric justifies violence when it operates as a corrective to actions which threaten the order of power and the unity of the group. Justice in this case is judged by the standards of power maintenance within the borders of a common world, and the rhetoric of violence appeals to this sense of justice when it imposes discipline within those borders. This is the kind of rhetoric that sustains the social violence that maintains order not simply in military units but society at large as a police function.

The rhetoric of violence is at its most complex, however, within the fluid borders between worlds and deserts, which is to say between coherent, self-identified groups organized as a powerful unit within a common world and other groups whose identities only partially overlap those borders. In these cases, it is not clear how much legitimacy any form of power holds across audiences that makes them respect the same authorities or acknowledge the same principles of order that constitute justice. Consequently, violence often finds justification in order to compensate for this lack of confidence in one's own authority or trust in the words of another. Consequently, speakers typically make eloquent appeals to fairness based on the legitimacy of some common commitments and shared identifications while, at the same time, indicating the strength of their position to use violence if necessary as a way to achieve what they believe to be a just outcome. This is precisely what we see in the negotiations with the ambassadors from Sinope. Xenophon begins by acknowledging their common Greek identity, and notes that whereas they have been pillaging villages of the enemy, "now that we have come among Greek cities and at Trapezus, where they gave us the facilities, we got our food and paid for it. We made the right sort of return to them for the honours they gave us and the gifts they gave to the army" (5.5.13–14). Having established the rules of fair dealing among Greeks, and appealing to their legitimacy as a Greek army among Greek cities, Xenophon then shifts not so subtly to the justification for further violence. If they are given no opportunities to buy food, then necessity will demand they take it by force, regardless of the identity of the city. Although Xenophon tells himself that it is his reputation for fair dealing that wins over his audience, it is quite clear to modern readers that the "gifts of friendship" sent by Cotyora were made to avoid being sacked.

That Xenophon is hardly constrained by his principles of fairness is made readily clear when he and his army actually arrive at Sinope. While in the process of negotiating for ships and supplies, it dawns on Xenophon that perhaps the best course of action might be to put down roots right next door. He reflects: "when Xenophon considered the numbers of Greek hoplites that there were, and the numbers of peltasts and archers and slingers and calvary, now, after all their experiences, in a very high state of efficiency, and when he considered that they were in the Euxine [the Black Sea], where such a powerful force could never have been assembled without the enormous expense, he thought it would be a fine thing to found a city there and so gain more territory and more power for Greece" (5.6.15). Not surprisingly, when the leaders of Sinope catch wind of this, they are not keen on having a huge military force camped right outside their walls, in effect preparing to dominate the entire south coast of the Black Sea. So they secretly send messengers to members of Xenophon's army "to accept a sum of money and take the lead in agitating for the army to sail away from the Euxine" (5.6.21). In any case, what is significant is how Xenophon clearly changes his calculus of the meaning of justice, considering now the degree to which the power of his army and their capacity for violence could dominate the entire area without concern for the opinions of the neighboring cities. Eventually he begins to question his plan when omens are not in his favor, and finally backs down when confronted by his soldiers, who in turn make a rhetorical appeal to a sense of justice within the common world of the army.

What we find in the rhetoric of violence, therefore, is a fluid conception of justice that adapts to the nature of the rhetorical situation. Within the context of a common world, justice appeals to a shared understanding of what is due according to the principles of order that guide the structure of legitimate power. In this case, violence is never accepted as a threat among equals, but it does do coercive work between hierarchies as a form of social violence and finds explicit justification according to the necessity to pay retribution to those who threaten that order. When, however, participants in this common world encounter those whose stand, from their perspective, completely outside these boundaries in the desert, violence becomes the primary means to attain practical ends and the only reasoning is purely instrumental. The only appeal to legitimacy is to those within the boundaries of the common world to ensure those inside that their acts of violence are legitimate according to their own internal standards. Lastly, the most complicated situation is one in which some form of negotiation must be had between worlds that only partially overlap. In these cases, such as between Xenophon and the ambassadors of Sinope, the appeal to legitimacy and common norms creates a hypothetical persuasive framework to allow for rhetorical interaction based on common understanding, but these agreements are almost always guaranteed by threats of violence on the one hand or "voluntarily" given "gifts" on the other. This delicate balance allows for two courses of action to follow. On the one hand, the positing of a possible solidarity under a common identity—for instance, all parties being "Greeks"—may allow for genuine solidarity to be created over time as the boundaries of world possibly blend together, as Xenophon undoubtedly imagined with his new city. On the other hand, any perceived violation of this agreement makes violent retribution appear "just" according to the original contract, the dominant party easily being able to claim the position of righteousness according to their own partial interpretation. The function of rhetoric in all of these cases is to give warrant for future actions and legitimacy and justification for past ones, thus generating in the minds of the actors a sense of their own virtue.

However, there is one other function of violence that Arendt recognizes that has become more significant over time, namely a protest violence that might "serve to dramatize grievances and bring them to public attention" (*Violence* 79). In this case, the justification of violence is found in a purely rhetorical sphere, to achieve publicity in order to reveal to a wider, potentially sympathetic audience the nature of an unjust system. This type of violence might include riots or even violence upon oneself, as in the tradition of self-immolation or the hunger strike. Xenophon, of course, cares nothing for such forms of violence. And yet, interestingly enough, he narrates an event which embodies its function. Xenophon narrates how they came upon the country of the Taochi, who "lived behind strong fortifications inside which they had all their provisions stored up" (4.7.1). Requiring provisions, the Greeks launch an assault and eventually overcome their defenses. Xenophon narrates what follows:

> Then it was certainly a terrible sight. The women threw their children down from the rocks and then threw themselves after them, and the men did the same. While this was going on Aeneas of Stymphalos, a captain, saw one of them, who was wearing a fine garment, running to throw himself down, and he caught hold of him in order to stop him; but the man

> dragged him with him and they both went hurtling down over the rocks and were killed. Consequently very few prisoners were taken, but they were great numbers of oxen and asses and sheep.
>
> (4.7.13–14)

If even the hard-edged character of Xenophon recognizes this as a "terrible sight," imagine the international condemnation which would have followed if it had been captured on video in a technological age. Rather than having his account of his expedition be deemed a "classic" of virtuous generalship to read and imitated by schoolchildren across the centuries, he and his band of marauders would have been condemned as war criminals and terrorists. But that is only because the boundaries of our common world now encompass the globe in which there are no more pure deserts; there are only overlapping worlds.

The *Anabasis* remains a classic of military history but its moral lesson has clearly changed; Xenophon today should be read as a case study in rationalization, exploring all the ways in which the rhetoric of violence justifies forceful discipline and the explication of those we condemn to the desert. Today our salvation is in a protest rhetoric that reveals the injustices legitimated and justified by the kind of rhetoric of violence we have inherited from the past. This is a violence not intended to harm but to expose, to express, to reveal through bodily acts the pervasive social violence that surrounds us every day. The end of all of this, of course, is not conquest or booty but peace. According to Crosswhite, "peace is a kind of sociality or community in which conflict has become one of the means by which individuals and groups are renewed and grow and achieve well-being. The form of this peace is justice" (145). Until this type of peace is achieved, of course, the traditional rhetoric of violence will continue—which means it will likely continue forever. Yet Xenophon's intuition is nonetheless correct. The more we can persuade without recourse to violent coercion and threats, the more it is possible to generate a true sense of power grounded in that feeling of trust, goodwill, and understanding the Arendt sums up in the simple word that, for her, forms the basis of politics, the promise.

Bibliography

Arendt, H. (1998), *The Human Condition*, 2nd ed., Chicago.
Arendt, H. (2005), *The Promise of Politics*, New York.
Arendt, H. (1968), *The Origins of Totalitarianism*, New York.
Arendt, H. (1965), *On Revolution*, New York.
Arendt, H. (1970), *On Violence*, New York.
Crosswhite, J. (2013), *Deep Rhetoric: Philosophy, Reason, Violence, Justice, Wisdom*, Chicago.

Flower, M. (2012), *Xenophon's* Anabasis *or* The Expedition of Cyrus, Oxford.
Marincola, J. (2017), "Xenophon's Anabasis and Hellenica," in: *The Cambridge Companion to Xenophon*, M. Flower, (ed.), 103–118, Cambridge.
Xenophon (1990), *Conversations of Socrates*, trans. High Tredennick/Robin Waterfield, New York.
Xenophon (1972), *The Persian Expedition*, trans. Rex Warner, New York.

Bogdan Burliga
Xenophon's βίαιος διδάσκαλος: Thinking War and Empire in the *Cyropaedia*

1 The Problem

'A fiction—says one of the main characters of the HBO 2016 tv series *Westworld*— which like all great stories, is rooted in truth'. This sounds somewhat paradoxical but seems to be relevant if applied to that *enfant terrible* of ancient Greek prose, the *Cyropaedia*, which has been called 'perplexing historical-novel-cum-guide-to-statesmanship'.[1] Xenophon's *opus vitae* was always regarded as a meditation on *iustum imperium* (Cicero's famous term),[2] a handbook of political theory, and an ancient predecessor of the *speculum regis*-genre.[3] As Cicero's judgment was based on a belief that the portrait of Cyrus is written *non ad historiae fidem*,[4] so, accordingly, the fictional and 'novelistic' features of the narrative as well as the utopian and idealized vision of Cyrus' state have been stressed.

Although still prevailing, this view is not commonly held now: nowadays the pendulum seems to tilt in the opposite direction, so that many experts on the Achaemenid Persia point to historical aspects of Xenophon's project;[5] some features are common with those of historical works, also his knowledge of Persian

---

I thank Dr. Aggelos Kapellos for inviting me to contribute to his project. I am also indebted to Professor P. J. Rhodes for reading an earlier draft of this version. The quotations are from W. Gemoll & J. Peters' Teubner edition, the translation being that of W. Miller, Loeb. All the dates, if not indicated otherwise, are B.C.

1 Lendon, 2006, 82. In Tuplin's 2010, 203, words, it is a 'strange compendium of putatively Achaemenid behaviour'; Breebaart, 1983, 115, calls it 'Cinderella'.
2 *Ad Q.* fr. 1. 1. 23; but Dionysius of Halicarnassus, *Pomp.* 4, locates the work among the historical ones.
3 Burliga, 2012, 11; Humble, 2017, 419; Tamiolaki, 2017. Cicero's interest in Xenophon's writings (his translation of the *Oeconomicus* is lost) and the figure of Cyrus 'the good herdsman' especially (his famous translation of *Cyr.* 8.7.1–22 in *Cat.* 22.79–81) is in itself telling: he apparently has found the tale of Cyrus' empire actual in the light of the Roman past and (what is more probable) recent Roman conquests and wars, cf. *Fam.* 1.1.23; 9.25.1. Particularly, I believe, he judged sound Cyrus' argumentation at *Cyr.* 1.5.13—regarding the notorious Roman claims of conducting 'defensive' wars, aimed at preventing any hostil eattacks; cf. Raaflaub, 2007; Dewald, 2013.
4 Cf. Breitenbach, 1966, col. 1706.
5 E.g. the problem of Xenophon's knowledge of the imperial court: Tuplin, 2010, 205–223.

customs and acquaintance with Oriental oral tradition are invoked.[6] In the following my goal will be to look at this work as a highly realistic piece. Leaving aside how careful was Xenophon's reconstruction of Persian *Realien* or how accurate is his picture in details,[7] my goal will be to explore one of the themes that barely appears in the work but nevertheless pervades it thoroughly: maintaining power and the use of violence. I will argue that in this respect the tale of Cyrus is far from idealistic; conversely, power (even if 'properly' used and based on a contrast between authority and brute force, as Xenophon aimed to show)[8] remains a basic foundation on which Cyrus' just imperium rests. But since the place of violence in the 'novel' overlaps with the topic of its (alleged) utopia and idealism, one needs first to determine how to take these terms?

2 Xenophon, an In-Depth Realist

The *Cyropaedia* has always confused readers. It is not so much the conundrum of its genre, although a part of the difficulty is due to this uncertainty. The work is often called a utopia. But in what sense?[9] If we think of it as an illustration of the main hero's *artificial* triumphs in his life long construction of the empire,[10] it may be labeled a utopian political vision. A journey through the work is like a realization of the premise from the prologue—to instruct in order to rule justly nothing counts more as the agent's character.[11] Such an unmasked, pedagogical assumption determines the way of presenting Cyrus—a literary construct and 'ideal' endowed with personal qualities and knowledge.[12] In effect, it is all too easy to realize that 'Cyrus' responds thus to the author's purpose: the portrait of the main

---

6 Hirsch, 1985; Tamiolaki, 2017, 178–179; on Cyrus the Great see Mallowan, 1972; Cataudella, 1998; Briant, 2002; Kuhrt, 1983; 2007a; 2007b, 47–103; 2007c; Brosius, 2005; van der Spek, 2014.
7 On this see Gera, 1993, 13–22.
8 There is a telling testimony of such a reading of the *Cyropedia*. In his *Anabasis*, 6.4.5, Arrian, apparently after reading Xenophon's work, scrutinises the conquests of Cyrus who, remarkably, Μήδους τε τὴν ἀρχὴν τῆς Ἀσίας ἀφείλετο καὶ ἄλλα ἔθνη τὰ μὲν κατεστρέψατο, τὰ δὲ προσχωρήσαντα οἱ ἑκόντα κατέσχεν.
9 Cf. Tuplin, 1997, 95–98.
10 Upon hearing of 'utopia' readers in the Middle and Eastern Europe could associate it with another utopian political project, so suggestively depicted by M. Heller and A. Nekrich in their book. But in the case of the *Cyropaedia* there is certainly no such sinister reality behind this word.
11 Too, 1998, 282; Due, 2002, 84; generally: Stadter, 2009.
12 Machiavelli, *Il prince*, 26.1: 'the greatness of spirit in Cyrus' (tr. P. Bondanella); cf. Nadon, 2001, 14; Rasmussen, 2009. The use of the figure of Cyrus could serve as an example of what

hero is sacrificed on an altar of overtly didactic instruction,[13] probably serving to prove the validity of the thesis set in advance; Xenophon's hero always wins and is right in his decisions.

The didacticism and artificiality of the hero's portrait has caused a great deal of embarrassment (to modern addressees, mainly); they are strictly connected with the way the narrative runs—the plot, being plainly didactic too, seems just somewhat naïve, so the readers' bafflement makes them hesitant to take the work seriously, rather than as an exercise in political utopia or a political fairy-tale.[14]

Xenophon's 'faith' in a man's virtues that suffice to solve all the dilemmas of ruling and maintaining power may be right or not. At any rate, he was by no means an exception in his belief in man's qualities,[15] for the majority of the then ancient Greek intellectuals agreed that what counts mostly in politics is the character of the men in power—tyrants, kings, statesmen, politicians, generals, and demagogues alike.[16] But inasmuch as the author's concern is with the ethical qualities of an eminent individual,[17] the epic tale remains for the same reason also a study in a personality *obsessed* with power and ruling,[18] 'tainted' by that baleful virus of an agonistic φιλοτιμία—the lust for being the first in order to be admired and respected by as many as possible.[19] If so, we come to one of the most interesting, perhaps, aspects of the novel that goes beyond its 'historical' level, tending to be a philosophical reflection both about power and about the proper ways of

---

Aristotle has observed (*Poet.* 1450a20–21) that 'it is not in order to provide mimesis of character that agents act; rather, their characters are included for the sake of their actions' (tr. S. Halliwell, Loeb).

13 Due, 1989, 14 and 2000; Gera, 1993, 280–284. Didactism pervades also the *Hiero*, written—as Delebecque, 1957, 411–424, thinks—not long after the *Cyropaedia*; cf. Gray, 2007.
14 Weathers, 1954.
15 Ferrario, 2014, 183–184. Gray, 2000, 146, and 2007, 13–14, on 'the importance of paradigms'; cf. Stadter, 2009, 457–458.
16 As Thucydides has shown depicting Themistocles (1.138) and Pericles (2.65). The most famous adherent of this view was Plato; cf. Gray, 2011, 2.
17 Stadter, 1991, 468; 2009, 456–470.
18 Stadter, 1991, 468, whilst rightly calling the work 'a novel of virtue', denies it to be 'a novel of imperial rule'. I think both problems, as inseparable, concerned Xenophon equally.
19 It was recognized by the elite of the *poleis* of archaic (*Il.* 11.784: αἰὲν ἀριστεύειν καὶ ὑπείροχον ἔμμεναι ἄλλων; Pindar, as quoted by Plutarch, *De cohib. ira*, 457b) and classical Greece (Euripides, *Phoen.* 531–532; Thuc. 2.44.4; 2.65.7; 3.82.8; 8.89.3; Xen. *Hiero* 7. 3–4; see Reisert, 2009 and Ludwig, 2009, 295; cf. Gill, 2003, 48; Brock, 2004, 251; van Wees, 2011a. It is believed that perhaps the most famous 'victim' of such a drive, Alexander of Macedon, in his royal propaganda to be the best and most invincible ruler ever, was *also* under the influence of the *Iliad* and Xenophon's work: Arrian, *Anab.* 1.12.1–3; cf. Ferrario, 2014, 326; Burliga, 2014a.

wielding it,[20] that is, just rule.[21] With this, one enters also into an intriguing issue, what was Xenophon's own attitude toward such 'natural' phenomena as might and force, empire and violence, a topic—popular among Greek intellectuals at that time—which he, the most competent person, after all[22]—must have been well familiar with.[23] From this point of view to speak of 'utopia' here would be misleading: again and again, Cyrus' παράδεισος, revealing its darker sides, is rather closer to a dystopian world (to retain the modern parlance),[24] in which relationships between states (conquests, then the administration of conquered territories) and groups or individuals within a state, rest on force and violence or compulsion.[25]

---

[20] Power is assumed by Xenophon as 'a natural' fact in social relations as 'natural' death is. As he once wrote, even heroes cannot avoid the latter since τοῦτο μὲν γὰρ ἡ φύσις (*Cyn.* 1.3; in Waterfield's, 1997 rendering: 'because that is what it is to be human'); see Dover, 1974, 314; Due 1989, 163; cf. Blundell, 1989, 26–59.

[21] It may be said that the work reconciles the two features recognized by Aristotle as appropriate for history and poetry (*Poet.* 1451b12–7).

[22] He lived in a world torn apart by many conflicts: he grew up in Athens during the bloody, Panhellenic war; as a hired hoplite of the Achaemenid prince who laid claim to the Persian throne, he participated in military upheaval in Persia; he saw atrocities of battle at Cunaxa in 401 BC; having retreated to the Black Sea across hostile territories with the army of 'the Ten Thousand', he continued to participate in campaigns under Agesilaus in Asia Minor. War did not let Xenophon go many years later when, living a peaceful life in Scillous, he lost in 362 his son Gryllus in battle. For many years the army was Xenophon's 'natural' *habitat*, so, understandably, warfare remained his constant companion, influencing his life, shaping his experience, and constituting a background to his literary output (cf. Kapellos, Introduction, in this volume). Xenophon always remained a man of practical mind, interested in specific issues (technical ones, or the duties of commanders) that warfare generates. He rather avoided engaging in *theoria*-philosophical speculations on the nature of armed conflicts and power. But assuming for sure that as a disciple of Socrates he either witnessed or heard many debates on this topic, and knew other people's reflections (including Herodotus' *apodexis* and Thucydides' *ktema es aiei*), it seems indisputable that he must have had his own views on this matter.

[23] Hippias of Elis (a hero of the two Platonic dialogues), figures prominently in *Mem.* 4.4. On these controversies see Gorgias, *Hel.* 6 (= Diels & Kranz, *FVS* II, 82B, fr. 11); Thuc. 1.76.2; 3.40.4; 4.60.1; 5.85–110, esp. c105; Plato, *Gorg.* 483c–d; *Legg.* 890a (of Callicles); *Resp.* 338c (of Thrasymachus); Sextus Empiricus, *Adv. math.* 9.54 (=Diels & Kranz, *FVS* 88, fr. 25–of Critias' *Sisyphus*).

[24] Our impression of this is strengthened by statements at *Cyr.* 1.1.3 and 8.8.1; cf. the ending of *Hell.* 7.5.26.

[25] Cf. *Mem.* 3.9.11; *Hell.* 6.3.15: ἀλλὰ μέντοι ὅτι μὲν πόλεμοι ἀεί ποτε γίγνονται καὶ ὅτι καταλύονται πάντες ἐπιστάμεθα; see Luccioni, 1947, 209; Dover, 1974, 315; Havelock, 1972, 72–74. Lendon, 2006, 82, says of Cyrus' 'trial' of Tigranes (*Cyr.* 3.) 'A single extended theoretical treatment of foreign relations survives from classical antiquity'; cf. Gera, 1993, 78–97; Pangle, 2015, 101–114.

Thus, taking the phenomenon of power for granted, Xenophon follows Thucydides, as if remembering the lesson of his predecessor that *αἰεὶ καθεστῶτος τὸν ἥσσω ὑπὸ τοῦ δυνατωτέρου κατείργεσθαι*,[26] a sentiment reappearing essentially in *Equit. mag.*[27] Although it is clear that what interests Xenophon especially is to what degree Cyrus' empire (and rule) can be *iustum*,[28] it is worth bearing in mind that what he is describing still is empire and hegemony, based on power and violence.[29] It is therefore legitimate, I think, to interpret the story of Cyrus in the manner Simone Weil once read Homer: being far from graphic gore of the *Iliad*, Xenophon's Oriental novel is implicitly a tale about the same phenomenon.[30]

That said, here a *caveat* is needed. As the politics of imperialism is now in Western societies out of fashion, officially at least,[31] one should resist criticizing Xenophon for paying insufficient attention to what nowadays seems to be the most important problem of hegemony—its human costs, depriving others of their freedom by imprisoning or enslaving them. Of course, it would be tempting to place such blame on him—the more so that in the Achaemenid (and Oriental, in

---

26 Thuc. 1.76.2; also 1.75.1 (cf. Andrewes, 1960; Lebow, 2003; Low, 2007, 222–231) to be compared with a sentence in *Hell.* 7.5.26, that sounds like a proverb: *τοὺς μὲν κρατήσαντας ἄρξειν, τοὺς δὲ κρατηθέντας ὑπηκόους ἔσεσθαι*. In their mutual relations both individuals and societies act in a certain way that seems to be unchangeable: a drive for economic advantages (in most cases a basis of power—*Mem.* 3.6.8; cf. Mann, 1986, 4) is common to all, regardless of one's ethnicity or political 'constitution'; many strive for prestige (fame). Although there is no direct evidence for this, I would like to suggest that Xenophon shared with Thucydides the same pessimistic view that human nature is in fact constant, and man's motivation is determined by the same factors: prestige (*τιμῆς*), fear (*δέους*), and profits (*ὠφελίας*), a conviction found later in Polybius, 3.4.11 (*πάντες δὲ πράττουσι πάντα χάριν τῶν ἐπιγινομένων τοῖς ἔργοις ἡδέων ἢ καλῶν ἢ συμφερόντων*). Moreover, he certainly would agree with the accuracy of the famous Thucydidean phrase that war teaches violence (3.82.2: *βίαιος διδάσκαλος*); on this topic see Rhodes, 2011, 26–28.
27 4.17: *ἀεὶ μέντοι <τῷ> ἰσχυροτέρῳ τὸ ἀσθενέστερον θηρᾶν* which reminds of Callicles' theory (Plato, *Gorg.* 483e; cf. Striker, 1996, 212), or Gorgias himself (*Hel.* 6: *πέφυκε γὰρ οὐ τὸ κρεῖσσον ὑπὸ τοῦ ἥσσονος κωλύεσθαι, ἀλλὰ τὸ ἧσσον ὑπὸ τοῦ κρείσσονος ἄρχεσθαι καὶ ἄγεσθαι, καὶ τὸ μὲν κρεῖσσον ἡγεῖσθαι, τὸ δὲ ἧσσον ἕπεσθαι*); cf. Burliga, 2011. The same tendency to dominate others is characteristic even of smaller communities: *Anab.* 5.5.7–10; *Hell.* 3.2.23; see Wickersham, 1994; cf. Bearzot in this volume.
28 Above all, an essential skill of a real statesman and just ruler is to punish enemies and lead policies of harming them; cf. *Cyr.* 1.4.25: *ἄνδρα ἔσεσθαι ἱκανὸν καὶ φίλους ὠφελεῖν καὶ ἐχθροὺς ἀνιᾶν*; also 1.6.11; 8.7.7; 8.7.38 (*μέμνησθέ μου τελευταῖον, τοὺς φίλους εὐεργετοῦντες καὶ τοὺς ἐχθροὺς δυνήσεσθε κολάζειν*) cf. *Mem.* 2.1.19; 2.1.28; 4.2.14–17; 4.6.14; Wood, 1991, 47; Blundell, 1989; see Lanni, 2008, 479; Thomas, 2009, xxii.
29 See Danzig, 2009, 293–294.
30 Weil, 1957, 24–55.
31 Cf. Pinker, 2011.

general) rulers were notoriously regarded as cruel despots,[32] whose behavior shocked—also because of the scale and scope of such acts—the Greek audience.[33] Such a dilemma is the result of the modern thinkers's tendency to censure imperial policies, rather than praise them.[34] Moreover, thanks to the didactic nature of the *Cyropaedia*, topics such as the costs of the policies of conquests and imperialism and the moral dilemmas they generate seem to be here less exposed.[35] Nevertheless, one must be fair and acknowledge that they are not totally omitted in the work: 'just' as it might be, Cyrus' state never ceases to be—as logic requires—oppressive, so feeding that voracious beast of empire always requires, more or less metaphorically, victims. So, failing to include in his novel reflections akin to modern sensibility, Xenophon adopts a soldier's look which may be taken as a mark of his sense of realism. I am deeply convinced that as a soldier too experienced to be unaware of the problems which maintaining power creates,[36] Xenophon presents thus a vision of a good kingdom in which justice is not to be taken in any absolute terms but as a matter of degree only. This means that if it was possible to rule in Cyrus' kingdom *more* justly than usual,[37] such justice had its strong constraints and did not exclude the use of coercion or violence. This is what I call a view of a realist which cannot be—otherwise—identified with Xenophon's personal promoting of the current 'might-is-right' theory.[38] Contrary to

---

[32] Excessive violence was a constant feature of Achaemenid policy, a means of securing authority, as Herodotus, Ctesias, or Curtius Rufus prove, and Xenophon himself confirms (*Anab.* 3.1.17); see Rollinger, 2004; cf. Wiesehöfer, 2009 and 2015.
[33] Although the Greeks themselves did not reftrain from committing bloody acts; cf. Kiechle, 1958; Lintott, 1992; Richer, 2005; Strauss, 2009; van Wees, 2011b and 2016; Raaflaub, 2014; Fisher, 2017, 99–141. See Kapellos in this volume for the slaughter of the Athenian captives at Aegospotami.
[34] Stadter, 1991.
[35] But they are not omitted; see below.
[36] In this respect Xenophon differs little, again, from Thucydides: see my commentary ad *Cyr.* 3.1.11, in Głombiowski et al., 2014, 151, n. 236.
[37] Ruling is a fact, yet there are still different styles of ruling: Lendon, 2006, 84.
[38] Burliga, 2011, and 2014b, 74. Here we are touching a problem that has already appeared in Thucydides (cf. also note 26, above): does the fact that Thucydides wrote about the role of violence mean that he was fascinated with or supported 'the law of stronger'?; see Xenophon's observation in *Poroi.*: at 5. 2, where he states that happy are those cities that live in peace as long as possible, while at 5. 13 he makes a concession that a city, if harmed, cannot avoid war (see *Cyr.* 1.5.3; 2.4.7). The two views are not mutually exclusive.

Clearchus, a psychopath obsessed with war,³⁹ or the perverse Menon of Thessaly,⁴⁰ Xenophon, although never promoting violence,⁴¹ remained nevertheless— as Thucydides did⁴²—a man without illusions about the inevitability of conflicts that presuppose and allow the use of βία.⁴³

3 Realities of War: A Distant Thunder

'Peaceful' as it might be, however, Cyrus' process of building the empire presupposes logically, as always, conquests (cf. 7.4.16: Προϊὼν δὲ τὴν ἐπὶ Βαβυλῶνος κατεστρέψατο μὲν Φρύγας τοὺς ἐν τῇ μεγάλῃ Φρυγίᾳ, κατεστρέψατο δὲ Καππαδόκας, ὑποχειρίους δ' ἐποιήσατο Ἀραβίους);⁴⁴ it always generates its own costs which in practical terms means expansion, conflicts, wars, annexation of territories,⁴⁵ with various forms of subordination and subjugation, including physical violence, enslavement and the killing of those who refuse to obey—before subjects are turned into a consenting and applauding flock, they must either be conquered by force or terrorized by the threat of using force (as in *Cyr.* 1.1.4;

---

39 See *Anab.* 2.6.1–15; cf. Braund, 2004, 97–107.
40 *Anab.* 2.6.21–29. Among the worst flaws of this pupil of Gorgias was a preference for cheating friends; see Rood, 2017, 180–186.
41 He was not blind to the fate of children (*Anab.* 4.8.27; 7.3.27) or civilians (*Mem.* 1.2.32; *Hell.* 4.4.1–4; 4.4.12; 5.4.12; *Conv.* 4.36); cf. Bearzot in this volume.
42 I fully agree with Flower's recent observation (2017, 307) that Xenophon sees history also '[...] in terms of Thucydidean Realpolitik'; cf. Ludwig, 2017, 515–530.
43 This may be seen in *Poroi* 5; see also his remark on Agesilaus' humanity towards prisoners: *Ages.* 1.21–22.
44 If necessary, Cyrus could be merciless: *Cyr.* 7.5.31–32. To the same category belongs boastful rhetoric in *Cyr.* 7.5.53: καὶ νῦν δὴ νενικήκαμέν τε τὴν μεγάλην μάχην καὶ Σάρδεις καὶ Κροῖσον ὑποχείριον ἔχομεν καὶ Βαβυλῶνα ᾑρήκαμενκαὶ πάντας κατεστράμμεθα; cf. 7.5.70; cf. the phraseology of pride as reward for conquests and power at 8.7.6 (σὺν τῷ χρόνῳ τε προϊόντι ἀεὶ συναυξανομένην ἐπιγιγνώσκειν ἐδόκουν καὶ τὴν ἐμὴν δύναμιν), and 8.7.6 (οὔτ' ἐπιχειρήσας οὔτ' ἐπιθυμήσας οἶδα ὅτου ἠτύχησα); see also 8.7.7 (τοὺς μὲν φίλους ἐπεῖδον δι' ἐμοῦ εὐδαίμονας γενομένους, τοὺς δὲ πολεμίους ὑπ' ἐμοῦ δουλωθέντας· καὶ τὴν πατρίδα πρόσθεν ἰδιωτεύουσαν ἐν τῇ Ἀσίᾳ νῦν προτετιμημένην καταλείπω·ὧν τ' ἐκτησάμην οὐδὲν [οἶδα] ὅτι οὐ διεσωσάμην). All this points to the observation that Xenophon understood Cyrus' ideology as similar to that professed by tyrants. Xenophon's Hiero stresses the hunger for prestige that makes men excellent, so that they are distinguished from common people and animals; see Gray, 2007; cf. Lendon, 2000; van Wees, 2011.
45 As the art of war is the art of acquiring something—according to Aristotle, *Pol.* 1256b; on Greek 'rules' of war see Ober, 1996, 51–71.

1.6.10; 3.1.3).⁴⁶ This topic—a 'darkside' of all imperial policies—one may agree now, is not especially stressed by Xenophon. Yet we must be honest with him, he does not forget about it altogether, so every reader of the *Cyropaedia* realizes it too, sooner or later, although the consciousness of this is—so to speak—like the experience of a distant thunder: here we only read about this, ocassionally, briefly and 'by the way'. Sometimes one is only briefly informed, as in *Cyr.* 8.6.1, where one reads about τὰ κατεστραμμένα ἔθνη.⁴⁷ As a student (and by the same teacher) of political ethics, Xenophon the soldier tries usually to avoid focusing on shocking accounts and things that eventually and inevitably happened 'on the way', when Cyrus constructed his ideal kingdom. Nevertheless, following the king's steps on his path to greatness, we have plenty of glimpses that atrocities occurred.⁴⁸ As in the case of the suggestive sentences from *Agesilaus* and *Hellenica*,⁴⁹ Xenophon, the man of arms, permits his readers- from time to time—to see terrifying details of battle, as it happens in *Cyr.* 7.1.31–7.1.40. Remembering these violent images is important to the extent that they are in contradiction with the idea that the *Cyropedia* is but an idyllic vision of paradise.⁵⁰ Rather, they help the reader to acknowledge that this is what real power and authority, even the most just, are about.

4 Why Empire?

Did such a philosophical question bother Xenophon?⁵¹ I assume he was conscious of it, although, to quote Professor Anderson, the writer 'is not at his best when discussing general ideas rather than illustrating them by particular examples'.⁵²

---

46 To cruel acts accompanying war also belong the murder of Gobryas' son (4.6.4); the castration of Gadatas (5.3.8); the suicide of Panthea and her servants (7.3.14–15). (I thank an anonymous referee for reminding me of these cases). See also Crick in this volume for Xenophon's use of the rhetoric of violence in the *Anabasis*.
47 Perhaps the most revealing instance is the way Cyrus becomes a ruler of Media: in Xenophon he simply inherits it, in all other sources—he conquers Media by force.
48 Of the atrocities and horrors accompanying warfare one learns more from reading the *Hellenica*.
49 *Ages.* 2.12: συμβαλόντες τὰς ἀσπίδας ἐωθοῦντο, ἐμάχοντο, ἀπέκτεινον, ἀπέθνῃσκον. καὶ κραυγὴ μὲν οὐδεμία παρῆν, οὐ μὴν οὐδὲ σιγή, φωνὴ δέ τις ἦν τοιαύτη οἵαν ὀργή τε καὶ μάχη παράσχοιτ' ἄν (= *Hell.* 4.3.19). Cf. Foster in this volume on deaths on the battlefield.
50 Cf. 7.3.8: a bit of a macabre detail (the mutilation of Gadatas' corpse).
51 Cf. Carlier, 2010, 334; see Danzig, 2012.
52 1974, 193.

As there can be no doubt, for Xenophon power and violence constitutes a substratum of Cyrus' 'ideal' kingdom, its core remains the proper use of power, in a way it can be distinguished from an improper one. This—by the same token—constituted also in Greek thought a fundamental line that separated tyranny from monarchy,[53] with a reservation that this rule applied to subjects only, the ruled. Outside, so to speak, the enemy was always present (cf. *Cyr.* 1.6.27).[54] Such a Greek distinction between enemies and friends remained fundamental for understanding the role of justice in the *Cyropaedia*—it may be said that Cyrus' constant desire, a mark of his political wisdom, was to turn enemies into friends—an endeavor that did not always succeed.[55]

It might be expected that as a disciple of Socrates, Xenophon would deal with Herodotean, Platonic, or Aristotelian-like dilemmas over which 'constitution' is the best. But nothing of this sort: the topic seems to have been irrelevant to him, for, as he declares from the outset, all the types of government—*including* monarchy—have serious flaws and faults.[56] Revealing no skin-deep fascination with force or violence, Xenophon thus takes for granted the ubiquity of power in social and political relations as a matter of fact since its source is just human nature, which is the subject of psychology now.[57] The core of the problem Xenophon puts before the eyes of his readers lies thus in a man's ἦθος which means that people, not equal in their natural capabilities, constantly try to excel by dominating others:[58] he who is

---

53 *Mem.* 4.6.12.
54 See *Cyr.* 1.6.30: a famous statement of how to use deceit and trickery against enemies; see 2.4.25; cf. 6.2.2; 6.2.9; 6.2.11—where Cyrus approves the trickery of the Indian envoys as double spies; earlier on, he sends to them Araspas as a spy (6.1.31; 6.3.15).
55 See *Cyr.* 4.4.10.
56 *Cyr.* 1.1.3; *Lac.Pol.* 1.1; see Gray, 2000, 146–147; also Dillery, 1995, 249.
57 A different interpretation is given by Lendon, 2006, analyzing the 'trial of the Armenian king', although elsewhere (Lendon, 2000, 1–2, 13–16) he observes that the two historians shared the same view of another propensity, common to all—revenge, a major factor in generating conflicts of various sort. Revenge, arising from one's sense of a violation of one's personal pride, falls under a broader category of prestige; cf. *Cyr.* 1.6.11; 7.5.32.
58 He held as obvious, probably following Socrates (*Mem.* 3.9.11), that the power of one over another is something natural (so Callistratus in *Hell.* 6.3.15: ἀλλὰ μέν τοι ὅτι μὲν πόλεμοι ἀεί ποτε γίγνονται καὶ ὅτι καταλύονται πάντες ἐπιστάμεθα; see a highly pessimistic observation in *Hiero* 2. 15: αἱ μὲν γὰρ πόλεις δήπου ὅταν κρατήσωσι μάχῃ τῶν ἐναντίων, οὐ ῥάδιον εἰπεῖν ὅσην μὲν ἡδονὴν ἔχουσιν ἐν τῷ ῥέψασθαι τοὺς πολεμίους, ὅσην δ' ἐν τῷ διώκειν, ὅσην δ' ἐν τῷ ἀποκτείνειν τοὺς πολεμίους, ὡς δὲ γαυροῦνται ἐπὶ τῷ ἔργῳ, ὡς δὲ δόξαν λαμπρὰν ἀναλαμβάνουσιν, ὡς δ' εὐφραίνονται τὴν πόλιν νομίζοντες ηὐξηκέναι, with Gray, 2007, 122 and Dayton, 2006, 75); cf. Luccioni, 1949, 209: 'les hommes sont gouvernés par d'autres hommes'.

more clever and superior to others gains power and authority.⁵⁹ For Xenophon, as a man's character was of key importance, the problem was not so much 'why empire' but how to be effective in governing.⁶⁰ Xenophon did thus not focus on the nature of power as such but on power used properly to ensure a stable and fair government.⁶¹ It was the author's deep conviction that Cyrus' use of power and violence, adequate and suitable, was the result of his character and wisdom in how to deal with subjects, that is to rule. What was crucial in this matter was based on authority, not despotism.⁶²

Accordingly, Cyrus' lifelong odyssey to achieve the status of a just king and to be considered by his subjects as the best ruler ever is presented by Xenophon as 'peaceful', that is, relatively moderate, rather than violent and tyrannical.⁶³ This has led some scholars to argue that Cyrus was meant to be a παράδειγμα of a good monarch, a moral example and benevolent, careful 'shepherd' of his flock,⁶⁴ while his striving for power and building the empire (a laborious task– ὑπερμέγεθες ἔργον: *Cyr.* 1.6.7–8; 7.5.73–80) was far from being a bloody and tyrannical process. Such a line of thinking may be interpreted as the main 'message' Xenophon wanted to confirm in his readers: it was (and still is) possible to reign justly, for the welfare of the ruled,⁶⁵ therefore with their willing consent⁶⁶ – a topic that became so popular, if not an obsession, later, in Hellenistic treatises *Peri basileias*.⁶⁷ Such an interpretation has made some researchers argue that the

---

59 So in *Cyr.* 3.1.24 we are told that it is possible to be happy even while being subjected. Later on, at 8.1.44, a notorious remark appears that Cyrus tried to make the slaves bear the fate of their slavery without opposition; cf. Gray, 2011, 282–283; Tamiolaki, 2012, 575.
60 E.g. *Poroi* 1.1.
61 Lendon, 2006, 83–84.
62 But see Wood, 1964, 51; on this topic see Newell, 1983, 889–906.
63 A point observed also by Plato *Laws* 694a–b.
64 In a quite literal sense—*Cyr.* 1.1.2; 8.2.14.
65 *Cyr.* 1.4.26; 1.6.8; 1.6.24. As Carlier, 2011, 329, notes, this might have been a polemics with Plato, *Resp.* 343c.
66 Cf. *Cyr.* 1.2.1: ψυχὴν δὲ φιλανθρωπότατος; cf. Danzig, 2012, 499; Tamiolaki, 2017: 176 'a benevolent despot'; cf. Tuplin, 1985, 360.
67 See Knauth und Nadjmabadi, 1975; Farber, 1979; Gray, 2011; Burliga, 2012. The origins of this genre go back probably to the last years of the Peloponnesian War, and their reflection is the dialogue between Socrates and Thrasymachus in the *Republic*, where the former refutes the latter's conviction that each form of goverrnment—despotic, democractic and aristocratic alike— *always* means ruling for the particular interest and profit of a single rulero faction thatactually wields power (it is, in fact, a rule of the stronger: 338c; 343c), thus taking no care of the ruled (338e). Socrates, on the contrary, argues (342e) that it ispossible to rule for the benefit of subjects.

Cyropaedia is a fairytale, set in a somewhat half-mythical, remote past, and separated carefully from the narrator's present by the frequently repeated formula *eti kai nyn*.

However, as I try to argue here, such a picture is too simple to be taken literally. The *Cyropaedia* is more complicated. First and foremost, one can find occasionally a few exceptions to this noble but one-sided vision.[68] The first occurs at *Cyr*. 8.4.8, where the following sentiment is expressed: when Gobryas praises Cyrus for being even better in his benevolence towards men than in strategy, Cyrus' reply is that 'I take much more pleasure in showing forth my deeds of kindness than ever I did in my deeds of generalship' (ἐπιδείκνυμαι τὰ ἔργα πολὺ ἥδιον φιλανθρωπίας ἢ στρατηγίας). His further explanation is somewhat surprising, namely that 'in one field (i.e. in generalship—B.B.), one must do harm to men; in the other, only good' (τὰ μὲν κακῶς ποιοῦντα ἀνθρώπους δεῖ ἐπιδείκνυσθαι, τὰ δὲ εὖ).[69] It may be a truism that war is evil,[70] as many agree; in this context the sentence remains important as

---

[68] Here a word must be said about a long controversy in modern *Cyropaedia* studies. Following the influential works of Leo Strauss, some scholars (e.g. Tatum, 1989; cf. Nadon, 2001) argued that the portrait of Cyrus is in fact that of a ruthless manipulator and deceiver, so Xenophon's praise must be pretended and ironical, at best. I think there is no discrepancy in Xenophon's thinking, and it was possible to glorify Cyrus and to see him at the same time as a shrewd, if not cunning politician who knows the techniques of a successful ruling; cf. 1.6.27–31, where it is acceptable to cheat friends for their own good; cf. in general Hesk, 2000. Perhaps the best instance of Cyrus' idealism and acute cleverness is his speech at 7.5.72–7.5.86, a fine exposition of specific solutions and general observations and recommendations that resemble the Athenian sentiments in Thucydides and concern their fitness to rule in the Aegean world. At 7.5.61 another interesting phrase appears: Cyrus is called 'a master who will be patron' (δεσπότου ἐπικούρου), which aptly describes the essence of the understanding of the king by Xenophon: to be sure he is *despotes* but is one who helps and provides care: where the modern reader feels an inconsistency, Xenophon did not. Additionally, the praise of Cyrus did not prevent Xenophon from stating (*Cyr*. 8.1.22) that 'the good ruler he regarded as a law with eyes for men' (τὸν δὲ ἀγαθὸν ἄρχοντα βλέποντα νόμον ἀνθρώποις ἐνόμισεν). As he adds in the same sentence, a ruler who is an embodiment of 'watchful law' can use force, and his vigilant eye may punish those who are disobedient. The same monitoring of the subjects was served by the notorious 'King's Eyes and Ears' (*Cyr*. 8.2.10–12; 8.6.16; *Oec*. 4.8). Gray, 2007, 11 rightly associated this idea with Aristotle's concept of *pambasileia*, while Breebart, 1983, 126 recalls another passage from *Politics*, 1310b–1315b, that 'mutual envy and espionage' leads to 'the promotion of anti-social distrust to be typically Persian and barbarian'. Be that as it may, the passage is, again, instructive in understanding that for Xenophon there was no contradiction in eulogizing Cyrus as a noble, lenient and moderate dynast, and highlighting *also* the fact that he tried to control everything in his kingdom, like an ancient prefiguration of king Louis XIV's alleged 'L'État, c'est moi'.
[69] W. Miller's Loeb tr.
[70] Cf. the famous, awesome diagnosis of the political situation in Greece after the Mantinea campaign: *Hell*. 7.5.26; cf. Dillery, 1995, 27–35.

it shows that Xenophon's views on war and empire, even in the case of his idealized Cyrus, were, in fact, more complicated and far from clear-cut.

It is only at *Cyr.* 7.5.80, therefore relatively late, that Xenophon makes his hero ask- by the way, however - a question why there should be conquests at all; what is the benefit of them (τί δή τα ἡμῖν ὄφελος καταπρᾶξαι ἃ ἐπεθυμοῦμεν)?[71] Additionally, in his final speech (8.7.12) Cyrus enters the details of what is to be a king by presenting a darker side of wielding authoritative power—a true other side of the coin. Handing over the satrapy to the younger son, the dying ruler frankly enumerates what the future king must expect (ταῦτα τῷ βασιλεύοντι ἀνάγκη). This includes τὸ δὲ δυσκαταπρακτοτέρων τε ἐρᾶν καὶ τὸ πολλὰ μεριμνᾶν καὶ τὸ μὴ δύνασθαι ἡσυχίαν ἔχειν κεντριζόμενον ὑπὸ τῆς πρὸς τἀμὰ ἔργα φιλονικίας. And - amid these inconveniences- one reads significantly about τὸ ἐπιβουλεύειν καὶ τὸ ἐπιβουλεύεσθαι [...]. But, despite these defects and the unpleasant aspects of ruling, something much more valuable lies behind such a picture, for the true answer as to why to strive for power and to rule at all appears earlier, in Cyrus' speech at 7.5.83: all the hardships in acquiring prestige and material goods retain their worth because thanks to them we can become better than we are; moreover, we are also better than those we rule. And finally, thanks to being better (and therefore distinguishing yourself from others) you can be happier. A logical conclusion that emerges from such a reasoning is, then, that ruling provides and leads to excellence, so therefore it can bring happiness. With such an argumentation the reader returns to what he has realized earlier on, when reading of Cyrus *philotimia*.[72] The latter finds its confirmation in Cyrus' proud and boastful words at 7.5.76 that μέγα μὲν γὰρ οἶμαι ἔργον καὶ τὸ ἀρχὴν καταπρᾶξαι, πολὺ δ' ἔτι μεῖζον τὸ λαβόντα διασώσασθαι.[73]

As we have seen, Xenophon did not face fully and comprehensively the most fundamental, simplest and perhaps the most intriguing problem: can any empire be just at all? After all, the Ciceronian phrase *iustum imperium* would not be an oxymoron to him, most probably. Being fully aware that—in modern terminology—

---

71 Cf. *Oec.* 1.15.
72 Remarkably, in one place, at least, Xenophon describes his hero as φιλοτιμότατος, ὥστε πάντα μὲν πόνον ἀνατλῆναι, πάντα δὲ κίνδυνον ὑπομεῖναι τοῦ ἐπαινεῖσθαι ἕνεκα: *Cyr.* 1.2.1; cf. 1.3.3 (φιλότιμος). In 7.5.37 one realizes that Cyrus accepts his exceptional position and dignity coming from achieving royal status (7.5.76: ὡς βασιλεῖ ἡγεῖτο πρέπειν) that is in turn based on possessing power: μέγα μὲν γὰρ οἶμαι ἔργον καὶ τὸ ἀρχὴν καταπρᾶξαι, πολὺ δ' ἔτι μεῖζον τὸ λαβόντα διασώσασθαι. Unsurprisingly, these sentiments remind us of the theme of prestige in *Hiero* 7.1–4: it is prestige which counts among the most important traits in tyrant's motivation; see Gray, 2007, 133.
73 Cf. Thuc. 2.61–64; see Balot, 2006, 141–42.

Cyrus used social engineering methods, Xenophon simply assumed that the king was right and his kingdom remained the greatest (8.8.1: καλλίστη καὶ μεγίστη τῶν ἐν τῇ Ἀσίᾳ ἡ Κύρου βασιλεία) which, of course, does not exactly fit modern standards and notions of what the justice of a state should be. But this does not mean, on the other hand, that Xenophon's aim was to create a utopian world. When talking about a discrepancy between reality and idealism in the tale of Cyrus one should be as far as possible from suggesting that Xenophon was naive, a noodle walking with his head in the clouds, even less a fool unable to see how brutal circumstances accompany the maintenance of power. However great the differences exist between the ancient Greek and modern understanding of what just rule is, one cannot doubt that Xenophon was not blind and deaf to what empire means. In this regard, it may be argued, Xenophon's 'idealistic' vision of Cyrus' kingdom appears to be highly ambiguous,[74] as it is deeply rooted in grim realities, occasionally allowing insight into a darker picture. The main reason for this is that the *Cyropaedia* remains, to simplify, a narrative about human nature, as was the case of Herodotus' and Thucydides' histories. In consequence, the following, memorable words of Hannah Arendt may be well applied to Xenophon's novel as matching this case:

> 'No one engaged in thought about history and politics can remain unaware of the enormous role violence has always played in human affairs, and it is at first glance rather surprising that violence has been singled out so seldom for special consideration [...]. This shows to what an extent violence and its arbitrariness were taken for granted and therefore neglected'.[75]

---

[74] I return to the scene of the trial of the Armenian king as an example of this ambiguity: the most troublesome phrase here is the Armenian's confession at 3.1.10: ἐλευθερίας ἐπεθύμουν· καλὸν γάρ μοι ἐδόκει εἶναι καὶ αὐτὸν ἐλεύθερον εἶναι καὶ παισὶν ἐλευθερίαν καταλιπεῖν. Although Xenophon adopts here the Persian point of view (a man's rebellion against his master is an injustice towards him), the impression of the inevitability of the power that the stronger can use is overwhelming (cf. 3.1.23 on fear of punishment). So is the conclusion of 3.1.7: ἐνταῦθα δὴ ὁ Ἀρμένιος γιγνώσκων τὴν ἀνάγκην καταβαίνει which reminds of Aeschylus, *Prometheus Bound* 103–105: τὴν πεπρωμένην δὲ χρὴ/ αἶσαν φέρειν ὡς ῥᾷστα, γιγνώσκονθ' ὅτι/τὸ τῆς ἀνάγκης ἔστ' ἀδήριτον σθένος (on the power of Zeus; cf. also v. 114). According to Lendon, 2006, 83, 'in Xenophon we witness—in contrast to, and perhapseven in reply to, Thucydides' pessimistic power-and-fear realism—a triumph of idealism'.

[75] Arendt, 1970, 8; See D'Huys, 1987.

Bibliography

Anderson, J.K. (1974), *Xenophon*, London.
Andrewes, A. (1960), "The Melian Dialogue and Perikles' Last Speech (Thucydides V,84–113; II,60–4)" in: *PCPhS* 186, 1–10.
Arendt, H. (1970), *On Violence*, Orlando.
Balot, R.K. (2006), *Greek Political Thought*, Malden/Oxford.
Blundell, M.W. (1989), *Helping Friends and Harming Enemies. A Study in Sophocles and Greek Ethics*, Cambridge.
Braund, D. (2004), "Xenophon's Dangerous Liaisons" in: *The Long March. Xenophon and the Ten Thousand*, R. Lane Fox (ed.), New Haven/London, 98–130.
Breebaart, A. (1983), "From Victory to Peace: Some Aspects of Cyrus' State in Xenophon's *Cyropaedia*" in: *Mnemosyne* 36, 117–134.
Breitenbach, H.R. (1966), *Xenophon von Athen*, Stuttgart.
Briant, P. (2002), *From Cyrus to Alexander. A History of the Persian Empire*, Winona Lake.
Brock, R. (2004), "Xenophon's Political Imaginery" in: *Xenophon and His World*, C.J. Tuplin (ed.), Stuttgart, 247–257.
Brosius, M. (2005), "*Pax persica*: Königliche Ideologie und Kriegführungim Achämenidenreich" in: *Krieg-Gesellschaft-Institutionen*, hrsg. B. Meissner/O. Schmitt/M. Sommer, Berlin, 135–162.
Burliga, B. (2011), "ἀεὶ μέντοι <τῷ> ἰσχυροτέρῳ τὸ ἀσθενέστερον θηρᾶν: The Meaning of the 'Hunting' Comparison in Xenophon's *Equit. mag.* 4.17" in: *Xenophon: Greece, Persia, and Beyond*, B. Burliga (ed.), Gdańsk, 131–152.
Burliga, B. (2012), "Do the Kings Lie? Royal Authority and Historian's Objectivity in Arrian's *Anabasis*" in: *Leadership in Antiquity. Language-Institutions- Representations* [Classica Cracoviensia 15], J. Janik/A. Klęczar (eds), Cracow, 5–59.
Burliga, B. (2014a), "Xenophon's Cyrus, Alexander φιλόκυρος: How Carefully Did Alexander the Great Study the *Cyropaedia*?" in: *MAeS* 15, 134–146.
Burliga, B. (2014b), "Did They Really Return upon Their Shields? The ὕβρις of the Spartan Hoplites at Lechaeum, 390 BC" in: *Iphicrates, Peltasts and Lechaeum*, N.V. Sekunda/B. Burliga (eds), Gdańsk, 66–83.
Carlier, P. (2010), "The Idea of Imperial Monarchy in the *Cyropaedia*" in: *Xenophon*, V.J. Gray (ed.), Oxford, 327–366.
Cataudella, M. (1998), "Vendetta e imperialismo nella monarchia achemenide" in: *Responsabilità perdono e vendetta nel mondo antico*, a cura di M. Sordi, Milano, 47–64.
Danzig, G. (2009), "Big Boys and Little Boys: Justice and Law in Xenophon's *Cyropaedia* and *Memorabilia*" in: *Polis* 26, 271–295.
Danzig, G. (2012), "The Best of the Achaemenids: Benevolence, Self-Interest and the Ironic Reading of *Cyropaedia*" in: *Xenophon: Ethical Principles and Historical Inquiry*, F. Hobden and C.J. Tuplin (eds), Leiden/Boston, 499–540.
Dayton, J. 2006, *The Athletes of War. An Evaluation of the Agonistic Elements in Greek Warfare*, Toronto.
D'Huys, V. (1987), "How to Describe Violence in Historical Narrative Subtitle: Reflections of the Ancient Greek Historians and Their Ancient Critics" in: *AncSoc* 18, 209–250.

Dewald, C. (2013), "Justice and Justifications: War Theory among the Ancient Greeks" in: *Just War in Religion and Politics. Studies in Religion and Social Order*, J. Neusner/B.D. Chilton/R.E. Tully (eds), Lanham, 27–50.
Delebecque, E. (1957), *Essai sur la vie de Xénophon*, Paris.
Dillery, J. (1995), *Xenophon and the History of His Times*, London/New York.
Dover, K.J. (1974), *Popular Morality in the Time of Plato and Demosthenes*, Oxford.
Due, B. (1989), *The* Cyropedia. *Xenophon's Aims and Methods*, Aarhus.
Due, B. (2000), "Utopia of Xenophon" in: *Proceedings of Danish Institute at Athens* 3, 97–105.
Due, B. (2002), "Narrator and Narrative in Xenophon's *Cyropaedia*" in: Noctes Atticae. 34 *Articles on Graeco-Roman Antiquity and Its Nachleben. Studies Presented to J. Mejer*, B. Amden et al. (eds), Copenhagen, 82–92.
Farber, J.J. (1979), "The *Cyropaedia* and Hellenistic Kingship" in: *AJP* 100, 497–514.
Brown, Ferrario S. (2014), *Historical Agency and the 'Great Man' in Classical Greece*, Cambridge.
Brown, Ferrario S. (2017), "Xenophon and Greek Political Thought" in: *The Cambridge Companion to Xenophon*, M. Flower (ed.), Cambridge, 57–83.
Fisher, N. (2017), "Socialisation, Identity and Violence in Classical Greek Cities" in: *Violence and Community. Law, Space and Identity in the Ancient Eastern Mediterranean World*, I.K. Xydopoulos et al. (eds), New York, 99–141.
Flower, M.A. (2017), "Xenophon as Historian" in: *A Cambridge Companion to Xenophon*, M. Flower (ed.), 301–322.
Gera, D.L. (1993), *Xenophon's* Cyropaedia. *Style, Genre, and Literary Technique*, Oxford.
Głombiowski, K./Burliga, B./Marchewka, A./Ryś, A. (2014), *Ksenofont, Wychowanie Cyrusa (Cyropaedia). With Introduction, Translation, and Commentary*, Wrocław.
Gill, C. (2003), "Is Rivalry a Virtue Or a Vice?" in: *Envy, Spite and Jealousy. The Rivalrous Emotions in Ancient Greece*, D. Konstan/N.K. Rutter (eds), Edinburgh, 29–52.
Gray, V.J. (2000), "Xenophon and Isocrates" in: *The Cambridge History of Greek and Roman Political Thought*, C.J. Rowe/M. Schofield (eds), Cambridge, 142–154.
Gray, V.J. (2007), *Xenophon on Government*, Cambridge.
Gray, V.J. (2011), *Xenophon's Mirror of Princes: Reading the Reflections*, Oxford.
Havelock, E.A. (1972), "War as a Way of Life in Classical Greece" in: *Valeurs antiques et temps modernes. Classical Values and the Modern World* [The G.P. Vanier Memorial Lectures], E. Gareau (ed.), Ottawa, 19–78.
Hesk, J. (2000), *Deception and Democracy in Classical Athens*, Cambridge.
Hirsch, S. (1985), *The Friendship of the Barbarians. Xenophon and the Persian Empire*, Hanover.
Humble, N. (2017), "Xenophon and the Instruction of Princes" in: *A Cambridge Companion to Xenophon*, M. Flower (ed.), Cambridge, 416–434.
Kiechle, F. (1958), "Zur Humanität in der Kriegführung der griechischen Staaten" in: *Historia* 7, 129–156.
Knauth, W./Nadjmabadi, S. (1975), *Das altiranische Fürstenideal von Xenophon bis Ferdousi. Nach den antiken und einheimischen Quellen dargestellt*, Wiesbaden.
Kuhrt, A. (1983), "The Cyrus Cylinder and Achaemenid Imperial Policy" in: *JSOT* 25, 83–97.
Kuhrt, A. (2007a), "Ancient Near Eastern History: The Case of Cyrus the Great of Persia" in: *Understanding the History of Ancient Israel*, H.G.M. Williamson (ed.), Oxford, 107–127.
Kuhrt, A. (2007b), *The Persian Empire. A Corpus of Sources of the Achaemenid Period I–II*, London/New York.

Kuhrt, A. (2007c), "Cyrus the Great of Persia: Images and Realities" in: *Representations of Political Power: Case Histories from Times of Change and Dissolving Order in the Ancient Near East*, M. Heinz/M.H. Feldman (eds), Winona Lake, 169–191.
Lanni, A. (2008), "The Laws of War in Ancient Greece" in: *Law and History Review* 26, 469–489.
Lebow, R.N. (2003), *The Tragic Vision of Politics. Ethics, Interests and Orders*, Cambridge.
Lendon, J.E. (2000), "Homeric Vengeance and the Outbreak of Greek Wars" in: *War and Violence in Ancient Greece*, H. van Wees (ed.), London, 1–30.
Lendon, J.E. (2006), "Xenophon and the Alternative to Realist Foreign Policy: Cyropaedia 3.1. 14–31" in: *JHS* 126, 82–98.
Lintott, A. (1992), "Cruelty in the Political Life of the Ancient World" in: *Crudelitas. The Politics of Cruelty in the Ancient and Medieval World*, T. Viljamaa/A. Timonen/C. Krötzl (eds), Krems, 9–27.
Low, P. (2007), *Interstate Relations in Classical Greece. Morality and Power*, Cambridge.
Luccioni, J. (1947), *Les Idées politiques et sociales de Xénophon*, Paris.
Ludwig, P. (2009), "Anger, Eros, and Other Political Passions in Ancient Greek Thought" in: *A Companion to Greek and Roman Political Thought*, R.K. Balot (ed.), Oxford, 294–307.
Ludwig, P. (2017), "Xenophon as a Socratic Reader of Thucydides" in: *The Oxford Handbook of Thucydides*, R.K. Balot/S. Forsdyke/E. Foster (eds), Oxford, 515–530.
Mallowan, M. (1972), "Cyrus the Great" in: *Iran* 10, 1–17.
Mann, M. (1986), *The Sources for Social Power I. A History of Power from the Beginnings to A.D. 1750*, Cambridge.
Nadon, C. (2001), *Xenophon's Prince. Republic and Empire in the Cyropaedia*, Berkeley/Los Angeles.
Newell, W.R. (1983), "Tyranny and the Science of Ruling in Xenophon's "Education of Cyrus" in: *Journal of Politics* 45, 889–906.
Ober, J. (1996), "The Rules of War in Classical Greece" in: Ober, *The Athenian Revolution. Essays on Ancient Greek Democracy and Political Theory*, Princeton, 53–71.
Pangle, L.S. (2015), "Moral Indignation, Magnanimity, and Philosophy in the Trial of the Armenian King" in: *In Search of Humanity. Essays in Honor of Clifford Orwin*, A. Radasanu (ed.), Lanham/Boulder, 101–113.
Pinker, S. (2011), *The Better Angels of Our Nature. Why Violence Has Declined*, New York.
Raaflaub, K.A. (2007), "Homer and Thucydides on Peace and Just War" in: *Experiencing War. Trauma and Society from Ancient Greece to the Iraq War*, M. Cosmopoulos (ed.), Chicago, 81–94.
Raaflaub, K.A. (2014), 'War and the City: The Brutality of War and Its Impact on the P.J. Community" in: *Combat Trauma and the Ancient Greeks*, P. Meineck/D. Konstan (eds), New York, 15–46.
Rasmussen, P.J. (2009), *Excellence Unleashed. Machiavelli's Critique of Xenophon and the Moral Foundation of Politics*, Lanham.
Rhodes, P.J. (2011), "Biaios Didaskalos? Thucydides and His Lessons for His Readers" in: *Thucydides – a Violent Teacher? History and Its Representations*, G. Rechenauer/V. Pothou (eds), Göttingen, 17–28.
Reisert, J.R. (2009), "Ambition and Corruption in Xenophon's Education of Cyrus" in: *Polis* 26, 296–315.
Richer, N. (2005), "La violence dans les mondes grec et romain. Introduction" in: *La violence dans les mondes grec et romain*, reunis par J.-M. Bertrand, Paris, 7–35.

Rollinger, R. 2004, "Herodotus, Human Violence and the Ancient Near East" in: *The World of Herodotus*, V. Karageorghis/I. Taifacos (eds), Nicosia, 121–150.
Rood, T. (2017), "Xenophon" in: *Characterization in Ancient Greek Literature*, K. De Temmermann/E. van Emde Boas (eds), Leiden/Boston, 172–190.
Stadter, P.A. (2010), "Fictional Narrative in the *Cyropaideia*" in: *Xenophon*, V. Gray (ed.), Oxford, 367–400.
Stadter, P.A. (2009), "Character in Politics" in: *A Companion to Greek and Roman Political Thought*, Balot (ed.), Oxford, 456–470.
Strauss, B. (2009), "Athens as Hamlet: The Irresolute Empire" in: *Enduring Empire. Ancient Lessons for Global Politics*, D. Tabachnick/T. Koivukoski (eds), Toronto/Buffalo/London, 215–226.
Striker, G. (1996), "Origins of the Concept of Natural Law" in: Striker, *Essays on Hellenistic Epistemology and Ethics*, Cambridge, 209–220.
Tamiolaki, M. (2012), "Virtue and Leadership in Xenophon: Ideal Leaders or Ideal Losers?" in: *Xenophon: Ethical Principles and Historical Enquiry*, Leiden/Boston, F. Hobden/C.J. Tuplin (eds), 563–590.
Tamiolaki, M. (2017), "Xenophon's *Cyropaedia*: Tentative Answers to an Enigma" in: *A Cambridge Companion to Xenophon*, M. Flower (ed.), Cambridge, 174–194.
Tatum, J. (1989), *Xenophon's Imperial Fiction. On the Education of Cyrus*, Princeton.
Thomas, D. (2009), "Introduction" in: *The Landmark Xenophon's* Hellenica, R.B. Strassler (ed.), New York, ix–lxvi.
Too Y. Lee (1998), "Xenophon's *Cyropaedia*: Disfiguring the Pedagogical State" in: *Pedagogy and Power. Rhetorics of Classical Learning*, Y. Lee Too/N. Livingstone (eds), Cambridge, 282–302.
Tuplin, C. (1985), "Imperial Tyranny: Some Reflections on a Classical Greek Political Metaphor" in: *Crux: Essays in Greek History Presented to G.E.M. De Ste. Croix*, P.A. Cartledge/F.D. Harvey (eds), Exeter, 348–375.
Tuplin, C. (1997), "Xenophon's *Cyropaedia*: Education and Fiction" in: *Education in Greek Fiction*, A.H. Sommerstein/C. Atherton (eds), Bari, 65–162.
Tuplin, C. (2010), "Xenophon and Achaemenid Courts: A Survey of Evidence" in: Der Achämenidenhof/The Achaemenid Court, hrsg. B. Jacobs/R. Rollinger, Wiesbaden, 189–230.
van der Spek, R.J. (2014), "Cyrus the Great, Exiles, and Foreign Gods: A Comparison of Assyrian and Persian Policies on Subject Nations" in: *Extraction and Control. Studies in Honor of Matthew W. Stolper*/M. Kozuh et al. (eds), Chicago, 233–264.
van Wees, H. (2011a), "Rivalry in History: an Introduction" in: *Competition in the Ancient World*, N. Fisher/H. van Wees (eds), Swansea, 1–36.
van Wees, H. (2011b), "Defeat and Destruction: the Ethics of Greek Warfare" in: *"Böser Krieg". Exzessive Gewalt in der antiken Kriegsführung und Strategienzuderen Vermeidung*, M. Linder/S. Tausend (eds), Graz, 69–110.
van Wees, H. (2016), "Genocide in Archaic and Classical Greece" in: *Our Ancient Wars. Rethinking War through the Classics*, V. Caston/S.-M.Weineck (eds), Ann Arbor, 19–37.
Waterfield, R. (tr.)/Cartledge, P. (1997), *Xenophon, Hiero the Tyrant and Other Treatises*, (intr.; notes), London.
Weathers, W. (1954), "Xenophon's Political Idealism" in: *CJ* 49, 317–330.
Weil, S. (1957), "The *'Iliad'*, Poem of Might" in: Weil, *Intimations of Christianity among the Ancient Greeks*, London, 24–55.

Wickersham, J. (1994), *Hegemony and Greek Historians*, Lanham.
Wiesehöfer, J. (2009), "The Achaemenid Empire" in: *The Dynamics of Ancient Empires. State Power from Assyria to Byzantium*, I. Morris/W. Scheidel (eds), Oxford, 66–98.
Wiesehöfer, J. (2015), "Rulers by the Grace of God", Liar Kings", and Oriental Despots": (Anti)Monarchic Discourse in Achaemenid Iran" in: *Antimonarchic Discourse in Antiquity*, H. Börm (ed.), Stuttgart, 45–65.
Wood, N. (1964), "Xenophon's Theory of Leadership" in: *C&M* 25, 33–66.

Aggelos Kapellos
The Greek reaction to the slaughter of the Athenian captives at Aegospotami and Xenophon's *Hellenica*

In *Hell.* 2.1.30–32 Xenophon reports that Lysander after the battle of Aegospotami captured the Athenian fleet and executed the prisoners. Some scholars have doubted the historicity of the slaughter, while Wylie doubts it on the grounds that such a decision would shock the Greek world.[1] It is the purpose of this paper[2] to argue that Xenophon leads his readers to realize that the Greeks would not have reacted against the slaughter and simultaneously to contribute to our understanding of his work as history.[3]

First of all, I may remark that Xenophon clarifies in these chapters the problematic relation of the Athenians and the other Greeks before the naval battle of Aegospotami. The historian reports two main accusations against the Athenians, both that they had already violated custom and what they had voted to do if they were victorious (2.1.31). This refers to: 1) Philocles' decision to throw overboard the crews of one Corinthian and one Andrian ship, which he had captured, and 2) Philocles' decree that if the Athenians were victorious, they would cut off the right hand of anyone captured alive. Since the second accusation is connected with the amputation of the Greeks, the violation of the Greek custom must be the killing of the crews of the Corinthian and Andrian ship.[4] Why the killing of these

---
[1] Ehrhardt, 1970, 225–228 and Will, 1972, 228, do not accept the historicity of Xenophon's account and prefer Diodorus. For Wylie, 1986, 139. Krentz, 1989, 180 seems to sympathize with Wylie, but he does not make his position clear. For an opposite view see Strauss, 1983, 24–35, especially 32–34, Gray, 1987, 78–79, Bleckmann, 1998, 572–580, Welwei, 1999, 241. I side with the second opinion.
[2] I express my gratitude to Prof. P.J. Rhodes who commented on an earlier draft of this version. Moreover, I express my warm thanks to Prof. J. Marincola who read my paper.
[3] In my approach I accept the opinion of Gray, 1989, viii that *Hellenica* must be understood as a literary work on its own terms, but I dissent from her view that Xenophon was not interested in the historical accuracy of his work (cf. Rhodes, 1994, 167). Unless stated otherwise, all references are to the *Hellenica*.
[4] Thus, the verb παρενενομήκεσαν must be connected with κόπτειν τῶν ζωγρηθέντων πάντων, καὶ ὅτι λαβόντες δύο τριήρεις, Κορινθίαν καὶ Ἀνδρίαν, τοὺς ἄνδρας ἐξ αὐτῶν πάντας κατακρημνίσειαν. We are also led to this interpretation by the phrase ὃς τοὺς Ἀνδρίους καὶ Κορινθίους κατεκρήμνισε, which Krentz, 1989, 74, 76 keeps in his edition, while it had been deleted by Cobet.

crews was considered a Greek crime is not easy to explain, but comparing Xenophon with Thucydides who defines the killing of the Theban captives by the Plataians, despite the latter's promise not to do so, as a *παρανομία* (3.66.2) and the Plataians' argument to the Spartans that the killing of men who had surrendered on their own accord is forbidden by the Greek law (3.58.3-cf. Diod. 13.26.2), I suggest that the Athenians surrounded the Andrians and the Corinthians and promised them that if they surrendered, they would not kill them, while the latter accepted this as they had no other choice in order to survive. After that, however, Philocles killed them.[5] It is obvious that, because of this brutal deed, all those who supported Sparta in this war considered the killing of the crews an action against all Hellas, not just against Sparta. Thus, Xenophon's mention of the two accusations against Athens allows the readers to think that for Sparta's allies the execution of the captives was something more than retribution for Philocles' treatment of enemy naval crews. Instead, it would be justified to say that the allies considered that justice would be served through the killing of these prisoners; that is why the decision was unanimous.

For such a stance there is another reason. Xenophon reports that the Spartans and their allies decided not to kill the non-Athenian captives who were sailors, that is, they let them live: ἔδοξεν ἀποκτεῖναι τῶν αἰχμαλώτων ὅσοι ἦσαν Ἀθηναῖοι. In this way the victors of the sea-fight did not consider the slaves, the metics[6] and even the allies of Athens who served in her navy as responsible for the two crimes,[7] but most important they gave the impression that Sparta still fought for the liberation of Hellas against Athenian imperialism. My point comes from Thucydides whose work Xenophon continued.[8] He says that in the beginning of the war the feeling of mankind was strongly on the side of the Lacedaemonians, because they professed to be the liberators of Hellas, while the general indignation against the Athenians was intense (2.9), although many Greeks supported the latter (1.1.1-2). As the war progressed, the general negative opinion about Athens continued to exist. Thus, during the Sicilian war the Syracusans thought that by defeating the Athenians they would earn glory among the Greeks, because they would free some of them and release others from fear (7.56.2). After

---

[5] Since Xenophon does not give any further information, I can claim that what I have already said constitutes just a plausible guess, but certainly not a proof. For a different interpretation of Xenophon's passage see Panagopoulos, 1978, 176.

[6] For the participation of mercenaries and metics in the Athenian fleet see Amit, 1965, 30-49.

[7] Notice that Xenophon has already mentioned that although Methymna, which supported Athens, refused to join Callicratidas, when the latter conquered the city, he released all her citizens (1.6.13-15).

[8] See MacClaren, 1979, 231-233, Rood, 2004, 341.

the destruction of the fleet in Sicily the Athenians were afraid that their allies would revolt against them (8.1.1). Thucydides proves in his narrative later on that the aim of Athens' subjects was to become free (8.48.5, 64.3). Thus, when Lysander defeated the Athenians, *immediately* after the naval battle the rest of Greece revolted from the Athenians except for the Samians, as Xenophon tells us (2.2.6), a fact which proves the testimony of Thucydides that Athens' allies were eager to revolt on every possible opportunity.[9] The thematic link between the two accounts[10] indicates that not only Sparta's allies but also the allies of Athens were against her and exploited this event in order to acquire their freedom. It is noteworthy that although the Samians were the only Greeks who did not revolt from Athens, we cannot fail to see that Xenophon does not even mention their reaction, but focuses on the subversion of the constitution in the island. Given these pieces of information it is difficult to believe that the Greeks would care about the execution of the Athenian captives at Aegospotami.

Xenophon also allows us to think that the Greeks would have liked to destroy Athens itself by narrating the Athenian reaction after the defeat in the Hellespont, i.e. from the viewpoint of the defeated. Thus, he says that after the report of the defeat the Athenians mourned much more themselves than those lost in the seafight, because they believed that they would suffer the same things they had done to the Melians, the Hestiaeans, the Scionaeans, the Toroneans, the Aeginetans and many other Greeks (2.2.3), that is they had killed the men and enslaved the women and children.[11] This impression is strengthened by a new reference to the Aeginetans, the Melians and all the other Greeks, who returned to their cities due to Lysander (2.2.9), and the increasing fear of the Athenians that their initial thoughts about punishment from these Greeks would soon become reality (2.2.10). Then, we read a clear proof of the real desire of the Greeks towards Athens when Xenophon says that in an assembly held in Sparta 'the Corinthians and the Thebans particularly, but *many other Greeks as well* urged the destruction of Athens' (2.2.19). If our author does not mean only the allies of Sparta but also those Greeks who revolted from Athens after the sea-fight at Aegospotami, i.e. her

---

9 Cf. Hornblower, 2008, 652, who comments on Thuc. 7.56.2 that the historian makes a metaphor from the Panhellenic games in order to show that the Greeks were spectators of the conflict/contest between Syracuse and Athens. Their revolt shows whom they applauded after the end of the 'game'.
10 For other links between the two works see the study of Rood, 2004, 341–396. I am much indebted to his approach of interpretation of the two historians.
11 See Rood, 2004, 347–348.

former allies,[12] this means that *the entire* Greek world would not even care about what had happened in the Hellespont.

Thus, it is no surprise that Xenophon does not mention that there were discussions between the ordinary citizens or in the public assemblies of the Greek cities about the various killings that occurred during the war. The only discussions that took place were the discussions in *Athens* about the destruction at Syracuse (Thuc. 8.1.1–4) and Aegospotami (Xen. 2.2.3–4), but these cannot be considered as Panhellenic, because they took place only in this city and not throughout the Greek world. The only reference to an incident of this kind can be considered the destruction of Melos because of the unjustified aggression of the Athenians, but the testimonies are not contemporary to the event.[13] The only evidence for a destruction which became a Panhellenic subject, but not relevant to the Peloponnesian War, is the destruction of Thebes by Alexander in the fourth century. It is noteworthy that after the destruction of the city by the King of Macedon the Greeks of that time compared this with the destruction of the Athenians at Aegospotami, but Arrian[14] points out that the Athenians soon recovered their strength (*An.* 1.9.3) and does not make any reference to the fate of the captives. It seems that this historian knew that there was no reaction among the Greeks of the 5th century in regard to acts of violence and in particular in regard to the fate of the prisoners in the Hellespont, so he did not give any different information than that of Xenophon.[15]

Someone could argue that our author chose not to report the reaction of the Greeks to the slaughter in the Hellespont perhaps from Spartan bias or because he had not really considered the consequences of violence for the Greek world, but this does not do justice to him. Once again we must bear in mind Thucydides, who says in the beginning of his *History* that the Peloponnesian War was a struggle attended by calamities such as Hellas had never known within a like period of time and that never were so many cities captured and depopulated, never were exile and *slaughter* more frequent (1.23.1–3). In order to prove this he includes several incidents in his work, which demonstrated the Athenian and Spartan

---

[12] For this point see Rood, 2004, 349. Isocr. 8.78 and Andoc. 3.21 explicitly say that Athens' former allies participated in this meeting and that they asked for its destruction.
[13] For the subsequent references to the destruction of Melos see Panagopoulos, 1978, 123 n.5. For Athens' inhumanity see Panagopoulos, 1978, 122.
[14] See Arrian *An.* 1.9.1–5. Cf. Diod. 17.13.5–6, Hyp. 6. ll.7–17 (ed. Jensen).
[15] The line of thought is the same in regard to the fate of the Athenians in the Sicilian expedition (*An.* 1.9.3).

atrocities.[16] Xenophon, writing in a similar vein, includes his own examples which would make the reader realize what this war was. Thus, in 1.1.20 we read that when the Cyzicenes admitted the Athenians into their city, Alcibiades took a lot of money from them and sailed back to Proconnesus without doing *any other harm* in the city. This is an implicit approval of Alcibiades' decision not to harm these people, but the obligatory deposit of money was a bad deed in itself. In the description of the invasion of Lydia we learn that the Athenians burned many villages, captured money, slaves and a great deal of other booty (1.2.4). The treatment of captives appears for the first time in 1.2.14, where we read that the Syracusan prisoners were held in the stone quarries of Peiraeus by the Athenians. Phanosthenes later on captured two Thurian triremes with their crews, arrested all of them, but showed pity on their commander Dorieus and released him without ransom (1.5.19). Such behaviour was better of course than the killing of the captives, but Xenophon does not tell us if these men ended up in the stone quarries like the Syracusans, so it would be an exaggeration to say that they were 'lucky'. Dorieus was an exception to the rule, although Xenophon avoids reporting what made the Athenians let him go. Spartan behaviour was not better, since Callicratidas did not sell the Methymnians as slaves, but he did do that to the Athenians (1.6.14–15).[17] At this particular instance it is noteworthy that it was the Greeks who had allied with Sparta that urged the selling of the Methymnians.[18] Last, Lysander enslaved the people of Cedreiai, who were half-barbarians (2.1.15), captured Lampsacus, but released all the free persons whom he captured (2.1.19), probably for political reasons.[19] From this list it becomes evident that the plundering of an area, the enslavement of a city and the execution of prisoners create a climax. It is also obvious that the Athenians and the Spartans never treated each other in a humane way, so Xenophon's message was that feelings and emotions were running so high that violence tended to become a banal fashion, while when pity was shown it was all the more remarkable.[20] Concerning the slaughter at Aegospotami, it is noteworthy that Xenophon does not dwell on the horror of what

---

16 For the behaviour of the Spartans towards the other Greeks see Thuc. 2.67.4, 3.32.1, 3.52–68, 7.3.4, 7.53.3 with Panagopoulos, 1978, 20, 38–41, 52, 127, 130 respectively. For the behaviour of the Athenians see Thuc. 3.34, 4.57.4, 5.32.1, 7.29–30 with Panagopoulos, 1978, 21, 58–59, 98–105, 118–123. See also Price, 2001, 213–216.
17 For Callicratidas see Higgins, 1977, 11, Panagopoulos, 1978, 165–167, Krentz, 1989, 148.
18 For this issue see Proietti, 1987, 18.
19 See Proietti, 1987, 24–25.
20 Although the severe punishment of the Athenian generals in the trial of Arginousae (1.7.14, 20; cf. Rhodes' analysis of the trial in the present volume) and the punishment of Sparta's allies

happened there and gives no details of the killing, but this is not coldness or aloofness. Despite its restraint and detachment the narrative nevertheless provides some insight into Xenophon's own feelings about what happened. Thus, instead of narrating the whole event of the massacre he selects one striking example out of the mass, that is the killing of Philocles by Lysander, and by using the verb ἀπέσφαξεν for the latter and showing that the Spartan commander did not wait to receive a reply from his captured enemy, the historian wants to shock the reader.[21]

Moreover, it is important to note that when Xenophon mentions the decision for the slaughter he chooses to mention that there could be some Greeks who would disagree with extreme acts of violence, but he makes it clear that these men were the exception to the rule. Thus, he says that while the Athenians had voted Philocles' decree to amputate their prospective Spartan prisoners after the final battle, the Athenian general Adeimantus alone objected to this brutal measure, but nobody agreed with him. Instead, some of his fellow citizens accused him after the defeat of betraying the fleet, without taking into consideration that his resistance to the dispassionate judgment of his colleague saved his life.[22] In this way, the historian proves that he was sensitive and perceptive in detecting human reactions to violence and that he had no reason to omit the Greeks' reaction against the slaughter, if there would be one.[23]

If the readers, ancient and modern, want to read a good treatment of captives and an interest by a victor for the creation of a good name among the Greeks due to his behavior towards the defeated, they should turn their attention to Xenophon's *Agesilaus*. Our author says that the Spartan king *often* told his men not to punish their prisoners as criminals, but to guard them as human beings, and that as a result of this he won the goodwill not only of those who heard of these facts,

---

in Chios by Eteonicus (2.1.2–5) are also examples of violence, the first incident shows the violence within Athens itself, while the second indicates Sparta's treatment of her allies. Thus, since they are not related to the violent behaviour between the two enemies, I have not included them in my analysis.

21 These points belong to Proietti, 1987, 31. I may strengthen his second argument by citing Plut. *Lys.* 13.1, where Lysander called Philocles to the Congress of the allies and *asked* him a possible punishment for having advised his fellow citizens against the Greeks, and the latter bade him boldly not accuse him of matters of which nobody was a judge, but to do to him, now he was a conqueror, as he would have suffered, had he been overcome.

22 See Kapellos, 2009, 257–258.

23 For a similar case see Diod. 13.19–31, where the general Hermocrates and particularly Nicolaus, who had lost two sons in the Sicilian war, urged their fellow citizens in the Syracusan assembly not to sell the allies of the Athenians as booty and make the Athenians labour as prisoners under guard, but the Syracusans did the opposite after Gylippus's speech.

but even of the prisoners themselves (1.21–22). This passage is no doubt part of the encomiastic fabric of the biography, but it is noteworthy that even in this case Xenophon remains realistic, since he makes a distinction between the king and his men: while the former remained humane, he could not always stop the latter from maltreating the prisoners, so he had to intervene many times and impose discipline on them. More importantly, however, what matters is that the Greeks paid attention to the treatment of captives. Thus, Agesilaus' treatment of his captives becomes a panhellenic issue and as such, perhaps it reflects what Xenophon hoped would happen one day in Greece, but did not happen during the Peloponnesian War, which he narrated in the first part of the *Hellenica*.

In conclusion, a connection between Thucydides' and Xenophon's work and a careful reading of the *Hellenica* itself does not permit us to say that Xenophon has omitted the reaction of his fellow Greeks during the Peloponnesian War in regard to the massacre at Aegospotami. If there was indeed such a different response to the slaughter, it is certain that we have no evidence of it.

Bibliography

Amit, M. (1965), *Athens and the Sea*, Brussels.
Bleckmann, B. (1998), *Athens Weg in die Niederlage. Die letzen Jahre des Peloponesischen Kriegs*, Stuttgart/Leipzig.
Ehrhardt, C. (1970), "Xenophon and Diodorus on Aegospotami" in: *Phoenix* 24, 225–228.
Gray, V.J. (1987), "The value of Diodorus Siculus for the years 411–386 B.C." in: *Hermes* 115, 78–79.
Gray, V.J. (1989), *The Character of Xenophon's* Hellenica, London.
Higgins, W.E. (1977), *Xenophon the Athenian: The problem of the individual and the society of the polis*, Albany.
Hornblower, S. (2008), *A Commentary on Thucydides*, Vol. III, Books 5.25–8.109, Oxford.
Kapellos, A. (2009), "Adeimantos at Aegospotami: innocent or guilty?" in: *Historia* 58, 257–275.
Krentz, P. (1989), *Xenophon*, Hellenica I–II.3.10, Warminster.
McClaren, M. (1979), "A supposed lacuna at the beginning of Xenophon's *Hellenica*" in: *AJP* 100, 228–238.
Panagopoulos, A. (1978), *Captives and Hostages in the Peloponnesian War*, Athens.
Price, J.J. (2001), *Thucydides and Internal War*, Cambridge.
Proietti, G. (1974), *Xenophon's Sparta: An Introduction*, Berkeley.
Rhodes, P.J. (1994), "In Defence of the Greek Historians" in: *G&R* 41, 156–171.
Rood, T.C. (2004), "Xenophon and Diodorus: Continuing Thucydides" in: *Xenophon and his World*, C.J. Tuplin (ed.), Stuttgart, 341–396.
Strauss, B.S. (1983), "Aegospotami Reexamined" in: *AJP* 104, 24–35.
Welwei, K.-W. (1999), *Das Klassiche Athen*, Darmstadt.
Will, E. (1972), *Le monde grecque et l'orient: Le Ve siecle (510–403)*, Paris.
Wylie, G. (1986), "What really happened at Aegospotami?" in: *AC* 55, 125–141.

Andrew Wolpert
Xenophon on the Violence of the Thirty

Xenophon probably remained in Athens during the rule of the Thirty and may even have served in the cavalry, which included some of the oligarchs' staunchest supporters and helped carry out some of the regime's more brutal acts of violence. The cavalry was, as a result, targeted for recrimination by the victims of the Thirty after the democracy was restored in 403 BCE.[1] Yet Xenophon's depiction of the Thirty in the *Hellenica* does not differ substantially from that of Lysias, who armed the democratic resistance after narrowly escaping an arrest by the Thirty that would have certainly resulted in his execution. The *Athenaion Politeia* and Diodorus Siculus offer a similar assessment of the Thirty. And while they agree with Xenophon on the nature of the oligarchy, their chronologies differ in striking ways that have been the focus of many studies on the Thirty.[2]

Until recently, Xenophon has generally been preferred because he was an eyewitness to the events that he describes and because his former association with the oligarchs did not prevent him from exposing their atrocities.[3] However, scholars have increasingly raised questions about Xenophon's portrayal of the Thirty for placing the installation of the Spartan garrison too early in their rule, for overlooking or downplaying the importance of the constitutional reforms that the oligarchs wanted to implement, or for exaggerating Critias' influence over his fellow oligarchs. Xenophon is thought to have made Critias, in particular, and the Thirty, in general, appear more extreme, so he could distance himself and other moderate oligarchs from their rule.[4] Thus, it is thought that Xenophon does not provide an accurate account of the vision or the long-term goals of the Thirty because he disregards their political efforts to transform Athens. He merely depicts them as brutal tyrants seeking to exploit the Athenian defeat for their own personal gain.

---

1 For Xenophon's service in the cavalry of the Thirty see Dillery, 1995, 280 n. 68; Rhodes in this volume. For subsequent reprisals against the cavalry of the Thirty, see Bugh, 1988, 129–143.
2 See Hignett, 1952, 378–389; Adeleye, 1976; Rhodes, 1981, 415–422; Munn, 2000, 340–344. Although Justin's brief overview mostly follows Diodorus, there are enough differences to suggest that it is derived independently from Ephorus.
3 For Xenophon on civil war more generally, see Pownall in this volume.
4 On the installation of the Spartan garrison: Krentz, 1982, 132–147; Ostwald, 1986, 481–483; contra: Munn, 2000, 413 n. 15. On the constitutional reforms of the Thirty: Osborne, 2003, 262–266; Shear, 2011, 167–180; cf. Whitehead, 1982/83, 129–130, who suggests that the Thirty could not model Athens after Sparta without violent purges of the population that ultimately led to their overthrow. On Xenophon's negative portrayal of Critias see Pownall, 2012, Danzig, 2014.

Although the differences in the accounts may sometimes stem from the biases of the authors or their sources, they also derive from the purpose of the individual works. Some are due to the politics of the restored democracy as Athenians attempted to rehabilitate specific individuals, such as Theramenes, or groups that had remained in Athens during the rule of the Thirty, such as the Three Thousand, or to denounce the Thirty and their supporters for what they had done.[5] There are also some more mundane reasons for the differences, such as honest mistakes, accidental omissions, or the composition and transmission of the individual works. Still the sources do not depict the oligarchy in significantly different ways, and we run the risk of fetishizing the chronological discrepancies if we overlook these similarities. Individually, the oligarchs may have had political commitments and long-term goals that they wanted to pursue, but they could not do so because, as a group, they created a brutal and violent regime, which, as a result, lacked legitimacy and called into question the very ideals that they individually espoused.

By comparing Xenophon's narrative in the *Hellenica* with Lysias' speech against Eratosthenes and the account of the Thirty in the *Athenaion Politeia*, I will show that they are largely in agreement on the nature of the oligarchy.[6] It has been noted that Xenophon focuses on the brutality of the Thirty and views the oligarchy primarily as an example of a "failed community" that was morally bankrupt.[7] As an authoritarian regime that depended on terror and violence to maintain its rule, its inhumanity cannot help but stand out. Xenophon calls attention to the moral vices of the oligarchs to explain the corrosive effects of tyrannical power. Yet, he also shows how the Thirty attempted to divide the Athenian people in order to prevent the opposition from overthrowing them, and in the process, they forced many to be complicit in their crimes. By recounting the different ways in which the Athenians responded to the Thirty, Xenophon helps us better understand the divisions caused by the civil war that would threaten to disrupt the subsequent reconciliation.

---

5 Wolpert, 2002, 75–118.

6 It is unnecessary to include Diodorus in the review. He provides the most favorable portrayal of Theramenes by claiming that Theramenes opposed the overthrow of the democracy and was chosen to be a member of the Thirty in order to serve as a check on their power (14.4.1). Otherwise Diodorus' account is sometimes in agreement with Xenophon and at other times with the *Athenaion Politeia* without providing much additional information.

7 See especially, Dillery, 1995, 138–163; cf. Ostwald, 1986, 481–485; Gray, 1989, 95–106.

1 Lysias against Eratosthenes

The civil war appears prominently or is mentioned in passing in many of Lysias' speeches. However, Lysias provides the most detailed account of the Thirty in his speech against Eratosthenes, and it best illustrates how and why Lysias' portrayal of the Thirty differs from Xenophon's. As a former member of the Thirty, Eratosthenes had to submit to an *euthyna* in order to live in Athens under the restored democracy and enjoy the privileges of the amnesty. If he passed his *euthyna*, Eratosthenes would have been immune from prosecution for all offenses committed during the civil war except murder by his own hands (*autocheiria*). Although Lysias devotes much of his speech to proving that Eratosthenes caused the death of his brother, Polemarchus, he does not attempt to establish that the killing was *autocheiria*. The speech, therefore, was most likely intended for Eratosthenes' *euthyna*.[8] Because Lysias did not receive citizenship and it is uncertain whether a metic would have been permitted to speak at an *euthyna*, it is possible that Lysias did not deliver the speech in court and instead circulated it as a political pamphlet.[9] For our purposes, it does not matter whether an Athenian court ever heard the speech because Lysias clearly intended for the published version to resemble what he would have said if provided the opportunity to speak at Eratosthenes' *euthyna*.

Lysias begins by recounting his family's plight under the Thirty. Like Xenophon (2.3.12) and the *Athenian Politeia* (35.2–3), he describes how the Thirty began with measures that appeared reasonable. They promised to rid Athens of wrongdoers, so the rest of the citizens would be good and law-abiding. However, Lysias asserts that this was an empty promise by base men acting as sykophants, and he immediately moves on without indicating how their first actions were received (12.5). It is not surprising that he passes over the arrests of those citizens who were a threat to the rule of the Thirty and discusses instead their attacks on metics. Although Athenian law permitted any citizen to initiate a public suit, prosecutors tended to do so only if they had a grievance against the defendant, and they regularly discussed how they had a personal stake in the outcome of the case in order to mitigate the suspicion that they had ulterior motives and to prevent the defendant from accusing them of sykophancy.[10] Even a citizen would

---

8 Cloché, 1915, 310–312; Todd, 2007, 13–16; Phillips, 2008, 154–156; contra: Loening, 1981, 285–287. For the date of Lysias 12 see Bearzot, 1997, 42–44, 47–50, 227.
9 Carawan, 1998, 194–195, 376–377; cf. Todd, 2007, 14.
10 Hunter, 1994, 125–129; Christ, 1998, 118–159; Rubinstein, 2005.

have needed to explain his reasons for prosecuting Eratosthenes. As a metic, Lysias was under enormous pressure to avoid the appearance of overstepping his place, so he first acknowledges that the Thirty had harmed everyone in the city. Then after showing how his family had been loyal to Athens in order to win the goodwill of the jury and establish his right to speak to the Athenian people, he immediately proceeds to recount how Eratosthenes was responsible for his brother's death.

It is unclear from Lysias' speech at what point the Thirty devised their plan to arrest wealthy metics in order to finance their government. According to Xenophon, the arrests occurred shortly after the installation of the Spartan garrison because the Thirty needed to pay Sparta the costs of the military support (2.3.21). At a meeting of the Thirty, Peison and Theognis suggested that they accuse metics of opposing the regime and include two poor metics in the round up, so they could plausibly deny that they were arresting them for their money (Lys. 12.6). This concern over public opinion reveals that the arrests were conducted at a point when the Thirty were still concerned about the appearance of their actions. Lysias thus gives the impression that these arrests mark the beginning of their reign of terror. After agreeing to the plan, the Thirty divided up the metics and went to their houses. Several men seized Lysias while he was entertaining guests and handed him over to Peison, who immediately accepted a bribe of one talent to let him go. In spite of their agreement, Peison seized all the contents of a chest that he was shown. Eventually, Lysias was taken to another house where Theognis was keeping watch over some other men. Fearing that Theognis might not accept a bribe, Lysias decided to flee. His brother was not as fortunate. On his way to Polemarchus' house, Eratosthenes found him in the street and dragged him off to prison. Polemarchus was executed without a trial, and all his property was confiscated. Lysias makes the shocking claim that Melobius had the audacity to seize earrings that Polemarchus' wife happening to be wearing when he entered the house to confiscate their property. The Thirty were unwilling to spare any of Polemarchus' cloaks or allow his family to use any of his homes for his funeral (12.8–19). Although financial difficulties led the Thirty to arrest the metics, Lysias presents their abuse of political power as rooted in their immorality, which would also be the cause of their downfall.

For the remainder of the speech, Lysias anticipates the arguments that Eratosthenes will use to justify his arrest of Polemarchus and defend his conduct under Thirty. He expects Eratosthenes to mention his association with Theramenes and his participation in the rule of the Ten in order to support his assertions that he had opposed the extreme policies of the Thirty. Because Theramenes twice assisted in the overthrow of the democracy and was a member of both the Four

Hundred and the Thirty, it was easy to criticize him and by extension his associates. Yet, he also helped overthrow the Four Hundred, and his execution by the Thirty could be used as proof that he was also working to end their rule. So, after the civil war, it was sometimes useful for Athenians complicit in the crimes of the Thirty to depict Theramenes positively in order to justify their own actions while those seeking redress against these men would need to respond by disparaging him. These competing agendas help explain how such radically different traditions emerged and why Theramenes is presented so differently in the ancient literature.[11] However, Theramenes acquired a greater importance in the historical accounts of the civil war than the lawsuits of post-war Athens. Because the Thirty were formally excluded from the amnesty and many Athenians were not directly involved in their government, it would not help the case of most litigants to mention Theramenes. It would be better for them to deny involvement in the oligarchy than to claim that they had supported the policies of the so-called moderates.[12] So Lysias discusses Theramenes in his speeches against Eratosthenes and Agoratus, but he is not mentioned in the other speeches that concern the civil war.

In order to preempt Eratosthenes' defense, Lysias presents the oligarchs as united in their opposition to the democracy, and he maintains that the conflicts that arose between them during their rule stemmed from personal rivalries and private animosities, not because of different political views. He claims that Eratosthenes plotted with Critias to overthrow the democracy after the battle of Aegospotami. Calling themselves "ephors" and aided by three other members of their *hetaireia*, they prevented the assembly from passing motions that could have saved Athens. Loyal citizens who would have stopped the conspirators and preserved the democracy were arrested and subsequently executed.[13] At the same time, Theramenes worked with Lysander to force Athens to surrender and hand over the government to the Thirty, ten of whom were selected by him, ten by the so-called "ephors," and ten by the assembly (12.69–76). Lysias thus buffers the Athenians from blame for the defeat by collapsing the meeting of the assembly to accept Sparta's terms of surrender with the meeting to install the Thirty and by making the specious claim that oligarchic conspiracies were hatched shortly after the battle of Aegospotami.[14] This dubious account of the surrender is also intended to cast Theramenes in an unfavorable light, so the jury is less likely to be

---

11 For the Theramenes myth, see Merkelbach and Youtie, 1968; Henrichs, 1968; Andrewes, 1970; Harding, 1974; Engels, 1993.
12 E.g., Lys. 16.4–5; 25.5–14. See Kapellos, 2014 for Lysias 16 and Murphy, 1992 for Lysias 25.
13 Lys. 12.43–49; cf. 13.20–36.
14 Wolpert, 2002, 120–129; see also Roisman, 2006, 72–85.

sympathetic to Theramenes as Lysias recounts his confrontation with Critias. Although the oligarchs executed him, Lysias insists Theramenes was put to death because they feared he would betray them, not because he was working to help the *demos* (12.77–78). Yet, Lysias fails to explain how Theramenes could betray the oligarchs unless he intended to restore the democracy.

Lysias had greater difficulty challenging Eratosthenes for his membership on the Ten than for his conduct under the Thirty because of the intended audience of the speech. On the one hand, it was easy to call into question the motives and actions of the Ten. They had requested troops from Sparta and asked for Lysander to be sent to Athens to serve as its harmost, so they could defeat the democratic exiles who had just gained control of the Peiraeus (12.59). On the other hand, many of the jurors had remained in Athens during the civil war. They had expelled the Thirty and elected the Ten. Although they could claim that they did not support the Thirty, they had greater difficulty denying that they had supported the Ten. So, if Lysias criticized the Ten in order to discredit Eratosthenes, he would be discrediting these jurors and would be implying that they had supported the oligarchy and only reluctantly accepted a reconciliation with the democratic exiles because of Pausanias' intervention. To avoid alienating them, Lysias claims that they had elected men to serve on the Ten, whom they believed were hostile to Critias and Charicles, but the Ten misled the men of the city and continued the fighting against their wishes. The civil war only ended after Sparta stopped supporting the oligarchs and interceded by brokering a peace between the warring factions.[15] Some of Lysias' assertions about the surrender, the trial of Theramenes, and the election of the Ten are dubious, intended mainly to discredit Eratosthenes and avoid alienating the jury. The exigencies of the *euthyna* required these conceits. Yet, his depiction of the Thirty as morally bankrupt individuals, who committed atrocities against the Athenian people, matches the description of their rule found in the other sources.

2 The *Athenaion Politeia*

The *Athenaion Politeia* differs from the other accounts mainly because it focuses, for obvious reasons, on constitutional developments and because it provides the fullest account of the reconciliation agreement. Other than Diodorus, it provides the most favorable assessment of Theramenes by presenting him as an opponent

---

15 Lys. 12.54–56, 60–61.

of the extreme policies of the other oligarchs even before the Thirty gained control of Athens and by distancing him from some of the more brutal acts of the oligarchy. It is likely that this positive portrayal of Theramenes is derived from the apologetic tradition that emerged after the restoration of the democracy as discussed above, and it may reflect some of the biases of that tradition. In contrast to Lysias, who insists that the Thirty gained control of Athens by secretly conspiring against the democracy even before the battle of Aegospotami, the *Athenaion Politeia* leaves the impression that the debate over the future of the democracy was conducted openly in public and without the conspirators needing to resort to the kind of violence depicted in Lysias.

Although the *Athenaion Politeia* claims that the Athenians surrendered to Sparta on the condition that they restore their ancestral constitution (34.3), it was likely that such a clause, if included in the peace treaty, was intended to guarantee Athens its autonomy and grant the Athenians the right to observe their ancestral laws. Debate over the constitution probably did not occur until after the surrender when the oligarchs used the terms of the peace to justify the changes that they were advocating.[16] The *Athenaion Politeia* remains problematic because it has Theramenes working with respectable citizens (ἄλλως δὲ δοκοῦντες οὐδενὸς ἐπιλείπεσθαι τῶν πολιτῶν) to restore the ancestral constitution, and it has him at odds with those men who had returned from exile and who were working with the *hetaireiai* to install an oligarchy. None of the individuals aligned with Theramenes became members of the Thirty. Archinus and Anytus, whom *the Athenian Politeia* specifically lists as Theramenes' associates, even later joined the democratic exiles. This makes Theramenes inclusion in the oligarchy puzzling. The *Athenaion Politeia* fails to explain why Lysander sided with the oligarchs, and therefore against Theramenes who had brokered the Athenian surrender, or why Theramenes joined the Thirty when he had initially opposed their plans and had even sided with men who clearly favored democracy.[17]

These difficulties are mitigated if the Thirty were appointed to draft new laws, as Xenophon states, or additionally to act as a provisional government until the new laws that they drafted were passed, as explained in Diodorus.[18] Although the defeat to Sparta may have caused some Athenians to rethink the merits of the democracy, the *Athenaion Politeia* suggests the Thirty feigned their own interest in restoring the ancestral constitution, so they could gain control of Athens. Once

---

16 Hignett, 1952, 285; Fuks, 1953, 52–58; Ostwald, 1986, 458; contra: McCoy, 1975, 133–141; Cartledge, 1987, 280–281.
17 Adeleye, 1976, 13.
18 Xen. *Hell.* 2.3.11; Diod. 14.3.7–4.1.

in power, they appointed councilors and some other magistrates, but they ignored the other instructions. They did, however, select the Eleven to oversee the prisons and three hundred lash bearers to serve as their attendants (*Ath. Pol.* 35.1). These moves were clearly intended to protect the Thirty against the opposition, which they expected to develop in response to their next actions, and are reminiscent of Peisistratus, who used club bearers to establish his first tyranny (*Ath. Pol.* 14.1). For the *Athenaion Politeia*, a real debate was taking place in Athens over the ancestral constitution after the Athenian surrender to Sparta, but it was hijacked by the Thirty, who used the political turmoil plaguing Athens to seize control of the city. In this account, Theramenes' involvement is only understandable if he was co-opted by the Thirty to mislead the Athenians about their goals and ambitions and to make it easier for them to seize greater power before the opposition could unite to stop them.

Tab. 1: The Rule of the Thirty in the Account of the *Athenaion Politeia*

Stage	Passage
1. After their election, the Thirty appoint councilors, the Eleven, and three hundred lash bearers, but they ignore the other instructions.	35.1
2. The Thirty abolish the laws of Ephialtes and controversial Solonian laws, remove ambiguities from some of the other laws, and prosecute sykophants.	35.2
3. The Thirty extend their prosecutions to include distinguished citizens and anyone who might challenge their rule.	35.3
4. Theramenes objects to how the Thirty rule Athens. The Thirty first ignore his criticism, but then make a list of Three Thousand to participate in their government. Theramenes objects to the limited number. Ignoring Theramenes' objections, the Thirty delay publishing the list of the Three Thousand.	36.1–2
5. After Thrasybulus and a band of democratic exiles seize Phyle, the Thirty pass two laws so they can execute Theramenes.	37.1
6. The Thirty disarm the Athenians, become more violent, and receive a Spartan garrison under the command of Callibius.	37.2
7. The democratic exiles defeat the Thirty at Munichia. The men of the city depose the Thirty and elect the Ten.	38.1

For the *Athenaion Politeia*, the violence escalated once the true intentions of the Thirty became known. As they resorted to violence because they did not have a legitimate agenda that they were seeking to promote, opposition and fear of opposition increased, which caused a further escalation in violence (see Table 1). The Thirty began by tearing down the laws of Ephialtes that stood on *stelai* before the Areopagus, by removing some "controversial" laws of Solon, and by limiting the ability of dikasts to interpret the laws (35.2).[19] They then purged the city of base politicians who had won the goodwill of the people but were up to no good (35.3: τοὺς τῷ δήμῳ πρὸς χάριν ὁμιλοῦντας παρὰ τὸ βέλτιστον καὶ κακοπράγμονας ὄντας καὶ πονηρούς). According to the *Athenaion Politeia*, these first measures were well received because the men killed by the Thirty were regarded as sykophants. However, once these politicians were removed, the Thirty then prosecuted whomever they thought could challenge their rule, or simply because they wanted their property. Their targets included Athenians distinguished for their birth, wealth, or reputation, so by the end of their rule they had killed more than 1,500 people (35.4). The reader of the *Athenaion Politeia* is left with the impression that the Thirty intentionally—and from the start—sought to rule Athens narrowly.[20] They feigned an interest in reforming Athenian law, so they could first isolate the democratic leadership, which would naturally be the first to oppose them. They then went after respectable Athenians, who might be expected to support their cause if allowed to participate and would not be content to be left out of their government.

Although the *Athenaion Politeia* presents Theramenes as an obstacle to the Thirty, in the short term he actually helped them by preventing the opposition from growing. Because Theramenes wanted to expand the government and, according to the *Athenaion Politeia*, his wishes were known to and had the support of the people (36.1), there was still the hope that the government could change peacefully. The Thirty, however, were not interested in allowing more Athenians to participate in their government. They promised to create a roll of three thousand citizens, but again their promises were empty. They kept delaying, and Theramenes continued with his objections to no avail. He insisted that the number was too small, and he warned the Thirty that they needed to expand the roll of citizens if they were to remain in power (36.1–2). It was only a matter of time until a clash with Theramenes would happen.

---

19 The Thirty presumably removed or corrected Solonian laws that were ambiguous to restrict the powers of the court, which were regarded as the hallmark of the democracy; cf. *Ath. Pol.* 9.2. For their efforts to rid the landscape of monuments celebrating the Athenian democracy, see Shear, 2011, 175–180.

20 The *Athenaion Politeia* even refers the Thirty as a *dunasteia* (36.1), which is a narrow authoritarian regime that must rely primarily on force to maintain its rule because it lacks legitimacy by restricting participation in the government to the narrow circle of leaders (cf. Ostwald, 2000, 25–26). The *dunasteia*, therefore, differs significantly from other forms of oligarchy, which often attempt to maintain power through both the repression and "co-optation" of the opposition (Simonton, 2017a, 107–147).

Once the Athenian exiles seized Phyle under the leadership of Thrasybulus, the Thirty were forced to act. If they expanded the government, there was the possibility that they could maintain their power, but Theramenes would most likely assume greater influence at the expense of his colleagues, and there was no guarantee that changes to their government would be enough to curtail the growing opposition. The Thirty chose instead to prevent Theramenes from challenging them. This time they had the council pass two laws that expanded their power and restricted the rights of everyone else. The first gave them the power of life and death over any person who was not enrolled in the Three Thousand. The second removed from the Three Thousand anyone who had helped demolish the fortifications of Eetionia or remove the Four Hundred (37.1).[21] It would be wrong to dismiss the second law as a thinly-veiled rhetorical attack on Theramenes or a hollow justification for their actions against him. Theramenes had sided with the enemies of the Four Hundred as they were facing increasing pressure from the opposition.[22] The Thirty were in a similar situation, and they had good reason to believe that he would do the same again in light of his criticism.

After they had Theramenes executed and had used the council to grant themselves even greater power, the Thirty could no longer disguise the nature of their rule or pretend that they would eventually allow more Athenians to participate in their government. Instead they more blatantly increased their control of Athens by disarming everyone except the Three Thousand. They requested and received a garrison from Sparta under the command of Callibius (37.2). The *Athenaion Politeia* does not mention the rounding up of the inhabitants of Eleusis and Salamis, but these massacres must also be dated to this final period of their rule. This sequence of events has the effect of removing Theramenes from the narrative before the more brutal acts of the regime (see Table 2).[23]

The *Athenaion Politeia*, for the most part, follows the same narrative as Lysias for the removal of the Thirty and the election of the Ten. However, the *Athenaion Politeia* states that the men of the city deposed the Ten for failing to peacefully end the war as instructed, and they elected another board of Ten, who made overtures to the men of Peiraeus even before the arrival of Pausanias (38.1–3). Although the second board of Ten should not be doubted simply because the other

---

[21] The *Athenaion Politeia* neglects to mention that the Thirty must have published the list of Three Thousand before they had the council pass the law that removed Theramenes from the Three Thousand.
[22] On the overthrow of the Four Hundred: Wolpert, 2017, 187–188. Teegarden, 2012; 2013, 17–53 places too much weight on the assassination of Phrynichus and overlooks the panic that occurred in Athens after Euboea revolted.
[23] Adeleye, 1976, 17–18; Rhodes, 1981, 422.

sources do not mention it, the *Athenaion Politeia* tends to place too much weight on constitutional maneuvers and legal proceedings to explain the developments of the civil war.[24] Since the second board lends credibility to claims about the Three Thousand wanting to restore the exiles, it is surprising that Lysias fails to mention the two boards of Ten when he praises the men of the city for their opposition to the Thirty. The second board seems doubtful because it provides a solution that is too convenient to the difficult questions about the role of the Three Thousand in ending the civil war. Perhaps Lysias and the *Athenaion Politeia* are misrepresenting the motives of the Three Thousand. They may have deposed the Thirty and elected the Ten because they had lost confidence in the ability of the Thirty to defeat the exiles. This would explain why the men of the city allowed the Thirty to retreat to Eleusis and why the Ten sought additional aid from Sparta and expanded their military operations immediately after their election.[25]

3 Xenophon's *Hellenica*

Although there are some notable differences in the chronologies of Xenophon and the *Athenaion Politeia* (see Table 2), the violence of the Thirty follows a similar trajectory in both accounts.[26] The Thirty become bolder as they accumulate greater power, and as their violence escalates, the opposition grows, causing them to resort further to violence. Theramenes is unsuccessful in his attempts to restrain his colleagues, and he is killed so he cannot hinder the Thirty from ruling as they please (2.3.23: οἱ δ' ἐμποδὼν νομίζοντες αὐτὸν εἶναι τῷ ποιεῖν ὅ τι βούλοιντο). Xenophon, however, is more equivocal in his assessment of Theramenes, and he provides a more vivid account of the violence perpetrated by the Thirty. Where the *Athenaion Politeia* emphasizes how the Thirty gained greater power first through deception and dissimulation and increasingly relied on violence once they could no longer conceal their goals, Xenophon shows how they

---

24 For the authenticity of the second board of the Ten, see Rhodes, 1981, 459–460.
25 Cloché, 1916.
26 According to the *Athenaion Politeia*, the violence escalated after Thrasybulus seizes Phyle. However, this does not mean that the Thirty ruled moderately until Thrasybulus launched his campaign to overthrow them or that the regime had a "good" and "bad" period. Even in the *Athenaion Politeia*, the reign of terror began once the regime extended the arrests beyond the so-called sykophants to include anyone who might oppose them, and these arrests occurred long before Thrasybulus seized Phyle (see Table 1).

co-opted the opposition and potential opposition by making Athenians complicit in their atrocities. He also includes speeches of the partisans and combatants of the warring factions to punctuate key moments in the civil war: the trial and execution of Theramenes (2.3.20–56), the mass conviction of the Eleusinians (2.4.9), the battle of Munichia (2.4.12–17, 20–22), and the victory procession of the democratic exiles (2.4.40–42). These speeches make the civil war less abstract and more personal than the *Athenaion Politeia*. By drawing in high relief the values and beliefs of the individuals who led the oligarchs and the democratic exiles, Xenophon emphasizes the moral implications of the conflict.

Tab. 2: Sequence of Events[27]

Xenophon, *Hellenica* 2	*Athenaion Politeia*
1. Arrival of the Spartan garrison (3.14).	1. Democrats seize Phyle (37.1).
2. Disarming of Athenians (3.21–22).	2. Trial of Theramenes (37.1).
3. Trial of Theramenes (3.23–56).	3. Disarming of Athenians (37.2)
4. Democrats seize Phyle (4.2).	4. Arrival of the Spartan garrison (37.2).

Xenophon provides less information than Lysias or the *Athenian Politeia* on the events leading up to the election of the Thirty. It has been suggested that Xenophon fails to mention Lysander's involvement in the overthrow of the democracy to avoid presenting him in a negative light.[28] However, he later describes how Lysander supported the oligarchs after the atrocities that they had committed and in spite of Pausanias supporting the democratic exiles (2.4.28–30). There is an interpolation at the beginning of Book 2, and Xenophon's discussion on the election of the Thirty is particularly compressed. These omissions, therefore, are probably not because of the author's biases, but the composition of the work. Still Xenophon fails to provide sufficient context for the initial stage of their rule that could help his reader understand the reasons for their first measures.

Like Lysias and the *Athenaion Politeia*, Xenophon mentions how the Thirty began their rule by arresting individuals whom they accused of sykophancy. Xenophon explains how many in the city approved of the arrests, but in contrast to

---

[27] Adapted from Adeleye, 1976, 17. The main difference in these chronologies is the placement of Theramenes in the escalation of violence and rising opposition. Both Xenophon and the *Athenaion Politeia* show the regime becoming increasingly more violent and the opposition increasing as the violence escalates (see Tables 1 and 3).

[28] See, for example, Krentz, 1995, 122–123.

the *Athenaion Politeia*, he qualifies this approval (2.3.12: οἵ τε ἄλλοι ὅσοι συνῄδεσαν ἑαυτοῖς μὴ ὄντες τοιοῦτοι οὐδὲν ἤχθοντο). Because Xenophon also indicates that the Thirty delayed enacting the legislation that they were appointed to draft (2.3.11), their request for a Spartan garrison so early in their rule is internally logical to his account (see Table 3). The Thirty had good reason to believe they would encounter resistance. Because they eliminated supporters of the democracy who were easy targets and were likely to oppose their rule, these actions caused other Athenians to worry that they might be next, and the Thirty failed to take the necessary steps to win over those Athenians who might be sympathetic to their cause.

So, after receiving the Spartan garrison, the Thirty widened the scope of arrests and continued to purge the city of possible opposition (2.3.14–15).[29] In the early clashes between Theramenes and Critias, Xenophon presents their arguments in stark terms that echo the language used in the Mytilenean debate and the Melian dialogue to describe the Athenian empire (Thuc. 3.37–40, 5.84–114). Critias tells Theramenes that he is foolish if he fails to recognize that their government is a tyranny simply because they are thirty and not one (2.3.16: εἰ δε, ὅτι τριάκοντά ἐσμεν καὶ οὐχ εἷς, ἧττόν τι οἴει ὥσπερ τυραννίδος ταύτης τῆς ἀρχῆς χρῆναι ἐπιμελεῖσθαι, εὐήθης εἶ). Theramenes warns Critias that they make themselves weaker if they continue to limit the number of people who enjoy privileges under their rule and continue to use force against subjects who outnumber them (2.3.19).

Tab. 3: The Rule of the Thirty in Book 2 of Xenophon's *Hellenica*

Stage	Passage
1. After the demolition of the Long Walls and the walls of the Peiraeus, the Thirty are elected to frame a new constitution.	3.11
2. The Thirty delay passing legislation, but they appoint councilors and other magistrates. They arrest sykophants, and the council condemns them.	3.12
3. The Thirty request and receive a Spartan garrison commanded by Callibius.	3.13
4. The Thirty arrest people who might oppose them. Theramenes objects.	3.14–15
5. As opponents to the Thirty begin to gather, the Thirty create a roll of Three Thousand citizens. Theramenes objects to the limited number.	3.17–19

---

29 Xenophon leaves his reader with the impression that the arrests of metics occurred after the execution of Leon and Niceratus; see Kapellos, 2018, 54–55.

Stage	Passage
6. The Thirty disarm the unprivileged and arrest metics to pay for the cost of the Spartan garrison. Theramenes objects to the new round of violence.	3.20–22
7. Theramenes is placed on trial and executed.	3.23–56
8. Violence increases after Theramenes' execution. All except the Three Thousand are prohibited from entering the city.	4.1
9. A band of Athenian exiles led by Thrasybulus seize Phyle and defeat the Thirty in battle.	4.2–3
10. The Thirty round up the Eleusinians to secure a place for retreat and force the infantry and cavalry to condemn them to death.	4.8–10
11. At the battle of Munichia, the Thirty are defeated and Critias is killed. The men of the city depose the Thirty and elect the Ten.	4.10–23

The reader cannot help but be sympathetic to Theramenes because of the way Xenophon portrays him at his trial and execution and for standing up to Critias who is depicted in the worst possible light. In the *Athenaion Politeia*, the Thirty pass two news laws in order to execute Theramenes. In Xenophon, Critias prosecutes Theramenes because he assumed that he would have no trouble convincing the council to convict him. However, the council actually applauded when Theramenes ended his speech, so Critias was forced to end the trial to prevent an acquittal. He then struck Theramenes' name from the roll of the Three Thousand so the Thirty did not need the council's consent to execute him (2.3.50–51). In the *Athenaion Politeia*, the Thirty must be devious and manipulative to execute Theramenes, but his execution is carried out without any opposition. In Xenophon, Critias must station guards before the council after expelling Theramenes from the Three Thousand to prevent the council from stopping the execution. Theramenes was praiseworthy in as much as Critias and his colleagues considered him a threat to their rule and because they were willing to take whatever steps were necessary to eliminate him.

At the same time, the trial also draws attention to Theramenes' weaknesses and raises questions about his character. Critias mentions Theramenes' role in the trial of the generals after the battle of Arginusae. He accuses Theramenes of being a traitor and reminds the council that he received the nickname *kothornos* for working to overthrow the democracy and then for helping to remove the Four Hundred and restore the democracy. Critias insists that Theramenes does not have serious political convictions. He merely does whatever it takes to serve his own interests (2.3.24–34). Since many of these criticisms echo those in Lysias, it would be wrong to dismiss them in Xenophon merely because they are spoken by Critias and failed to sway the council. Xenophon still allows them to appear in his work, and they impact how his reader perceives Theramenes' reply. Although Xenophon ends his discussion of Theramenes by praising him for the lighthearted manner in which he accepted his death (2.3.56: ἐκεῖνο δὲ κρίνω τοῦ ἀνδρὸς ἀγαστόν, τὸ τοῦ θανάτου παρεστηκότος μήτε τὸ φρόνιμον μήτε τὸ παιγνιῶδες ἀπολιπεῖν ἐκ τῆς ψυχῆς), Xenophon does not praise him for his political convictions or for what he had done to protect Athens and help his fellow citizens. Theramenes certainly appears better than Critias at the trial, but he falls far short of Thrasybulus who has the last word in Xenophon's account of the civil war and who best demonstrates what it means to be a good citizen (2.4.40–42).

After Theramenes' execution, the violence continued to escalate just as in Lysias and the *Athenaion Politeia*. However, Xenophon reveals how the Thirty made the Three Thousand complicit in their murders and how this in turn created dissension among the men of the city even after the Thirty had been deposed and the Ten elected. Critias' plan to have the council approve Theramenes' execution may have backfired, but it taught him an important lesson, which he used to carry out the execution of the Eleusinians. First, he had the cavalry arrest the residents of Eleusis. Then the Thirty summoned the cavalry and hoplites to the Odeum, which was stationed with guards. Critias demanded that they condemn the Eleusinians in order to prove their loyalty, and they ordered Lysimachus, a hipparch, to deliver the prisoners to the Eleven (3.4.8–10). The troops were forced to be present and to declare their consent, so they could not later claim that had attempted to stop the Thirty from carrying out the murders.

After the battle of Munichia, the men of the city deposed the Thirty and agreed to the election of the Ten, but they were at odds with each other. Some wanted to end the war because they had not participated in the crimes of the regime. Others were aware of their guilt and feared reprisals should the democrats be restored (2.4.23). Thus, in contrast to the accounts of Lysias and the *Athenaion Politeia*, the Ten did not contravene their instructions. Xenophon shows that there were divisions within the ranks of the men of the city, and at least some of them wanted to continue the war because they feared retaliation. This makes more sense than to believe that the Ten duped the men of the city. After the Thirty retired to Eleusis, these fears remained and caused the atrocities to continue. The cavalry conducted patrols in Attica to prevent the men of Peiraeus from securing resources. When Lysimachus came upon residents from Aexone, he killed all of them in spite of the protests of many in the cavalry. This act caused the men of Peiraeus to retaliate by killing a knight whom they had captured (2.4.26–27). Once the violence began, it was not easy to stop.

4 Conclusion

Authoritarian regimes are inherently violent. As Dahl explains:

> Since all opposition is potentially dangerous, no distinction can be made between acceptable and unacceptable opposition, between loyal and disloyal opposition, between opposition that is protected and opposition that must be repressed. Yet if all oppositions are treated as dangerous and subject to repression, opposition that would be loyal if it were tolerated becomes disloyal because it is not tolerated. Since all opposition is likely to be disloyal, all opposition must be repressed.[30]

It is irrelevant whether the Thirty requested the Spartan garrison after they assumed power as reported by Xenophon or they waited until after the democrats seized Phyle as stated in the *Athenaion Politeia*. Repression and opposition were inevitable once the Thirty refused to extend power beyond a narrow clique of individuals. One must avoid fetishizing the chronological narratives of the ancient sources. Violence was systemic to their rule.[31] Modern studies have also shown how violence has a constitutive force for authoritarian regimes. These regimes use violence to terrorize the population. Through violence, they attempt to isolate, silence, and traumatize the population so it loses the will to fight back and must passively accept its new role as political subject.[32] Of course, violence does not occur only in authoritarian regimes, and there are differences in the methods and modes of violence that states employ to assert and maintain its control. One could draw distinctions about structural, physical, and symbolic violence perpetrated by states that would extend beyond the focus of this study. So, there are also differences in the ways in which states voluntarily restrain, restrict and put limits on themselves. Regimes of violence set no limits on their power or their authority over the population that they rule. Anyone for any reason can be subjected to their violence. Justice and legality are irrelevant. Terror defines such regimes in much the same way as the rule of law defines democracies.

Modern authoritarian regimes are frequently totalitarian, and therefore differ significantly from authoritarian regimes of ancient Greece, but their use of violence corresponds in important ways to that of the Thirty. They disarmed the population, banned the unprivileged from the city, hindered their victims from burying their dead, and tore down landmarks of the democracy. They made a mockery of democratic laws and procedures, illegally invaded people's homes,

---

30 Dahl, 1971, 13. For ancient Greece see Simonton, 2017b.
31 Wolpert, 2006.
32 Corradi, 1982; O'Donnell, 1986; Perelli, 1994.

killed their opponents without trials, and forced Athenians to become complicit in their atrocities. They violated practically all traditional norms that ancient Greeks generally embraced regardless of whether they supported democracy or oligarchy. This is why Xenophon's language to describe their actions is so stark. We cannot expect him to use the vocabulary of a modern political scientist. Instead he used ancient Greek political terminology to describe their actions and concluded that their turn to violence was evidence of their moral weaknesses. Critias perhaps perhaps voices this best. Although they were thirty, their regime was nonetheless a tyranny.

Bibliography

Adeleye, G. (1976), "Theramenes: The End of a Controversial Career" in: *MusAfr* 5, 9–22.
Andrewes, A. (1970), "Lysias and the Theramenes Papyrus" in: *ZPE* 6, 35–38.
Bearzot, C. (1997), *Lisia e la tradizione suTeramene: Commento storico alle orazioni XII e XIII del corpus lysiacum*, Milan.
Bugh, G. (1988), *The Horsemen of Athens*, Princeton.
Carawan, E. (1998), *Rhetoric and the Law of Draco*, Oxford.
Cartledge, P. (1987), *Agesilaos and the Crisis of Sparta*, Baltimore.
Christ, M.R. (1998), *The Litigious Athenian*, Baltimore.
Cloché, P. (1915), *La restauration démocratique à Athènes en 403 avant J.-C.*, Paris.
Cloché, P. (1916), "Les Trois-Mille et la restauration démocratique à Athènes en 403" in: *REG* 29, 14–28.
Corradi, J.E. (1982), "The Mode of Destruction: Terror in Argentina" in: *Telos* 54, 61–76.
Dahl, R.A. (1971), *Polyarchy: Participation and Opposition*, New Haven.
Danzig, G. (2014), "The Use and Abuse of Critias: Conflicting Portraits in Plato and Xenophon" in: *CQ* 64, 507–24.
Dillery, J. (1995), *Xenophon and the History of His Times*, London.
Engels, J. (1993), "Der Michigan-Papyrus über Theramenes und die Ausbildung des 'Theramenes-Mythos'" in: *ZPE* 99, 125–155.
Fuks, A. (1953), *The Ancestral Constitution*, London.
Gray, V. (1989), *The Character of Xenophon's* Hellenica, Baltimore.
Harding, P. (1974), "The Theramenes Myth" in: *Phoenix* 28, 101–111.
Henrichs, A. (1968), "Zur Interpretation des Michigan-Papyrus über Theramenes" in: *ZPE* 3, 101–108.
Hignett, C. (1952), *A History of the Athenian Constitution to the End of the Fifth Century B.C.*, Oxford.
Hunter, V. (1994), *Policing Athens: Social Control in the Attic Lawsuits, 420–320 B.C.*, Princeton.
Kapellos, A. (2014), "In Defence of Mantitheus: Structure, Strategy and Argumentation in Lysias 16" in: *BICS* 57, 22–46.
Kapellos, A. (2018), "Lysias Interrogating Eratosthenes on the Murder of Polemarchus (Lys. XII,25)" in: *Erga-Logoi* 6, 51–64.
Krentz, P. (1982), *The Thirty at Athens*, Ithaca.

Krentz, P. (1995), *Xenophon:* Hellenika II.3.11–IV.2.8, Warminster.
Loening T.C. (1981), "The Autobiographical Speeches of Lysias and the Biographical Tradition" in: *Hermes* 109, 280–294.
McCoy, W.J. (1975), "Aristotle's *Athenaion Politeia* and the Establishment of the Thirty Tyrants" in: *YCS* 23, 131–145.
Merkelbach, R./Youtie, H.C. (1968), "Ein Michigan-Papyrus über Theramenes" in: *ZPE* 2, 161–169.
Munn, M.H. (2000), T*he School of History: Athens in the Age of Socrates*, Berkeley.
Murphy, T. (1992), "Lysias 25 and the Intractable Democratic Abuses" in: *AJP* 113, 543–548.
O'Donnell, G. (1986), "On the Fruitful Convergences of Hirschman's Exit, Voice, and Loyalty and Shifting Involvements: Reflections from the Recent Argentine Experience" in: *Development, Democracy, and the Art of Trespassing: Essays in Honor of Albert O. Hirschman*, A. Foxley, M.S. McPherson/G. O'Donnell (eds), 249–268, Notre Dame.
Osborne, R. (2003), "Changing the Discourse" in: *Popular Tyranny: Sovereignty and its Discontents in Ancient Greece*, K.A. Morgan (ed.), 251–272, Austin.
Ostwald, M. (1986), *From Popular Sovereignty to the Sovereignty of Law: Law, Society, and Politics in Fifth-Century Athens*, Berkeley.
Ostwald, M. (2000), *Oligarchia: The Development of a Constitutional Form in Ancient Greece*, Stuttgart.
Perelli, C. (1994), "*Memoria de Sangre*: Fear, Hope, and Disenchantment in Argentina" in: *Remapping Memory: The Politics of Timespace*, J. Boyarin (ed.), 39–66, Minneapolis.
Phillips, D.D. (2008), *Avengers of Blood: Homicide in Athenian Law and Custom from Draco to Demosthenes*, Stuttgart.
Pownall, F. (2012), "Critias in Xenophon's *Hellenica*" in: *SCI* 31, 1–17.
Rhodes, P.J. (1981), *A Commentary on the Aristotelian* Athenaion Politeia, Oxford.
Roisman, J. (2006), *The Rhetoric of Conspiracy in Ancient Athens*, Berkeley.
Rubinstein, L. (2005), "Differentiated Rhetorical Strategies in the Athenian Courts" in: *The Cambridge Companion to Ancient Greek Law*, M. Gagarin/D. Cohen (eds), 129–145, Cambridge.
Shear, J.L. (2011), *Polis and Revolution: Responding to Oligarchy in Classical Athens*, Cambridge.
Simonton, M. (2017a), *Classical Greek Oligarchy: A Political History*, Princeton.
Simonton, M. (2017b), "Stability and Violence in Classical Greek Democracies and Oligarchies" in: *CA* 36, 52–103.
Teegarden, D.A. (2012), "The Oath of Demophantos, Revolutionary Mobilization, and the Preservation of the Athenian Democracy" in: *Hesperia* 81, 433–465.
Teegarden, D.A. (2013), *Death to Tyrants! Ancient Greek Democracy and the Struggle against Tyranny*, Princeton.
Todd, S.C. (2007), *A Commentary on Lysias, Speeches 1–11*, Oxford.
Whitehead, D. (1982/83), "Sparta and the Thirty Tyrants" in: *AncSoc* 13/14, 105–130.
Wolpert, A. (2002), *Remembering Defeat: Civil War and Civic Memory in Ancient Athens*, Baltimore.
Wolpert, A. (2006), "The Violence of the Thirty Tyrants" in: *Ancient Tyranny*, S. Lewis (ed.), 213–23, Edinburgh.
Wolpert, A. (2017), "Thucydides on the Four Hundred and the Fall of Athens" in: *The Oxford Handbook of Thucydides*, R.K. Balot/S. Forsdyke/E. Foster (eds), 179–191, Oxford.

Notes on Contributors

Cinzia Bearzot is Professor of Greek History in the Catholic University of Milan. Her main interests focus on political and institutional history of ancient Greece, on history of ancient political thought, and on history of ancient historiography (Thucydides, Xenophon, fragmentary historians). She has published many books and papers on these topics: among them, *Federalismo e autonomian elle Elleniche di Senofonte*, Milano 2004; *Come si abbatte una democrazia. Tecniche di colpo di stato nell'Atene antica* (2013); *Manuale di storia greca* (2015^3).

Bogdan Burliga is Associate Professor of Classics at University of Gdańsk. He is mainly interested in ancient Greek historiography and technical writings. Among his publications there are the editions (with translations, introductions and commentaries) on: Aeneas Tacticus (Warsaw 2007), Xenophon's *Cyropaedia* (Wrocław 2014: co-author) and Frontinus' *Stratagems of War* (Wrocław 2016). He is also an author of "Arrian's *Anabasis*. An Intellectual and Cultural Story" (Gdańsk 2013), as well as an editor of "*Xenophon: Greece, Persia, and Beyond*" (Gdańsk 2011) and co-editor of "*Iphicrates, Peltasts and Leachaeum*" (Gdańsk 2014).

Nathan Crick is a Professor of Communication at Texas A&M University. Dr. Crick's work explores the relationship between rhetoric and power throughout different periods of political and social change, focusing specifically on those factors which are result of conscious strategies of persuasion by individuals or groups. This goal requires research into a variety of diverse topics, roughly including classical rhetorical theory, social media, the structure of news, religious rhetoric, modern propaganda, the rhetoric of science and technology, the power of aesthetics, the dynamics of social movements, and the history of philosophy. His first book, *Democracy and Rhetoric: John Dewey on the Arts of Becoming*, uses Dewey's philosophy to construct a view of rhetoric, logic, and aesthetics that is consistent with an ethics of democracy that promotes creative individuality. His second book, *Rhetoric and Power: The Drama of Classical Greece*, explores through the texts of canonical authors like Aeschylus, Gorgias, Thucydides, and Plato how rhetoric was conceptualized as a means of constituting and transforming power in Greek political culture. His third book, *The Keys of Power: The Rhetoric and Politics of Transcendentalism*, interprets the writing and thought of figures like Ralph Waldo Emerson, Henry David Thoreau, and Margaret Fuller as active rhetorical engagements with the political controversies of their time.

Edith Foster works on ancient Greek prose writers, primarily historiography. She published a monograph called *Thucydides, Pericles, and Periclean Imperialism* with C.U.P. in 2010 (paperback 2013), and co-edited (with Donald Lateiner) a volume on Thucydides and Herodotus, published with O.U.P. in 2012. Another co-edited volume (with Christina Clark and Judith Hallett), *Kinesis: Essays for Donald Lateiner on the Ancient Depiction of Gesture, Motion, and Emotion*, appeared with the University of Michigan Press in 2015. She is also a co-editor (with Ryan Balot and Sarah Forsdyke) of *The Oxford Handbook of Thucydides* (2017) and (with Emily Baragwanath) of *Clio and Thalia: Attic Comedy and Historiography*; HISTOS Supplement 6, 2017). Finally, she is a co-editor (with Dominique Lenfant and Christian Wendt) of *Interprétations de la défaite d'Athènes dans la guerre du Péloponnèse* which appeared as *Ktèma* 42 in December, 2017. She is presently working on a study of the battle narratives of Herodotus, Thucydides, and Xenophon and preparing a commentary on book four of Thucydides for the Cambridge Greek and Latin Classics series.

Edward M. Harris is Emeritus Professor of Ancient History at Durham University and Honorary Professorial Fellow at the University of Edinburgh. He is the author of *Aeschines and Athenian Politics* (Oxford University Press), *Democracy and the Rule of Law in Classical Athens* (Cambridge University Press), and *The Rule of Law in Action in Democratic Athens* (Oxford University Press). He has recently co-edited with David Lewis and Mark Woolmer, *The Ancient Greek Economy: Markets, Households and City-States* (Cambridge University Press. He has translated Demosthenes, *Speeches 20–22* and Demosthenes, *Speeches 23–26* (University of Texas).

Aggelos Kapellos has written *Lysias 21: A Commentary* (De Gruyter, Berlin) and a string of papers on Xenophon's *Hellenica* 1-2 and the Attic orators. Moreover, he has completed a monograph on *Xenophon's Peloponnesian War* for which he was awarded a visiting scholarship at the University of Heidelberg in 2012 and will be published in De Gruyter, *Trends in Classics*. He is presently working on a new commentary on Hyperides' *Funeral speech* for which he was a visiting fellow at the CHS-Harvard, Washington D.C. in 2014.

Frances Pownall (Professor, University of Alberta) is the author of *Lessons From the Past: The Moral Use of History in Fourth-Century Prose* (Michigan 2004), *Ancient Macedonians in the Greek and Roman Sources* (co-edited with Tim Howe, forthcoming with the Classical Press of Wales), and many historical commentaries on fragmentary Greek historians in *Brill's New Jacoby*. She has published widely on Greek history and historiography of the classical and Hellenistic periods.

P.J. Rhodes was Professor of Ancient History at the University of Durham and is now Emeritus Professor and Honorary Professor. He is author of *The Athenian Boule* (1972, rev. 1985), *Greek Historical Inscriptions, 359–323 BC* (1972, rev. 1986), *A Commentary on the Aristotelian Athenaion Politeia* (1981, rev. 1993), *The Athenian Empire* (1985, rev. 1993), *The Greek City States: A Source Book* (1986, rev. and enlarged edition 2007), (with D.M. Lewis) *The Decrees of the Greek States* (1997), *Ancient Democracy and Modern Ideology* (2003), (with R. Osborne) *Greek Historical Inscriptions, 404-323 BC* (2003, corr. 2007), *A History of the Classical Greek World, 478-323 BC* (2005, 2nd ed. 2010) and *Alcibiades* (2011). He has translated *The Athenian Constitution* for Penguin Classics (1984), has produced editions of Thucydides, Books II (1988), III (1994), and IV.1–V.24 (1998), and *The Old Oligarch* (with J.L. Marr, 2008), and has edited (with L.G. Mitchell) *The Development of the Polis in Archaic Greece* (1997), D.M. Lewis's *Selected Papers in Greek and Near Eastern History* (1997), *Athenian Democracy* (2004), and (with E.E. Bridges and E.M. Hall) *Cultural Responses to the Persian Wars: Antiquity to the Third Millennium* (2007).

Paolo A. Tuci is research fellow in Greek History in Università Cattolica del Sacro Cuore of Milan. His main topics of interest are history of classical Greek institutions, Greek historiography. He has been contributor for *The Encyclopedia of Ancient History* and *Brill's New Jacoby Online*. Among his works: *La fragilità della democrazia. Manipolazione istituzionale ed eversione nel colpo di Stato oligarchico del 411 a.C. ad Atene*, Milano 2013.

Andrew Wolpert is an Associate Professor of Classics at the University of Florida. He has written primarily on Athenian social memory and political culture, focusing on democratic discourse, civil war, and internal political conflicts. He is the author of *Remembering Defeat: Civil War and Civic Memory in Ancient Athens* (Johns Hopkins University Press, Baltimore) and co-author (with Konstantinos Kapparis) of *Legal Speeches of Democratic Athens: Sources for Athenian History* (Hackett Publishing Company, Indianapolis).

Index of Sources

Aeschylus
Prometheus Bound
103–105   155 n.74
114   155 n.74

Andocides
1.96–98   119 n.36
3.18   56 n.66
3.21   164 n.12
3.26–27   56 n.66

Androtion
F 48   57 n.69
FGrH 324   57 n.69

Antiphon
5.69   47 n.18

Aristides
1.266 (Lenz)   52 n.44
10.29 (Lenz)   52 n.44

Aristophanes
Acharnians
54–58   114
723–24   113
968   114
Equites
665   114
Ecclesiazousai
143   114
258–259   114
Lysistrata   108
Pax
734–735   113
Thesmophoriazousai
933–934   114

Aristotle
Poetics
1450a20–21   145 n.12
1451b12–7   146 n.21
Fragments
611–642 [Rose])   106

[Aristotle]
Athenaion Politeia
9.2   177 n.19
14.1   176
16.10   121
34.3   48 n.22
35.1   176
35.2   177
35.2–3   171
35.3   177
36.1   177
36.1–2   177
37.1   178
37.2   68 n.7, 178
38.1–3   178
40.4   49 n.28

Arrian
Anabasis
1.9.3   164
1.9.1–5   164 n.14
1.12.1–3   145 n.19
6.4–5   144 n.8

Cicero
Ad Quintum Fratrum
fr. 1.1.23   143 n.2
Ad Catilinam
22.79–81   143 n.2
Ad Familiares
1.1.23   143 n.3
9.25.1   143 n.3

Craterus
FGrHist 342 F17   109

Demosthenes
18.204   107 n.18
22   114
22.51–53   115
22.55   116

22.59–62	115	16.21.4	49 n.20
22.63	115	16.65.2–6	57 n.73
24.114	105	17.13.5–6	164 n.14

[Demosthenes]

Diogenes Laertius

47.52–61	115	2.56	46 n.9
59.66	105	2.58	46 n.9
59.66–70	105 n.9	2.59	46 n.9

Diodorus Siculus

Dionysius of Halicarnassus
Ad Pompeium

12.78.5	108	4	143 n.2
13.19–31	66 n.23		
13.26.2	162		
13.76.2	28 n.7	**Euripides**	
13.101	47 n.14	*Phoenician Women*	
14.3.2–7	48 n.22	531–532	145 n.19
14.3.7–4.1	175 n.18		
14.4.1	48 n.23	**Etymologicum Magnum**	
14.13	51 n.42	s.v. *alytarches*	112
14.4.30–3	68 n.7		
14.32.6	68 n.7	**Gorgias**	
14.86.1–3	56 n.66	*Helen*	
14.92.1	56 n.66	6	146 n.23, 147 n.27
14.92.1–2	57 n.69		
14.99.4	31	fr. 11	146 n.23
15.5	61 n.86		
15.12	61 n.86	**Harpocration**	
15. 20.1–2	58 n.74	ξ 2 Keaney	
15.25–7	59 n.78	ξενικὸν ἐν Κορίνθῳ	57 n.69
15.29.5–6	55 n.60	*Hellenica Oxyrhynchia*	
15.38	55 n.63	(ed. Chambers)	
15.49	57 n.71	18.4	33 n.24
15.50.4–6	55 n.63	19.2–4	59 n.77
15.58	57 n.71	20.1–2	59 n.77
15.59.1	62 n.90		
15.67.1	50 n.34	**Herodotus**	
15.70.3	63 n.94	5.71	120
15.72.4	62 n.90	5.90–93	121
15.76. 3	57 n.72	5.97.2	121
15.77.1–4	62 n.92	5.92	71
15.78.1–3	62 n.92	6.72	108
15.82.1–3	62 n.92	6.75.1	115
15.82.4–89.2	62 n.93	9.4–5	49 n.31
15.84.4	62 n.93	9.4.1–5.3	106
15.29.5–6	55 n.60		
15.50.4–6	55 n.63		
15.67.1	50 n.34		

Homer
Iliad
10.482–490	85 n.7
11.784	145 n.19

Hyperides
6. ll.7–17 (ed. Jensen)	164 n.14

Inscriptiones Graecae
v. ii 1	62 n.90
vii 2418. 11, 24	60 n.81
IG I³ 250, lines 9–11	113
IGVII 3078	113
LSS 18, lines 9–11	113
IG V 1 1390, LSCG no.65	113
LSAG no. 83, lines 23–26	113
Meiggs and Lewis 1969	no. 13 108
SEG 26	72, lines 14–16
	116 n.31
Gauthier and Hatzopoulos 1993	
lines B 8–10	112
lines B 21–23	112
B 69–70	112
B 97–99	112
Rhodes & Osborne	
32	60 n.81
57.11, 24	60 n.81

Isocrates
8.78	164 n.12
16.26	108

Istrus
FGrH 334 F 32   46 n.9

Justin
5.8.11	68 n.7
9.14	68 n.7

Lycurgus
1.122	107
124–126	119 n.36

Lysias
1.28	105 n.10
1.32	19 n.34
1.49	105

12.5	171
12.6	172
12.8–19	172
12.43–49	173 n.13
12.54–56	174 n.15
12.59	174
12.60–61	174 n.15
12.69–76	173
12.77–78	174
13.20–36	173 n.13
16	173 n.12
16.4–5	173 n.12
22.5	48 n.19
25	173 n.12
26.5–14	173 n.12
28	48 n.20
29	48 n.20

Nepos
Epaminondas
6.1–3	62 n.91

Timoleon
1.3–6	57 n.73

Nicolaus of Damascus
FGrHist 90 F 60   108

Pausanias
3.9.10	33 n.24
3.9.11	33 n.24

Philochorus
F 150	57 n.69
FGrH 328	57 n.69

Plato
Apology
32B	47 n.16

Gorgias
483c–d	146 n.23
483e	147 n.27

Laws
694a–b	152 n.63
890a	146 n.23
936c	114

Protagoras
338a	113

Republic
338c	146 n.23
342e	152 n.67
343c	152 n.65

Plutarch
Agesilaus
4.3–6	53 n.50
6.6	29 n.11
9.1–3	29 n.12
23.6–24.2	58 n.74
26.2	55 n.61
27.5–28.4	55 n.63
28.5–8	55 n.65

Aristides
23.1–3	114
23.11	114

De cohib. Ira
457b	145 n.19

Lysander
19.1–21.1	53 n.50
27.3	29 n.11

Moralia
162A–C	108
291f–292A	106
834A	109

Pelopidas
5.1–6.2	58 n.74
6.3–12	59 n.78
27.3	29 n.11

Themistocles
11.2–3	112

Timoleon
4.4–5.4	57 n.73
22.1–3	109

Regum et Imperatorum Apophthegmata
193 C–D	62 n.91

Pollux
3.153	113

Polybius
3.4.11	147 n.26

Scholion on Aristophanes' *Lysistrata*
273	108

Sextus Empiricus
Adv. math.
9.54	146 n.23

Solon
fr. 32 [West]	120

Supplementum Epigraphicum Graecum
xi 1051

Thucydides
1.1.1–2	162
1.19	79
1.23.1–3	164
1.75.1	147 n.26
1.76.2	146 n.23, 147 n.26
1.95.1	114
1.126.2–11	120
1.131.1	53 n.50
1.138	145 n.16
2.9	162
2.12.1–2	103
2.22.1	25 n.2
2.42.3	99
2.43.1	98
2.44.4	145 n.219
2.59.3	25 n.2
2.65	145 n.16
2.61–64	143 n.73
2.65.1	25 n.2
2.65.3–4	25 n.2
2.65.7	145 n.219
2.67.4	165 n.16
3.32.1	165 n.16
3.34	165 n.16
3.36–50	72 n.25
3.37–40	181
3.40.4	147 n.26
3.42.1	25 n.2
3.52–68	72 n.25, 165 n.16
3.58.3	162
3.66.2	162
3.81–83	70
3.82. 2	147 n.26
3.82.8	145 n.219
3.93.3	88 n.18

3.96.3–98	88 n.17	1.5.8	37
4.5.17	89	1.8.15	45 n.5
4.32.4	88 n.18	1.8.27	13 n.9
4.32–36	88	1.12.1–3	145 n.19
4.33–35	89	2.3.11	114
4.34.1	89	2.5.37	45 n.5
4.32.1	85 n.7	2.5.41	45 n.5
4.34.3	89	2.6.1–15	149 n.39
4.40.2	98	2.6.9	37, 41 n.41
4.57.4	165 n.16	2.6.21–29	149 n.40
4.60.1	147 n.26	3.1.14	13 n.9
4.127.2	90 n.20	3.1.17	148 n.32
5.10.9	97 n.44	3.1.21	13
5.38.1–3	59 n.77	3.1.24	131
5.49.1–5	112	3.1.29	13 n.9
5.50.1–2	112	3.1.4–47	45 n.5
5.50.4	112	3.4.12	13
5.84–114	181	4.7.1	139
6.101.6	97 n.44	4.7.13–14	140
7.3.4	165 n.16	4.8.27	149 n.41
7.53.3	165 n.16	5.2.18	129
7.56.2	163 n.9	5.2.24	130
8.1.1	163	5.2.25	129
8.1.1–4	164	5.2.27	129
8.48.5	163	5.3.5	45 n.7
8.63.3–70	46 n.11	5.3.6	45 n.6
8.64.3	163	5.3.7	45 n.7
8.84.2–3	111, 114	5.5.6	134
8.89.3	145 n.219	5.5.7–10	147 n.27
		5.5.11	13
Tyrtaeus		5.5.13–14	138
8.11–14	92 n.29	5.5.16	13
		5.5.18	13
Xenophon		5.5.19–21	134
Agesilaus		5.5.20	13
1.14–17	29 n.12	5.5.25	135
1.20	18	5.6.2	135
1.21–22	149 n.43	5.6.15	138
2.12	150 n.49	5.6.21	138
3.3	14	5.7.8	13
10.2	14	5.7.24–30	103
11.11	20	5.7.27–30	104
Anabasis		5.7.29	133
1.2.26	37	5.8.1	11 n.1
1.3.2	13	5.8.1–26	103
1.4.4	13	5.8.2–3	110
1.4.5	13	5.8.3	13

5.8.5	110	1.6.27	151
5.8.6–11	110	1.6.30	151 n.54
5.8.14–17	111	2.4.7	148 n.38
5.8.11	137	2.4.25	151 n.54
5.8.13	111, 137	3.1.3	150
5.8.13–26	111	3.1.10	155 n.74
5.8.18–19	111	3.1.11	148 n.36
5.8.19	13	4.4.10	151 n.55
5.8.21	111	5.4.35	39, 41 n.41
5.8.22–23	13	5.5.21	38
5.8.25	111	6.1.31	151 n.54
6.4.2	13 n.9	6.2.2	151 n.54
6.4.5	144 n.8	6.2.9	151 n.54
6.6.15	13	6.2.11	151 n.54
6.6.25	13	6.3.15	151 n.54
7.1.18	125	7.1.31–40	150
7.1.12–31	125	7.5.32	151 n.57
7.1.16	125	7.5.37	154 n.72
7.1.17	125	7.5.61	153 n.68
7.1.19	13	7.5.72–86	153 n.68
7.1.21	126	7.5.73–80	152
7.1.29	126	7.5.76	154
7.1.30	132	7.5.80	154
7.1.31	13	7.5.83	154
7.1.36	133	8.1.22	153 n.68
7.3.3	13	8.2.10–12	153 n.68
7.3.5	135	8.4.8	153
7.3.27	149 n.41	8.6.1	150
7.3.48	136	8.6.16	14 n.13, 20, 153 n.68
7.7.24	13		
7.8.11	13	8.7.7	147 n.28
7.1.25	40	8.7.12	154
7.3.27	149 n.41	8.7.38	147 n.28
7.7.41	135	8.8.1	155
Apology		*Equites*	
19.5	14	6.13	41 n.41
Cynegeticus		9.5	21 n.39
1.3	146 n.20	9.7	21 n.39
3.10	41 n.42	*Eq. mag.*	
12.9	14	5.14	14
Cyropaideia		*Hellenica*	
1.1.3	146 n.24	1.1.34	45 n.2
1.1.4	149	1.2.1–3	83
1.5.3	148 n.38	1.2.4	165
1.6.7–8	152	1.2.13	108
1.6.10	153	1.5.19	165
1.6.11	151 n.57	1.6.1–12	54 n.54

Index of Sources

1.6.7	27	2.3.23	48 n.25
1.6.13	28	2.3.23–52	68
1.6.13–15	162 n.7	2.3.23–55	51 n.38
1.6.14–15	165	2.3.24	69
1.6.28	28	2.3.24–34	182
1.7	36 n.31, 46 n.12	2.3.26	69
1.7.5	46 n.13	2.3.28	73
1.7.14	165 n. 20	2.3.32	69
1.7.15	37 n.32	2.3.34	69
1.7.34	37 n.32	2.3.41	69
1.7.35	41 n.41	2.3.45–46	69
2.1.2–5	166 n.20	2.3.48	46 n.10
2.1.9	20	2.3.50	48 n.25
2.1.15	165	2.3.50–51	182
2.1.19	165	2.3.53	70
2.1.31	161	2.3.54	70
2.1.30–32	161	2.3.55	48 n.25
2.2.1.6–7	54 n.54	2.3.56	70, 71
2.2.3	163	2.4.1	45 n.4, 46 n.10
2.2.3–4	164	2.4.4	85
2.3.11–13	48 n.23	2.4.4–7	83, 84, 85 n.9, 96 n.40
2.3.13–56	48 n.25		
2.2.6	163	2.4.5–7	45 n.4
2.2.9	163	2.4.6	84 n.5
2.2.10	17, 163	2.4.8–10	49 n.27
2.2.15	49 n.30	2.4.9	180
2.2.16–23	45 n.4	2.4.10–22	45 n.4
2.2.19	163	2.4.12–17	180
2.2.23–3.3	48 n.22	2.4.17	15
2.3.11–2.4.43	67	2.4.23	15
2.3.11	175 n.18	2.4.28–38	54 n.55
2.3.11–13	48 n.23	2.4.28–30	180
2.3.12	171	2.4.31–33	91 n.32
2.3.13	85	2.4.32	28 n.8
2.3.13–14	84 n.6	2.4.32–33	83, 85 n.9, 96 n.40
2.3.14	84 n.6		
2.3.13–14	85	2.4.33	84 n.5, 91 n.32, 97
2.3.15	68		
2.3.14–15	181	2.4.34	97 n.44
2.3.15–56	45 n.4, 48 n.25	2.4.35	28
2.3.16	181	2.4.35–43	45 n.4
2.3.17	68	2.4.38–43	49 n.28
2.3.19	15	2.4.26	71
2.3.20	48 n.25, 68	2.4.26–27	183
2.3.20–22	180	2.4.28–30	180
2.3.20–56	180	2.4.30–34	45 n.4
2.3.21	48 n.25, 68, 85	2.4.35–43	45 n.4

2.4.40–42	180	4.1.16–19	83, 85 n.9, 96 n.40
2.4.42	45 n.4		
2.4.43	49 n.28	4.1.17–19	86 n.11
3.1.1	53 n.50	4.1.19	84 n.5
3.1.4	180	4.2.9	52 n.44
3.1.8	28	4.2.9–23	87 n.13
3.1.17	28	4.2.21–22	95
3.1.21	16	4.3.1	95
3.2.2–5	83, 84, 85 n.9, 96 n.40	4.3.19	95, 150 n.49
		4.3.21	45 n.7
3.2.3	84 n.5, 88 n.14	4.3.22–23	84 n.4, 85 n.9, 87 n.12, 96 n.40
3.2.4	96 n.43		
3.2.5	84 n.5, 87	4.3.23	97 n.44
3.2.6	53 n.51	4.4.1	74
3.2.12	53 n.51	4.4.2	74
3.2.15–16	94	4.4.3	74
3.2.21	112	4.4.1–4	149 n.41
3.2.21–31	33 n. 24	4.4.10	97 n.44
3.2.23	52 n.44, 147 n.27	4.4.1–13	56 n.66
3.2.25	52 n.44	4.4.5	75
3.2.27	72	4.4.6	46 n.10
3.2.31	19	4.4.9–12	87 n.13
3.3.1–4	51 n.41	4.4.10	84 n.4, 85 n.9
3.3.4–11	52 n.43	4.4.11–12	75
3.3.5	52 n.43	4.4.12	96, 149 n.41
3.3.8	52 n.43	4.4.15	60 n.82
3.3.36	52 n.43	4.4.16–18	88 n.14
3.4.2–3	53 n.52	4.5.1	56 n.67
3.4.2–10	55 n.56	4.5.6	29 n.11
3.4.4	29	4.5.7–18	83, 96 n.40
3.4.8	36 n.29	4.5.9–18	91
3.4.8–10	183	4.5.10	29 n.11, 79, 98
3.4.12	38	4.5.11–12	96 n.40
3.4.20	55 n.56	4.5.12	87, 88
3.4.27–9	53 n.53	4.5.13	88
3.5.1	74	4.5.14	88 n.14, 98
3.5.5	19, 29 n.11	4.5.15–16	89 n.18,19
3.5.6	52 n.44	4.5.15	88
3.5.6–7	55 n.57	4.5.16	88
3.5.8	34	4.5.17	84 n.5, 89
3.5.12	73 n.32	4.5.17–18	85 n.9
3.5.13	73 n.32	4.6.3	52 n.45
3.5.17–20	83, 85 n.9	4.7.1	52 n.44
3.5.17–25	55 n.57	4.8.6	39 n.34
3.5.18–20	93 n.34	4.8.7	31
3.5.24	19	4.8.15	56 n.67
4.1.2	16		

4.8.17–19	83, 85 n.9, 96 n.40, 97	5.3.3	93
4.8.18	90	5.3.4	93
4.8.18–19	90	5.3.5	93
4.8.19	84 n.5, 91	5.3.6	84 n.5, 93, 97 n.44
4.8.30	31	5.3.7	27, 35, 41, 94 n.35
4.8.32	91		
4.8.33–39	83, 85 n.9	5.3.8	94 n.35
4.8.34	56 n.67, 91	5.3.10–17	60 n.84
4.8.34–39	90	5.3.12	16
4.8.35	91	5.3.13	16, 52 n.44, 109
4.8.38	84 n.5, 92	5.3.21–5	61 n.85
4.8.39	92, 97 n.44	5.3.24	30
4.32–36	88	5.3.25	30
4.34.3	89	5.4.1	46 n.10
4.33–35	89	5.4.1–2	58 n.76
5.1.7	77	5.4.1–9	118
5.1.10–12	83, 85 n.9	5.4.12	149 n.41
5.1.11	84 n.5	5.4.13	52 n.44
5.1.12	84 n.5	5.4.1–18	59 n.78
5.1.19–24	27	5.4.9	46 n.10
5.1.20	93 n.33	5.4.13	46 n.10
5.1.24	93 n.33	5.4.13–18	55 n.57
5.1.29	52 n.44	5.4.20–33	55 n.60
5.1.31	95	5.4.22–34	51 n.39
5.1.34	56 n.67	5.4.12	77
5.1.35–36	95	5.4.16	77
5.1.36	52 n.44, 56 n.67	5.4.17	77
5.2.1–7	61 n.86	5.4.35	52 n.44
5.2.3	52 n.44, 55 n.57	5.4.35–37	55 n.61
5.2.5	36 n.29	5.4.38–40	83, 85 n.9, 96 n.40
5.2.8–10	60 n.83		
5.2.25	75	5.4.39	84 n.5
5.2.25–36	58 n.74	5.4.39–40	86 n.11
5.2.27	58 n.75	5.4.42–45	84 n.4, 85 n.9
5.2.28	27, 36 n.30	5.4.43–45	27
5.2.29	75	5.4.45	84 n.5
5.2.33	54 n.55	5.4.46	59 n.79
5.2.34	18	5.4.47	52 n.44
5.2.37	27	5.4.56	84 n.4, 85 n.9, 96 n.40
5.2.38	19		
5.2.38–39	93 n.33	5.4.57	91 n.25
5.3.1	27 n.5, 93	5.4.58–61	55 n.62
5.3.1–6	92	5.4.59	52 n.44, 84 n.4, 85 n.9, 96 n.40
5.3.6	94		
5.3.1–7	83, 85 n.9, 96 n.40	5.4.63	32
		5.4.64–65	32

6.1.1	59 n.79	7.1.34	29 n.11
6.1.7	17	7.1.41	84 n.4, 85 n.9, 96 n.40
6.1.15	16		
6.2.3	94	7.1.41–3	60 n.80
6.2.5	94	7.1.44–6	63 n.94
6.2.5–7	94	7.1.46	46 n.10
6.2.15–19	114	7.2.4	32
6.2.17	94	7.2.11–15	118
6.2.17–24	83, 85 n.9, 96 n.40, 97	7.2.23	94
		7.2.24	95
6.2.19	36 n.31, 94	7.3.2	118
6.2.20	94	7.3.2–3	118
6.2.20–24	92	7.3.4–5	118
6.2.22	92	7.3.6	118
6.2.24	84 n.5	7.3.7–11	118
6.3	55 n.63	7.3.7	46 n.10
6.3.3	54 n.55	7.3.8	46 n.10
6.3.8	17	7.3.9	19
6.3.15	146 n. 25, 151 n.58	7.3.10	46 n.10
		7.3.11	60 n.81
6.4.7	12	7.3.12	119
6.4.17	52 n.44	7.4.2–3	62 n.91
6.4.20	49 n.30	7.4.4–10	57 n.72
6.4.21	18	7.4.12–40	62 n.92
6.4.32	46 n.10	7.4.13–14	83
6.4.34–35	46 n.10	7.4.20–25	83, 85 n.9, 96 n.40
6.5.3–5	61 n.87		
6.5.4–5	78	7.4.21–25	95 n.38
6.5.5	30	7.4.26	83
6.5.6	78	7.4.25	84 n.5
6.5.7	78	7.4.37	31 n.18
6.5.7–8	78	7.5	62 n.93
6.5.9	78	7.5.10	97 n.46
6.5.10	52 n.44, 78	7.5.26	146 n.24, 147 n.26, 153 n.70
6.5.26	84 n.5, 97		
6.5.26–27	83, 85 n.9	7.5.27	80
6.5.28	97 n.46	8.4.17	90 n.24
6.5.33–49	50 n.32	*Hiero*	
6.5.37	50 n.33	1.33	12
6.5.46	12	2.15	151 n.58
6.5.47	12	4.3	20
7.1.1	50 n.37	7.1–4	154 n.72
7.1.1–14	50 n.34	7.6	12
7.1.14	50 n.36	7.7	20
7.1.15–17	83, 85 n.9, 96 n.40	8.9	20
		10.2	14
7.1.17	84 n.5	10.4	20

7.3–4	145 n.19	3.5.12	12 n.7
Lac.Pol.		3.6.8	147 n.26
1.1	151 n.56	3.7.6	109
3.2	14	3.9.10	18
4.6	39	3.9.11	151 n.58
5.6	14	3.10.5	14 n.13
9.1–2	93 n.29	3.11.11	14
Memorabilia		4.2.14–17	147 n.28
1.1.18	37, 38, 47 n.16	4.4	146 n.23
1.2.10	17	4.6.12	151 n.53
1.2.12–13	17 n.25	*Oeconomicus*	
1.2.19	14	1.15	154
1.2.32	149 n.41	4.8	20
1.2.41	18	*Poroi*	
2.1.5	13	1.1	152 n.60
2.1.19	147 n.28	5	149 n.43
2.1.28	147 n.28	5.2	148 n.38
2.3.13–14	84 n.6	5.5	18
2.4.6	14	5.7	18
2.4.31–33	93 n.32	5.13	148 n.38
2.6.9	13, 14	*Symposium*	
2.6.24	16	8.20	19

General Index

Accountability 122
Adeimantus 8, 166
Agesilaus 2, 4, 14, 16, 20, 29–31, 34, 36, 38, 45, 51–54, 57–58, 60–61, 73–74, 79, 84, 86, 90, 146, 149, 167
Alexander (the Great) 145, 164
Anger 2, 4–5, 25–31, 33–40, 83, 92–94, 126
Arginousae 1, 37, 45, 68, 165
Argos 5, 32, 56–57, 62, 64
Assembly 1, 30, 33, 37, 46–57, 59, 61, 63, 106, 108, 114, 163, 166, 173
Athens 1–5, 8–9, 12, 21, 28, 30, 34, 45–51, 54–55, 57–59, 63–64, 68, 71, 73–74, 79, 84–85, 90, 95, 103, 105–108, 116, 118, 146, 162–164, 166, 169–178, 183
Battle(s) 1–2, 6–8, 15, 19, 26–28, 37, 45–46, 49, 53–55, 61–62, 64, 67, 73, 78–80, 83–84, 86–89, 91–93, 95, 98–99, 107, 146, 150, 161, 163, 166, 173, 175, 180, 182–183
Cadmea 58–59, 75–77
Callibius 67–68, 78, 84, 176, 178, 181
Captives 1, 8, 148, 161–63, 165–166
Corinth 5, 29, 46, 50, 56–57, 64, 75, 87–88
Court (s) 13, 58, 105–106, 108–109, 115, 143, 171, 177
Cyrus 1, 14, 20, 27, 30, 37–39, 45, 54, 125, 143–144, 146–155
Civil strife (*Stasis*) 2, 5, 16, 67, 72–76, 78–80, 83, 96
Council (ors) 46–51, 56, 58, 69–70, 78, 106, 109, 115, 118–119, 176, 178, 181–183
Democracy 6, 45, 49, 57, 63, 106, 109, 117–18, 121–22, 169–175, 177, 180–182, 184–185
Dercylidas 16, 28, 30–31, 53, 72, 86–87
Discipline 6, 11, 14, 76, 92, 104, 110–112, 114, 126–127, 133, 137, 140, 167
Eleusis 49, 71, 108, 178–179, 183

Empire 1, 2, 7, 73, 77, 136, 143–144, 146–150, 152, 154–155, 181
Ephor(s) 33, 39, 52–55, 60, 173
Euphron (of Sicyon) 6, 19, 46, 63–64, 103, 117–120, 122
(the) Four Hundred 46, 173, 178, 182
Force (s) 1–3, 6–7, 11–14, 16, 18, 27, 32, 50, 52–54, 56–57, 68, 73, 84–92, 94–95, 97, 103, 110–114, 116–119, 122, 126–130, 132–136, 138, 144, 146, 149, 151, 153, 177, 181–182, 184
Gerousia (Spartan) 51–53, 55
Hoplites 5–6, 26, 49, 84–90, 93–94, 114, 138, 183
Hybris 4, 11–14, 16–17, 19–21, 109, 116
Justice 6, 8, 14, 70, 103–109, 118, 122, 127, 132–138, 140, 148, 151, 155, 162, 164, 184
Law 39, 48, 61, 63, 103, 105, 110, 115–116, 119, 121–122, 131, 136, 175–178, 182, 184
Lechaeum 75, 84, 87–88, 95, 98
Leuctra 6, 12, 32, 49, 53, 55, 57, 59, 61, 67, 77–78, 92, 99
Lysander 1, 28, 34, 36, 48, 51, 53–54, 73, 84–85, 93, 97, 117
Massacre 5, 56, 72, 74–75, 77, 125, 166–167, 178
Metic(s) 48, 56, 68, 162, 171–172, 181–182
Monarch (y) 120, 151–152
Oligarchy 8–9 49, 64, 69, 169–170, 173–175, 177, 185
Persia 2, 72, 95, 125, 143, 146
Rule (of law) 6, 111, 121–122
(the) Thirty 1–4, 8–9, 15, 20, 45, 48–49, 51, 54, 67–74, 76, 79–80, 84–85, 119, 121, 169–184
Critias 5, 9, 45, 48, 51, 68–71, 146, 169, 173–174, 181–183, 185
Elite 69, 71, 109, 136, 145
Official(s) 3, 6, 48, 51, 54, 103, 105, 111–114, 116, 118–122
Persuasion 4, 14, 17–20, 53, 126, 131

Philocles 8, 161–162, 166
Phyle 68, 85, 87, 89, 119, 176, 178–180, 182, 184
Physis (nature) 2, 8, 11, 29, 58, 74, 109, 126, 128–131, 135, 138–139, 146–148, 152, 155, 169–170, 178
Phlius 5, 12, 16, 21, 29–30, 32, 34, 50, 60–61, 109, 117
Power 4, 7–9, 12–13, 18–21, 50, 53, 56, 59, 64, 79, 90, 95, 99, 103, 113, 115, 119, 121–122, 125–128, 130–138, 140, 144–152, 154–155, 170, 172, 176–179, 184
Procedure(s) 1, 5–6, 45, 47, 51–53, 64, 111, 122, 184
Punishment 4, 6, 21, 77, 103–108, 112, 116, 119, 122, 135, 155, 163, 165–166
Sicyon 5–6, 19, 46, 56, 63–64, 87, 103, 117, 119
Slaughter 1, 5, 8, 31, 73–75, 77, 83, 90, 111, 148, 161, 164–167
Slave(s) 37, 111, 113, 116, 133, 136, 152, 162, 165
Socrates 8, 14, 17, 37, 47, 68, 113, 126, 135, 146, 151–152
Solon 99, 120–122, 177
Soldier(s) 15, 26, 31, 36–41, 53, 62, 83–84, 86–87, 91–92, 99, 103–104, 110–111, 125–126, 129, 133, 137–138
Sparta 1–2, 5–6, 16–17, 26, 29–30, 32–35, 45–46, 49–64, 73–74, 78, 80, 83–84, 87, 92, 94–99, 117–118, 133, 162, 165, 169, 172–176, 178–179

Sphodrias 5, 32, 51, 64
Stick(s) 111
Stoning 106–108
Thrasybulus 9, 15, 31, 34, 45, 49, 68, 71, 85, 176, 178–179, 182–183
Three Thousand 9, 15, 48, 170, 176, 178–179, 182–183
Ten Thousand 2, 39, 62, 104, 110–112, 114, 116, 146
Thebes 2, 5–6, 12, 18, 46, 50, 52, 54–63, 75–77, 118–119, 164
Theramenes 5, 9, 15, 45–49, 51, 68–71, 74, 76, 170, 172–183, 185
Thibron 90–92, 95, 97–99
Threat 3, 7, 13, 18, 50, 52, 128, 132–133, 138–140, 149, 171, 182
Thucydides 3, 5–6, 8, 25, 35–36, 46, 49, 72, 79, 80, 88–89, 99, 111, 120, 125, 145–149, 153, 155, 162–164, 167
Trial(s) 1, 9, 37, 41, 45, 47–49, 51, 54, 62, 68, 75–76, 104–105, 107, 109, 120, 122, 146, 151, 155, 165, 172, 174, 180, 182–183, 185
Trierarch(s) 115–116
Tyrant(s) 4, 6, 15, 20, 46, 54, 56–58, 63, 67–68, 73, 75–76, 85, 108–109, 117–122, 145, 149, 154, 169
Violence 4–9, 11–21, 25, 28, 32–35, 40, 45, 51, 55–56, 62–64, 67–72, 74–78, 80, 83, 103–111, 114, 116, 118–120, 122, 125–140, 144, 146–152, 155, 164–166, 169–170, 175–176, 179, 181–185
Whip 33, 112–114

www.ingramcontent.com/pod-product-compliance
Lightning Source LLC
Chambersburg PA
CBHW021730220426
43662CB00008B/788